The New
Single
Woman

The New Single Woman

E. KAY TRIMBERGER

BEACON PRESS
BOSTON

Beacon Press
25 Beacon Street
Boston, Massachusetts 02108-2892
www.beacon.org

Beacon Press books
are published under the auspices of
the Unitarian Universalist Association of Congregations.

Text design by Bob Kosturko
Composition by Wilsted & Taylor Publishing Services

Library of Congress Cataloging-in-Publication Data

Trimberger, Ellen Kay
The new single woman / E. Kay Trimberger.
p. cm.
Includes bibliographical references and index.
ISBN 0-8070-6523-4 (pbk. : acid-free paper)
1. Single women—United States—Identity. I. Title.

HQ800.2.T75 2005
306.81′53—dc22   2005004102

The poem reprinted on page 42 appears by permission of the author,
Sondra Zeidenstein. It was originally published in the essay
"The Naked Truth," *Ms.*, August/September 1999, p. 59.

Author's Note

All the women portrayed in this book are real people, not composites. Although I have changed their names and other identifying characteristics to protect their privacy, the details of their stories and their words are accurate, gleaned from transcripts of taped interviews. Both first names and surnames are fictional; any resemblance to people living or dead is unintentional.

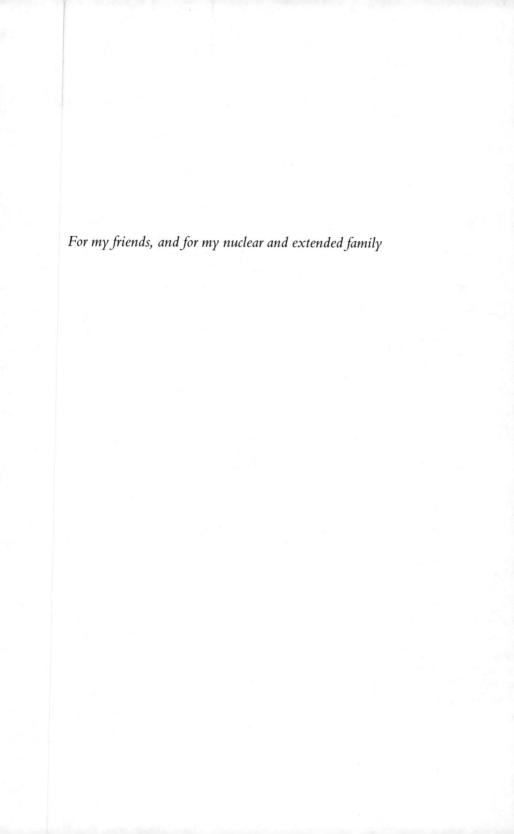

For my friends, and for my nuclear and extended family

Contents

The new single woman can answer affirmatively the question:
"Are you somebody?" She no longer is bothered by the question:
"Why aren't you with somebody?"
Inspired by NUALA O'FAOLAIN's *Are You Somebody?*

I'm sitting in a park on a warm June afternoon talking with Janice Belmont, an artist, a teacher, and an ever-single woman whose life I have been following for some years.[1] Now in her early fifties, Janice looks much as I remember her when we met almost nine years ago. She is slim, serious, and soft-spoken. Her attractive face is partly hidden by big glasses and set off by short black hair, cut in a chic but casual style. I ask Janice how her life has changed since she took part in a 1994 discussion I organized with three other divorced and never-married women. Back then, she was the unhappy, ever-single mother of a troubled teenager. She yearned to find a partner. Now she is still single, but her son is a college graduate, about to enter a prestigious graduate school, and she is a proud grandmother.

Janice tells me that for years she has been longing, and always looking, for a deep personal connection with a man. A year ago she decided to no longer look but just live in the present. "I now know that finding someone is not the route to happiness," Janice said. "It is an odd thing when all your life you long for that and then you realize that it is not necessary. I'm not saying that I decided I don't want a relationship. But it's been so freeing not to look, not to think about it. Just to let it go. In letting go, I realized I have a really full life with a lot of joy."

Is it possible to be a single woman in one's fifties with a full life and a lot of joy? Not if you listen to the cultural messages beamed at us. Whereas single women in their twenties and early thirties have gained visibility and social acceptance, single women over the age of thirty-five are still stigmatized. They live in a culture that tells them that finding a partner, preferably a soul mate, is absolutely necessary for their happiness. Only in an intimate couple, the culture tells us, will we find emotional satisfaction, sexual fulfillment, companionship, security, and spiritual meaning.[2] This emphasis on the romantic couple implicitly demotes all other types of human relationships, especially friendships, extended family, colleagues, mentors, neighbors, and community. Women who find intimacy, security, and human warmth, as well as contented solitude, in all or some of these relationships are culturally invisible.

Recently, the romantic standard for coupling has been elevated to a more idealized height. A 2001 national Gallup Poll of unmarried women and men between the ages of twenty and twenty-nine found that 94 percent were seeking a soul mate to marry and 87 percent were confident they would find one. Fully 80 percent of women in this poll felt that a husband who can communicate his deepest feelings is more desirable than one who makes a good living.[3] This soul-mate ideal, I discovered, affects older single women too, legitimating single life as long as these women are searching for *the one,* but undermining any conception of a satisfying life outside a couple.

The idea that you need to couple to be happy has spawned a multimillion-dollar industry of online matchmaking, personal ads, and dating services. Innumerable television, film, and book plots revolve around people who find their soul mates after struggling for years in the harsh, unsatisfying wilderness of singleness. If a single woman, no matter what her age or how long since she was partnered, is not looking for or is not successful at finding someone, then something must be wrong with her. Although the word *spinster* is no longer used, some of the negative attributes attached to it linger. The older single woman is often seen as an isolated loner, an unhappy striver who overinvested in work, or a neurotic loser who again and again fails at relationships.

If you are older than thirty-five and not coupled, it is easy in this cultural milieu to internalize the belief that you can't love, are neurotic, and have *issues*. This cultural message is reinforced by family and friends. In January 2004 Richard Roeper, a bachelor and columnist for the *Chicago Sun-Times,* wrote about pressures from his friends to couple. He received holiday cards from two longtime female friends who waxed rhapsodic about the joys of married life and who expressed confidence that he would soon find a partner. Although Roeper was not offended by their words, he envisioned how negatively they would react if he penned a similar note expressing his worldview: "To my dear, dear friend: I know you've been married for the last 12 years and you CLAIM to be happy, but for 2004 my greatest wish for you is that you open your eyes to the possibility of a commitment-free existence! Dump your husband and get back in the game! I don't want you to wake up at 60 one day and wonder why you didn't live the single life."[4] Three days later, Neil Steinberg, another *Sun-Times* columnist, wrote a rebuttal column, "Single Life Is Fine Till About 30, Then Normal People Marry" (January 23).

In a similar vein, a thirty-year-old woman called in to a radio show where I was discussing my research to say that her friends find it disturbing that she is happier when she is single. Her friends say, "Don't turn your back on love; you will be so much happier with someone." Another caller—a forty-seven-year-old never-married woman—thought she had a personal flaw: "I feel my life is fine and I'm generally very happy, but I think that I and a lot of single people have deep-seated trust issues." There is no research that validates her position, and none that shows that those who couple are more trusting. But this combination of having a satisfying life, yet feeling that something is wrong with being single, is common among midlife single women.

Within this cultural context, I decided in the mid-1990s to conduct a study of single women between the ages of thirty and sixty. As an ever-single woman myself—and a single mother—I had been thinking about the issue of singleness for about ten years, looking at what meager social and psychological literature existed, giving a few talks on my preliminary thoughts on the subject, and trying to decide whether I wanted to focus intellectually on an issue of such personal concern. As a sociologist, I was interested to find out how the increase in the numbers of single women related to the marriage crisis and its impact on the family, but now as a never-married woman in my midfifties, the mother of a teenage son, I was also looking for personal direction. I had only recently accepted the probability that I would never be coupled. Because I had no role models and no cultural road map for my ever-single life, I decided to interview long-term single women in the hope that I would find women who had achieved a satisfying single life with less stress than I had experienced. This is not what I found.

In 1994–95, through a widely distributed letter to colleagues, friends, and acquaintances, I collected a diverse group of middle-class white, African American, and Latina women over the age of thirty; some had never married, others were divorced, and half of them had children. I included heterosexual, lesbian, and bisexual women. I interviewed forty-six women, all of whom live in northern California but grew up in various geographic regions, social classes, and family types. All of the women had worked outside the home for most of their adult lives, in all kinds of jobs and professions. The diversity of these women, and of their aspirations, perceptions, and values, convinced me that their experiences would speak for and to a large number of American women. Some of these women participated in, and were profoundly influenced by, the social movements of the 1960s and 1970s, but an equal number were largely unaware of and unaffected by feminism, black power, civil rights, the New Left, or the counterculture. Many were in religious or conservative families during that period and were influenced by the values of these movements—and the backlash against them—as they spread later, in the 1980s and 1990s.

Among those I interviewed, I did *not* find primarily contented single women. Most of them were more conflicted than I was about being single, even though they were not isolated and were leading active, productive lives. Most had strong family ties and/or supportive networks of friends. But it struck me that the new cultural norm of looking for a soul mate, and then becoming an egalitarian couple combining family and work—norms advocated by second-wave feminism—seemed to be taking a heavier toll on the self-confidence of single women today than the older ideal—that a career and conventional family life do not mix for women. Almost all of the women, even those in their fifties, whether heterosexual, lesbian, or bisexual, still hoped to find the "right one."

These findings were disconcerting. How could I write about these single women without reinforcing negative cultural stereotypes about them? This dilemma, combined with the demands of work and single motherhood, led me to put the study aside. When I reinterviewed the women seven to nine years later, in the early twenty-first century, I discovered that more than half of those who were not cohabiting in 1994–95 were still single (two of them had died recently).[5] Their lives were full of often unpredictable changes—in their lives, their relationships, and their attitudes.

Most of these women, I discovered, went through a series of personal struggles that led them to accept their singleness and be more satisfied with their lives. The stories of these twenty-seven single women (including the two who died), and my own story, form the basis of this book. Although our numbers are small, the depth and richness of the stories, as they were revealed to me over time, capture the essence of the lives of middle-class single women at the beginning of the twenty-first century. We are pioneers creating viable and satisfying lives as long-term single women. Our fears, struggles, and anxieties, as well as our triumphs, represent those of many other women.

New single women, during their thirties, forties, and sometimes into their fifties, create the structures that support a viable single life *before* they are able, usually from their midforties to their late fifties, to discard the cultural ideal of the couple as the only route to happiness, as the only protection against loneliness. Given the heavy dose of cultural stigma and the invisibility of alternative models, how and why did most of the women in my study become more accepting of their single lives? Some might say that as we age, we become more ready to accede to whatever life has dealt to us. But I think this is an inadequate explanation. We can all think of single women in their fifties or even sixties who continue to frantically search for a partner and who seem genuinely unhappy. There were a few such women in my study. But a number of factors converge in this historical period to make single life for middle-class women more viable.

Sheer numbers help. In 2000, 42 percent of all women in the United States over the age of eighteen were unmarried—44 million women (compared with 38 million men). Only about 6 million of these unmarried women were cohabiting.[6] Thus, perhaps 38 million women were not coupled. Twelve million of these uncoupled women were between the ages of thirty-five and fifty-nine (25 percent of the women in this age span). The percentage of single-person households (25.8) is now greater than that of households with a married couple and one or more children (23.5). This increase in the percentage of single women is due primarily to those who postpone marriage and those who are divorced.[7] The divorce rate is holding steady at about 50 percent for first marriages and higher for subsequent ones.[8] In 1950 two-thirds of divorced women remarried, but today only half of them marry again or are cohabiting after five years.[9]

Women's economic advances make single life possible for more women. Increasing numbers of women in the United States are able to support themselves and their children. Today, never-married and divorced women over the age of thirty-five have higher personal earnings than married women.[10] Despite a justified concern about the economic plight of single mothers, 68 percent of these mothers are above the poverty line, and almost 40 percent are well off.[11] But economic self-sufficiency does not by itself lead to satisfaction with single life.

The middle-class women who volunteered to be interviewed for my study did not know in their twenties or early thirties that they would be single at forty-two, fifty-five, or sixty. Though they never made a conscious decision to be single, on looking back many women see that they did make concrete choices that led them to become more autonomous and to create alternative structures of support. They chose to leave a marriage, end an unsatisfactory relationship, focus on building a career, pursue unconventional adventures, or become a mother without a partner. Second-wave feminism, as I demonstrate, did not sanction single life but, along with the counterculture and movements for racial, ethnic, and gay liberation, supported women's break with conventional expectations for women.

By their forties and fifties, these divorced and ever-single women had good jobs, homes, and a strong network of family and friends. They were active in their neighborhoods, voluntary organizations, churches/synagogues, or political organizations. In various ways, they had come to terms with their sexual needs. But often a personal crisis was necessary for them to fully accept the disconnect between their full lives and the cultural message that they needed to be coupled to be happy. Only then could they discard the cultural norm and come to appreciate the life they had created. They implicitly agree with author Alice Koller: "I drifted into a situation that I in time acknowledged and then turned to my own account."[12] Turning to one's own account a life not envisioned or chosen is not passive acceptance but a process of *active* exploration and change. I found that creating a satisfying single life—like building a good marriage—is a process of development, self-discovery, and work.

New cultural messages that slowly began to contest the dominance of the ideal that women need to be coupled to be happy also facilitated single women's acceptance of their lives. They could patch together scraps of alternative values—gleaned from feminism, from the increasing acceptance of divorce and of women's career successes, and from changing sexual norms. Nancy Dean, one of my subjects, commented: "I was looking at a magazine in the dentist's office that had a big ad for diamonds for your right hand geared to the single woman who wants to indulge herself. You can tell you've made the grade when you become a marketing tool."

During the years between the interviews, a trickle of popular literature and media began to affirm single life. Television shows (for example, *Golden Girls, Friends,* and *Sex and the City*) and films (*Wait-

ing to Exhale, The First Wives' Club, and *Divine Secrets of the Ya-Ya Sisterhood*) emphasized the importance of friendship networks in providing intimacy and sustaining a viable single life for women whether they are in their twenties, thirties, forties, or older. In the 1990s, vice presidential candidate Dan Quayle denounced the TV character Murphy Brown's decision to have a baby as a single woman in her thirties. But more than ten years later, the same decision by a single woman in *Sex and the City* elicited no such controversy. In both cases, media attention undoubtedly led more women to consider this as an option. The last episode of the six-year HBO hit *Sex and the City* aired in February 2004. By then three of the four women protagonists, now in their late thirties and early forties, were married or had a committed boyfriend. However, Carrie, the central character, had an ambiguous future. She concluded that she had made a mistake in abandoning her job, her friends, and the city she loved to move to Paris with a famous artist absorbed in his work. She left him before an old boyfriend, the commitment-phobe Big, came galloping to Paris to bring her back to New York. But what their future held was left ambiguous. Carrie affirmed that her happiness depended most on knowing, loving, and being true to herself.

Last, taking part in the research interviews may have facilitated a shift in attitude for many of these single women, as it did for me. The first interviews were with groups of three to five single women, all similar in age and all either single mothers or childless. A three-hour group interview with other single women—like a women's consciousness-raising group—permitted them to articulate their dissatisfaction with how society viewed them. Telling their life stories in a sympathetic environment led to a reevaluation. In written comments after the group interviews, women indicated how that experience led to a process of personal change. Jane liked "the opportunity to talk about issues not usually discussed." Joyce, a childless woman in her late forties, in contrast, had been afraid that the interview might bring up an unconscious regret. But afterward she wrote: "I learned I am comfortable being child free." Thirty-one-year-old Linda remarked: "I left [the interview] recognizing what a good choice I made being single up to this point in my life." Eight years later

I found her still single and trying to become pregnant through artificial insemination, encouraged by an e-mail discussion group sponsored by the national organization Single Mothers by Choice.

Thus, the group interviews, and the subsequent individual interviews with me, allowed many of the women to see the more positive aspects of their lives, to talk about being single with their friends, and to be receptive to new ideas. In the same way, I hope readers of this book will talk about singleness with others, and in so doing begin to see their lives differently and to be more self-aware about the choices they are making.

A New Type of Single Woman

The process of change in my life and my subjects' lives leads me to articulate the emergence of a new type of single woman, one quite different from the traditional spinster or single girl in her twenties. For many of us, becoming a new single woman was a long and complex task. But an increase in cultural visibility and an acceptance of a long-term single life may make this an easier route for many women in the future.

The *new* single woman is content and happy with her life and the prospect of remaining single. She is satisfied with her accomplishments, relationships, and identity. She cannot be classified as having a specific personality; she is not a loner or an aberrant individual.[13] She has erected six pillars of support that allow her to lead a satisfying life:

1) The new single woman has a home that nurtures her, whether she lives by herself or with other people.

2) She has satisfying work that provides her with economic autonomy and a psychological identity but is not her whole life. Because a new single woman integrates her work with other aspects of her life, she may be less free to move than a coupled woman when career opportunities arise.

3) The new single woman is satisfied with her sexuality. What constitutes *satisfying* varies widely. I did not find much sexual frustration. The single women in my study who lead active sex lives do not see a permanent partner as necessary to their sexual satisfaction, and they do not restrict their sex lives to a soul mate. Contrary to stereotypes, many women were content with celibacy, and some had found other outlets for their sensuality.

4) A new single woman enjoys some connection to the next generation, which can take many forms: relationships with her own children and grandchildren, nieces and nephews, stepchildren, and younger protégées and volunteer work with the young.

5) A new single woman finds intimacy within a network of friends, or of family and friends, that provides companionship and people she can rely on in times of trouble.[14] Because friendship is not an exclusive relationship, and because American culture stresses the importance of equity and mutuality in a friendship, friends are more supportive of women's autonomy than most family members and romantic partners. Single women over the age of forty are especially good at forming and maintaining friendships and often create large networks of friends.

6) A new single woman creates and maintains a community primarily through her friendship networks. Friends made in diverse organizational settings (at school, college, work, church, politics) are linked together to form the basis of a contemporary community. Thus the single woman is not alone, not on her own.

While articulating these supports for a long-term single life, I thought of them as applicable only to satisfied *singles*. When I outlined these features during a talk at a community college, however, a woman raised her hand and said: "But these are the things all people need to lead a good life, whether single or coupled." I quickly admitted that she was right. I had not yet liberated myself from the erroneous notion that single and coupled/married people lead very different lives. It was the beginning of my awakening to what is another theme of this book—the continuum between single and married women, despite the cultural messages driving us apart. Many women today are not married or cohabiting, but they are not completely single either. Moreover, a majority of women spend one part of their lives married or cohabiting and another part as singles. This diversity of experience gives rise to a more complicated view of what it means to be single and to connections between women who, whatever their current living situations, can understand and emphathize with each other's lives. I will demonstrate how friendship networks incorporate both single and married women—as well as those who are in between—providing intimate connections and security for all.

Another important finding of my research—again one I had not anticipated—is that about half of the long-term single women I interviewed grew up with parents who were in stable, often good, marriages, some with large families. Perhaps I should not have been surprised, since it is true of my background too, but the social science and popular literature overwhelmingly assumes that the experience of parental divorce and unstable family life leads to increases in singleness. Although my sample is too small for any definitive analysis, my exploration of the family backgrounds of the single women in my study counters the idea that the rise in divorce is the only factor in the increase in singleness.

In the following chapters, I present detailed stories about how single women use and then free themselves from the soul-mate ideal. Through the long process of crafting a viable single life, many of them become more autonomous and find value in that. I address several questions and issues: How do single women separate themselves from the conventional motherhood mandate in order to remain childless or to accept single motherhood? What are the contours of a life lived without a primary commitment to a partner but in which a woman uses her considerable emotional capacities to connect to many others? How do single women resolve conflicts with friends when friendship is a major source of intimacy, companionship, and care? We meet women who are coupled but not cohabiting and women who have found viable alternatives to living by themselves. We experience the distinct ways in which single women die.

I identify the similarities in single women's lives that lead to satisfaction, but I also find many differences. Some of these women are strong and autonomous, and others never make a decision by themselves. Some value long periods of solitude, and others are always on the phone and with friends even if they live by themselves. Sexual expression is very important for some, and they seek and usually enjoy active sex lives. Others embrace celibacy.

This model of a new single woman in her prime, as distinct from the *single girl* who is supposed to marry by her midthirties, has positive implications for younger single women. Single women in their twenties and thirties who are increasingly anxious about combining autonomy and career ambitions with marriage now will have another framework for life after the age of forty. Despite all the opportunities for education, careers, dating, and living that they have in their twenties, young women today have only *one* culturally sanctioned option for life after the age of thirty-five—as an egalitarian couple sharing work and family life. Within this couple, there is the option to have children or not, and how many. But young single women have not been able to envision a positive single life for after the age of forty. Journalist Peggy Orenstein has found that these women believed they would become isolated and live alone if they were still single in their forties, without "the comfort and satisfaction of a home life."[15] They thought they would have only a work, and no personal, life.

The mothers of single women over the age of thirty-five often impose the coupled ideal on their daughters. Today it is commonplace for a mother to brag about the educational accomplishments and career advancement of her twenty-seven-year-old single daughter. But the mother of a fifty-year-old ever-single daughter often has very different feelings. She frequently says: "I worry about Janet's being alone. I wish she would meet someone and settle down." How often do we hear a mother say, "I'm so proud of Janet; she bought her own home, won a teaching award last year, and has more friends than anyone I know"? Nor are we likely to hear Irene's mom brag about her forty-year-old divorced daughter who is raising her son in cooperation with a single woman friend who has adopted her own child. Rather, Irene's mother will say: "I wish she would find someone and remarry. That child needs a father."

The Tenacity of the Romantic Ideal

Despite my own long-term singleness and the change in my perception attained through this study, I still find myself slipping back into the conventional cultural elevation of romantic love, which demonstrates its tenacious hold on all of us. When I contacted Anne Rosetti in 2003, six years after I last interviewed her and eight years since the first group interview, she said: "You just caught me before I move permanently to Tucson; I'm moving for a matter of the heart." I immediately assumed that she had met someone. But it turned out that this attractive, very successful entrepreneur who had been divorced for twenty years was moving to the Southwest at the age of fifty-five not for a man but because she had spent part of her childhood there and loved the climate, the skies, the art, and the aesthetics of both the landscape and the art. She had friends and family in Tucson, would find some sort of job, and felt that a smaller city offered more opportunities for community. These were what her *heart* sought, not romance or a partner.

But not everyone's desire to couple is driven only by cultural norms. Not all long-term single women, including some of my friends, want to remain single. They have built viable lives and are relatively happy, but they still hope to be coupled. They want the daily closeness, touching, and routine of living as a couple. Although changing our culture will not alter their desire or cure the pain of not finding someone, even these women, as some admitted to me, will feel better in a culture that views their lives as normal and acceptable. Reading about the women portrayed in the chapters ahead may help less content single women better discern how to continue to look for a partner without undermining the supports they have built for a single life.

With the new perspective provided here, more single women, even those who want to couple, can avoid putting their lives on hold while they experience the painful ambiguity of continuing to look for a partner year after year. Indeed, Kate Zernike, in a recent *New York Times* article ("Just Saying No to the Dating Industry," November 30, 2003), finds that some singles in their thirties reject the social pressure to look for a partner. The few women in my study, who, well into their fifties, focused most of their energy on finding a partner, were also the most unhappy and the least successful at building the social supports necessary for a single life. In chapter 5 we will meet Rachel Brown, who at the age of fifty-nine spent so much time on finding a mate that her friends slipped away, and she had little energy to deal with serious conflicts in her family and at her workplace. She attended numerous workshops on how to couple, but she did little to mend her other relationships.

Toward a New Cultural Model

The New Single Woman identifies a cultural change that is in process and aspires to make it visible and coherent. Historian Ann Douglas recently told a reporter, "the possibility for women to sustain a single life is one of the most important social shifts going on and it is largely unaddressed except by scare tactics."[16] I hope to change that. I seek to create a story about long-term single life—a cultural narrative that does not center on romance, marriage, or being coupled but that emphasizes intimacy and support in friendship networks; personal fulfillment in family, work, and community; and, for some, satisfaction in sensuality/sexuality and/or in mothering. With a changed cultural perspective that values friendship as a major source of intimacy, single women often have lives that are very rich.

Unlike many contemporary analysts of the marriage crisis who castigate singleness, and contrary to the defenders of singleness who critique marriage, I argue that an increase in long-term singleness is compatible with stronger and more stable marriages. A culture that normalizes long-term single life might decrease the divorce rate as people marry for positive reasons and not to escape the stigma of being single. Peggy Orenstein wisely proclaims: "If women can't see single life as a viable alternative with its own set of costs, rewards, and challenges, then they remain as controlled by marriage as previous generations, equally vulnerable to making choices negatively—out of fear instead of authentic desire."[17] Rather than having the highest marriage *and* divorce rate among economically advanced countries,[18] the United States could come to have a smaller, but more stable, married population living in harmony with a stable group of single people. The friendship networks that are so important in single women's lives incorporate coupled and married women and provide them with intimacy, as well as security in case of divorce, the death of a partner, or severe illness. The portraits in this book provide a vivid testimony to the possibility of leading a fulfilling life as a single person, a life that is parallel with, and not very different from, those of our married and coupled counterparts.

When we embark on adulthood, most of us don't know where we will end up. Given this reality, single women in their twenties, thirties, and forties must more consciously create the pillars of support for a viable life whether they will couple or not. This is the route to a richer life, and one with more options later on. Conversely, to focus primarily on finding a partner while other parts of life are neglected is a recipe for unhappiness.

Reading about the struggles of single women to accept and relish their lives will, I hope, help other women short-circuit the process. Singleness will come to be seen as more than just an empty way station between coupled relationships. It will become a way of life, one with many variations, but a satisfying life path with its own demands and rewards.

The New
Single
Woman

CHAPTER I

"We Don't Have to Settle"

Soul Mates and Singleness

On a chilly February day in 2003, I'm sitting in a California college classroom with twenty-eight women students, most of whom are in their early twenties. We begin a discussion of single women's lives today. I ask the students if they agree with an author's contention that hardly any women choose to be single.[1] They do. Then Michelle blurts out: "But we do choose not to settle." Lisa adds that she chose to leave a bad relationship. Both of them—like many of their contemporaries—are looking for a soul mate.

The ideal of a soul mate, someone with whom one can combine love, fidelity, emotional intimacy, and togetherness,[2] is a contemporary reinterpretation of romantic love. At least at the level of ideology, finding a soul mate has replaced other reasons for long-term partnerships and marriage. To support my point, I present an expanded version of the statistics I provided in the introduction.

A 2001 national Gallup Poll of unmarried women and men between the ages of twenty and twenty-nine found that 94 percent were seeking a soul mate to marry and 87 percent were confident they would find one. Young people do *not* see marriage as a source of economic security or as important for having children. In the Gallup Poll only 16 percent of young adults agreed that the main purpose of marriage is to have children. More than two-thirds of young women (equal to the number of young men) believe it is important for them to be economically secure *before* marriage.

Although sexual attraction is part of being soul mates, sexual pleasure is not central to the ideal.[3] Black feminist writer bell hooks emphasizes that love that consists of a "mysterious connection between our soul and that of another person" does not necessarily involve a shared sexual passion.[4] "Ultimately, most of us would choose great love over sustained sexual passion if we had to," hooks concludes.[5] Sexologist Pepper Schwartz concurs that soul-mate relationships are often lacking in sexual passion. Such closeness, she concludes, obliterates one of the key ingredients of passionate sex, "The desire to bridge the gap of intimacy between partners, the desire to reduce or extinguish distance and hierarchy."[6]

The women students in my class agreed that love is more important than sex. All of them *disagreed* with the statement "I would marry a man I did not love if he met my criteria in every other way." However, more than half said that they "would form a permanent partnership with a soul mate even if the sex wasn't very good." Because casual and consensual sex is so readily available to young people and the divorce rate is so high, the search for a soul mate implies the need for a deeper and presumably more permanent bond. One of my students noted: "The ideal of a soul mate is finding emotional stability, support, and comfort."

The idea of a bond that seems predestined rather than something you have to work for is attractive too. Philosopher Thomas Moore writes: "A soul mate is someone to whom we feel profoundly connected, as though the communicating that takes place between us were not the product of intentional efforts, but rather a divine grace."[7] In a country where people work longer hours than anywhere else in the world, and in a culture that extols us to work on our relationships, we are relieved to be told that we will find a soul mate without effort. The spiritual appeal also resonates in a society in which religion is more important than in other advanced industrial countries.

Once the Gallup Poll and my students had alerted me to the saliency of the soul-mate ideal, I started seeing references to soul mates everywhere, in both popular culture and in highbrow venues. Here are a few examples:

The HBO hit *Sex and the City,* about the lives of four single women, began its fourth season in 2001 with an entire show devoted to the topic of soul mates. The four protagonists debated whether soul mates exist and, if so, whether their happiness depends on finding one. Charlotte offered a solution: "Maybe we could be each other's soul mates. Then men just could be great, nice guys to have fun with."

The popular TV show *Friends* aired this exchange on February 28, 2002: Phoebe asked Rachel if she believed in soul mates. Rachel replied: "Oh yes, I do. I do. I believe there is one perfect person out there for everyone. You know how you find them. You stop looking. I know he'll find me."

Later that spring, the new reality show *Bachelor* was launched, in which a single man meets, dates, and rejects a large number of single women. In the final episode, Alex, the bachelor, said, "Can you find your soul mate through this process? I believe you can."

It is not only white middle-class women who want soul mates. Journalist Alex Kotlowitz, in the TV documentary "Let's Get Married," which was aired on PBS's *Frontline* series on November 14, 2002, interviewed an African American single mother with seven children. The mother introduces the father of her last child as "my soul mate." She will wait to marry him, however, until he gets a good job. In 1999 *Essence* magazine featured an article that discussed the importance for black women of finding a soul mate.[8]

Lesbians too have bought into the soul–mate ideal. In 2001 Dian Katz, in *Lesbian News,* wrote:

> Your soul mate will love you regardless of any character flaws you have. You will feel a sense of being understood and loved like never before as you discover you and your soul mate share the same value and belief systems and feel strongly about the same goals and ideals. It's as if someone took a mirror of your heart and placed it in front of you and your soul mate's matched yours perfectly.[9]

References to soul mates proliferated in more elite sources as well: Katha Pollitt, in an essay in *The New Yorker* (July 22, 2002), wrote, "I did not realize that the man I lived with, my soul mate, made for me in Marxist heaven, was a dedicated philanderer." The *New York Times Book Review* titled a review "Seeking Soul Mate: Must Like DeLillo."[10] In a late 1990s memoir, Michele Wallace, a 1970s radical black feminist, writes about her "hubby bear Gene, the love of my life and my soul mate."[11]

Implications for Single Women

Social scientists who document the prevalence of a soul-mate ideal are concerned primarily with its implications for marriage. I, however, ask how it affects single women. I posit that the cultural emphasis on finding a soul mate leaves a particularly difficult and contradictory legacy for us. The contemporary soul-mate ideal originates in the idealism and egalitarianism of second-wave feminism, but it reinforces the idea that only through coupled love can one be truly fulfilled. For some women, at certain stages in their lives, the search for a soul mate—and refusing to settle for less—provides a rationale for their current singleness. But such a justification does not help them envision or find support for a long-term single life.

Since the soul-mate ideal is both a very high and quite vague standard, it can justify remaining single in one's twenties or putting off a permanent attachment to one's current partner. It seems suited to an era when the average age of marriage is twenty-five for women and twenty-seven for men; these figures are even higher for the college-educated.[12] In the summer of 2000, Sasha Cagen, a San Francisco writer in her late twenties, wrote an article about being a "quirkyalone"[13] in which she characterized herself and other "quirkyalones" as romantic women who would like to find soul mates but realistically think that this is unlikely. These women would rather remain uncoupled than compromise just to be married.[14]

Acceptance of the soul-mate ideal, however, leads to anxiety and despair among single women in their late twenties and early thirties who do not consider themselves *quirky* and do not want to be *alone*. Journalist Peggy Orenstein found that high-achieving young single women were terrified by the prospect of ending up middle-aged and single. Orenstein reported:

> When I ask the young, ambitious women I meet in the New York publishing firm—the ones who'd been so vocal about their myriad possibilities—how they would feel about being unmarried at forty, they look horrified. "That's just not an option," Leslie says with a little frisson. "Do we have to have this conversation?" Tracy says, grimacing. "I don't want to think about it." Abbey goes so far as to rap her knuckles against the table. "God forbid," she says, shaking her head. "God forbid."[15]

How did the soul-mate ideal affect the single women I studied who were over the age of thirty-five? Although only a few of the never-married and divorced women I interviewed in the mid-1990s used the term *soul mate,* many of them espoused an ideal similar to it.[16] Whether divorced or never married, these women looked for a deep bond. They wanted to find a "life partner," someone who really engaged them "mentally and emotionally."

Let me illustrate how two single women who participated in my study, one Latina and the other African American, articulated and used the soul-mate ideal as they moved from their late thirties into their midforties. Although one can find some differences from white women in their lives, I was struck by the similar themes in the stories of the white and nonwhite middle-class single women I interviewed.

Maria Cardoza: A Divorced Single Mother

I was immediately drawn to Maria Cardoza, an attractive, articulate, and bubbly Latina. Arriving for the group interview on a warm summer night in sandals and a simple blouse and skirt, her thick brown hair swinging loose, Maria still looked girlish at thirty-eight. She talked with intensity, using her hands to make a point.

This divorced single mother, who was born and raised in Puerto Rico, specified what she was looking for in a new partner. "I'm hopeful that I will meet somebody who could be a soul mate to me. He'll understand where I am, will walk in my shoes for a few miles, and I could do the same for him. I haven't lost hope, even though I don't meet many men about whom I can say: 'This person is together; this person had done some personal growth; he's looking at himself and his issues; he can be honest and not play games.'" I was surprised by Maria's explicit espousal of the soul-mate ideal. But I soon learned that she had been heavily involved for many years in the U.S. counterculture, both in Puerto Rico and after she came to the mainland.

By the time she was eighteen, Maria was a vegetarian and involved with Buddhism and yoga. For years she dreamed of leaving the island to pursue an alternative lifestyle in a more accepting environment. So in the late 1970s, the twenty-one-year-old Maria took the money she had saved, dropped out of her Puerto Rican college, and flew to Florida ready for travel and adventure. She soon ended up at a large communal farm in Tennessee. In this alternative community of more than a thousand people, Maria did some translation, worked with children in the school, and helped with the farm. Soon after, she left for a sister commune in Michigan where she picked organic apples. Maria reminisces: "It was really fun, we were just picking apples, smoking pot, and being young."

But Maria's attraction to this alternative lifestyle did not obliterate the religious values with which she was raised. At the age of twenty-five, Maria married her English boyfriend, a man she had met in the commune, because she wanted to have a baby. "I was raised as a Catholic girl, who needed to get married before being pregnant," she explained. Despite her adventuresome spirit, Maria yearned for the conventional family life she never had. Although she had reservations about her boyfriend, she knew he was stable and reliable (unlike her own father), and she loved his mother. Maria's decision to marry and start a family came after she and her boyfriend had spent eight months living with John's mother, helping her through radiation and chemotherapy treatments after her bout with cancer.

Maria thought her new husband was "kind of a sad person," but she believed she could "cheer him up." After they had the baby, when they were living alone for the first time, she woke up. "We didn't connect," she said. "We really didn't talk a lot about things. There was not this spirit there to share." After only three years of marriage, Maria left John when their son, Ethan, was two.

Maria picked up her "hippie" (in her words) lifestyle again in the 1980s, after her divorce. For several years she lived in a yoga center and then moved to a rural town in California. Maria worked at many jobs—as a house cleaner, carpenter, yoga teacher, home health aide, and preschool teacher. In her midthirties, however, she went on welfare for about eight months so she could go back to college full-time.

Earning a BA in psychology and a master's degree in social work marked Maria's move away from the counterculture, which for her always expressed personal and spiritual values. She never spoke about participating in any organized political activity and never referred to herself as a feminist. When she was twenty-eight, however, Maria decided to change her last name to her mother's maiden name. This was an expression of her anger at men but was also meant to assert that, as she said, "I'm my own person." Again, her choice implied a personal rather than a political value.

Maria's ability to define, redefine, and pursue her own goals depended on whether she could obtain help with raising her son. As she had foreseen, John proved to be a good father. Even after he moved to the East Coast to be with another woman, he kept up his relationship with Ethan. When Maria wanted to go to school full-time and was having trouble coping, John took the nine-year-old Ethan east to live with him for a year. He became even more involved during their son's troubled teenage years.

In 1995 John (now single again) accepted Maria's offer to move into her two-bedroom apartment and help raise their thirteen-year-old son. Maria and John made it clear to Ethan that they were not getting back together, and both dated others. Despite her preoccupation with her son, living with her ex-husband, and a demanding work and graduate school schedule, Maria yearned to be coupled again. But rather than desiring the traditional values that she articulated when marrying John, now she wanted a soul mate.

I found Maria again in 2002, still single at the age of forty-six. The woman I met at her office in the small social work agency where she worked looked different from her younger self. I could still recognize her face, her slim figure, and the gentle lilt in her voice. She greeted me warmly, but her style had changed. She wore makeup, and her hair was shorter and stylishly cut. Her attractive suit was adorned with a smart scarf, and heels had replaced the sandals. There was no trace of the erstwhile hippie.

Before our interview, I had sent Maria a transcript of what she had said eight years earlier. With an embarrassed smile, she immediately zeroed in on her comments about wanting to find a soul mate. She now thought that the soul-mate ideal was silly and overly romantic. "I'm done with that," she said. "I think that relationships need good chemistry, good rapport, and similar views, but they are a decision we make. I don't think anymore that love is something that happens. I think it is something that you work at. If there are enough of the qualities I am looking for, then both he and I have to make a decision—one that often involves compromise."

Maria wanted very much to find a marriage partner and refused to cohabit. She had advanced professionally and was financially secure. Her son, in his early twenties, had an independent life, and her ex-husband—still a friend—had remarried. An attractive woman in her midforties, Maria dated a lot, meeting men mainly through friends. She used these dates to "interview candidates"—using skills she had learned in her professional training. Maria had been dating one man for about five months and had high hopes for the relationship. He was her age, divorced, also an immigrant, professionally successful, and financially secure. Maria was relieved that he did not have, and did not want, children. He was nurturing and supportive of her spirituality. Rather than use the vague language of a soul mate to describe this man, Maria talked in much more concrete terms of why they were a good match.

The differences in Maria's aspirations in the two periods illustrate how the search for a soul mate provides a rationale to a single woman who desires to be coupled but whose situation precludes it. When she was seeking a soul mate, Maria was in no position to find a satisfying partner. She was the poor single mother of a difficult teenager, with a demanding schedule as she obtained the training to become a professional. She had experienced an unsatisfactory cohabitation with two different men; one of them did not accept her son, and the other turned out to be a "second child." She lived with her ex-husband, a situation that was not conducive to attracting a potential mate. Now that she was in a position where coupling was possible, she replaced the search for a soul mate with more specific and realistic goals.

Despite her clear preference to marry, Maria accepted the possibility that she might continue to be single. "If I don't find the right person for me," she said, "I'll remain single." Maria has work she likes, a family, good friends, hobbies, and a spiritual community, and she is saving money to buy a house. She has no trouble finding a sexual partner. But Maria cannot refer to a set of values that justifies her single life to her family and friends and, more important, to herself. She has nothing to replace the search for a soul mate to affirm single life.

Lanette Jones: A Single Career Woman

The search for a soul mate sustained a woman like Maria who wanted to couple but whose situation at the time made it unlikely that she would find a man. It also serves those who are happy with single life. Meet Lanette Jones. A petite, perky, and light-skinned African American woman, Lanette walked into a 1995 group interview organized by one of her former classmates in graduate school. At thirty-seven, she was only one year younger than Maria Cardoza and lived within one hundred miles of her. But as a never-married, professionally successful administrator with no children, Lanette had a very different life.

Lanette grew up in a middle-class, professional family in Los Angeles. Her parents divorced when she was seven, but unlike Maria, she maintained a solid relationship with her father, which continues to this day. Lanette is close to her two sisters and her mother, all of whom live nearby. She has a large extended family and friends all over the country. Lanette was not attracted to the counterculture; she was a cheerleader in high school and joined a sorority in college. Now, having completed her dual MBA and master's of public policy degree, she was heading for a job on the East Coast.

Although she is extroverted, attractive, and usually has a boyfriend, Lanette said she had never had a relationship that had lasted more than seven months. At that time Lanette did not hold to the soul-mate ideal. "Maybe I buy into this fairy tale of marriage," she said. "But I think about a partner as somebody who is going to be around; somebody whom I could talk to, somebody who I could do things with, who I could sleep with. Seeing my friends couple up makes me think I'd be missing out on something if I didn't end up with a partner." The imperative to couple—because all her friends were doing so—seemed more compelling for Lanette than an ideal that she recognized as probably "a fairy tale."

Lanette was dating only black men and preferred it that way. But she knew the dismal demographics documenting the dearth of equally credentialed black men for professionally successful African American women.[17] She quipped: "I always said that if I wasn't in a relationship by thirty-five, I'd start dating white men, and if I'm not coupled by forty, I'll start dating women." But neither seemed to be a real possibility.

I found Lanette more than seven years later, now forty-five and still single. She had recently moved back to the Bay Area for a high-powered executive position and to be closer to her family. Like Maria, her appearance had changed a lot since her graduate-school days. As I walked into her office, I barely recognized this elegantly dressed, confident woman. But she proved to be still open and friendly.

Lanette quickly gave me an update on her personal life during the intervening years. She dated a lot in the East, which led to a serious relationship with an African American man who was several years older and in the same profession. "He was a wonderful man," she said, "sensitive, romantic, and committed." Nor was he intimidated by her assertiveness. They lived five hundred miles apart when Lanette was in the East, with three thousand miles between them after she moved back to California. Lanette didn't mind the long-distance relationship: "You fly in, you fly out, you do your thing. You get more time and space, and you can postpone those levels of intimacy that would occur if someone is around all the time."

He wanted to get married. He was willing to relocate and to have children. But Lanette started to feel claustrophobic. She worried that she would always be more successful than he and make more money. She didn't want to take the responsibility of asking him to move to California. So she broke up with him. In justifying her decision, Lanette used language that invoked soul-mate rhetoric, although she did not use the term.

She "chose not to settle" because he was "not the one." In doing so, she realized that being married and having a family were not as important to her as being with "someone exciting with whom I can really connect." She told a friend: "I just want to have that feeling one more time before I die, whether the feeling turns into someone I spend fifty years with or not. I just want to be excited when that person walks into the room." When I asked if having these feelings was more important than a permanent relationship, she replied in the affirmative.

Lanette's responses demonstrate how, for a woman who prefers single life to settling down, the search for an idealized love helps rationalize her choice in a culture that idealizes couples and denigrates single people. By professing such a high, but vague, standard for love, and by justifying personal feelings as taking precedence over desires for family or marriage, Lanette can defend her singleness in order to keep looking for "the one."

Lanette admits that she likes her single life and does not hesitate to call herself single. Seven years ago she said that sometimes she was lonely. When I asked her if she would say that now, she replied no and began talking about "nesting" in her own home. She owns her house, loves her work, and has many friends, an active social life, and strong family ties.

Although she has not given up her desire to have children, Lynette still adamantly refuses to be a single mother. From an early age on, she recoiled at the denigration of black single mothers. Lanette admits now that having children is not her highest priority. She points with pride to the many pictures of friends' children on her desk. She does not say that relationships with any of them could take the place of having her own child (adopted or biological), but she says that she soon may have to consider how to make some of these children a more active part of her life.

Thus, Lanette at the age of forty-five seems to be the epitome of a successful single woman. I heard from another informant that shortly after this interview, Lanette moved to Southern California for a better job. In the fall of 2004, as this book was nearing completion, I was reading the newspaper one evening, casually perusing the personal portrait of a powerful person in the Bush administration, when I came across several quotes from Lanette. She had been interviewed because the high official was her mentor and friend. I was amazed. Lanette had said she had friends all over the United States but never mentioned ones of this political stature. Reading the article, however, reinforced my belief that I had interviewed an interesting and diverse group of single women, all broadly middle class but, as we will see, very different in their values, lifestyles, and politics.

Despite her career success, Lanette, within our current cultural context, can easily be branded as someone who must have problems with trust and intimacy. By one's midforties, one is supposed to have found a soul mate, and if not, to have settled for a good man, like the one Lanette rejected. To her credit, Lanette did not say anything negative about herself, and I found her to be a very happy and satisfied woman. But without any cultural legitimacy for her long-term single life, Lanette fears she will be alone in the future.

"I'm a total planner. I've already signed up for long-term care," Lanette told me. "But whenever I pick up the paper at Christmastime and see a story about an older woman who has no relatives, who needs a couple of hundred bucks so that her lights don't get turned off, I say to my mother, 'That's my fear. I'll be eighty-five years old and all my family and friends will have passed on, and because I have not partnered myself, I'll end up here.'" I wondered why she used the phrase "not partnered" rather than "childless." Probably because for Lanette they go together, and because a woman without a partner is more stigmatized than one without a child.

Feminism, Soul Mates, and Singleness

Where did the ideal of a soul mate come from? Do its origins help explain both its appeal and its limitations? In tracing the trajectory of ideas about single and coupled life from the mid-twentieth century on, I discovered that radical feminist writers whom I had read with admiration in the early 1970s articulated ideals similar to those of a soul mate.[18] In hindsight, I could still see the appeal of their critique of the power imbalance found in heterosexual love and the alternative they advocated: a more equal love relationship based on greater intimacy and sharing of feelings. But I also discovered that although most of these radical feminists were single, they had no vision for a single life.

In the late 1960s and early 1970s, many young women activists broke with their male comrades in the civil rights movement, the New Left, the antiwar movement, and the counterculture to form an independent women's liberation movement. Some of the most radical groups and individuals initially rejected heterosexuality and marriage and critiqued the family. Early participants in radical and socialist-feminist circles remember times when they felt embarrassed to be married or in a heterosexual relationship.[19] The alternative, however, was not to be single but to become a lesbian. But this rejection of heterosexuality and marriage was short-lived. It was countered quickly by other radical feminists who defended the reform of marriage initiated by more moderate feminists like Betty Friedan. By the early to mid-1970s, the egalitarian couple—whether heterosexual or lesbian—was highly valued by all feminists, but younger feminists stressed the emotional content of the relationship.

Shulamith Firestone, one of the most influential early radical feminist theorists, and initially one of those most critical of marriage, changed the dialogue from marriage to love.[20] Firestone's chapter on love, from her groundbreaking 1970 book, *The Dialectic of Sex*,[21] was reprinted in a popular pamphlet and succinctly laid out how heterosexual love could be "obstructed, distorted, or poisoned by an unequal balance of power."[22] But Firestone wanted to reform, not reject love. She foresaw the possibility of a healthy love based on "an exchange of selves" when women and men were truly equals. "Love between two equals could be an enrichment, each enlarging himself through the other.... [Each] could participate in the existence of another—an extra window on the world."[23]

Firestone's view of love did not emphasize sexuality, and her vision of the perfect couple did not extend to a consideration of any alternatives if the woman did not find such a man. Firestone's belief in the possibility of such an equal and ideal love is in sharp contrast to her disparagement of the life of single women whom she saw as exploited by a sexual revolution for men.[24] Single women were "consigned forever to the limbo of 'chicks'... [or to being] the 'other woman' for the rest of one's life, used to provoke his wife, prove his virility and/or independence, discussed by his friends as his latest 'interesting' conquest."[25]

Another book, *Combat in the Erogenous Zone*, published in 1972 and written by Ingrid Bengis, a twenty-six-year-old woman with no formal connection to feminist groups, went beyond Firestone in articulating an ideal even more similar to the contemporary notion of a soul mate. *Combat* was embraced by feminists, but it also reached a wider audience and was reprinted as late as 1991. Bengis sought authenticity in sex and love. She wanted "someone who would be lover, friend, confidant, companion, mentor and advocate, someone with whom making love would be an act of transcendent beauty."[26] Bengis spelled out what this would mean in practice:

> We wanted love that was intense but not consuming. We wanted to be cared for, thought of, and valued, not abstractly, as men often value women, but in the accumulation of daily minutiae that make life dense and intricate and worthy of infinite consideration. We were seeking in men what we were seeking in ourselves, a combination of strength, diversity, commitment, passion and sensitivity, seeking an equivalent humanity.[27]

Although Bengis recognized the difficulties of meeting her ideal, she refused to compromise. She asked: "How can I possibly compromise on things like warmth, communication, a passionate sense of life, a healthy capacity for commitment to the requirements of intimacy as well as to an outside purpose?"[28]

Bengis, however, recounted many negative experiences with men in which she felt exploited. Rather than writing about power differences between women and men and how such inequality distorts love, Bengis discussed how changes in social norms, and the disparity between her own ideals and her experience, led to conflicts in herself and to insecurity.

> I cannot be the completely feminine woman of the fifties, the emancipated, sexually free woman of the sixties, and the militant, anti-sexist woman of the seventies.... The woman I've continued to be is a contradictory and uncertain human being. Believing in love, I am also terrified of it. Believing in stability, I live a thoroughly unstable life. Believing in marriage, I have never risked it.... I long for liberation and don't know what it is. I hate when I would prefer to love, and love when I would prefer to hate.[29]

Despite her idealism, her unwillingness to compromise, and her personal conflicts, Bengis never envisioned herself remaining single.

She too wanted to combine marriage, children, and work.[30] In an introduction to a new edition of *Combat* written almost twenty years later, we learn that Bengis has not had children, has experienced long periods of celibacy, and has become a "reasonably independent woman." She admits that this is not how she thought she would end up.

> [U]ntil I was almost forty, I believed despite that fact that all the evidence of my life seemed to mitigate against it, that any day now I would find myself in a house with a wonderful husband and five children and we would all sit around the dining room eating the bountiful meals which I had just prepared from scratch for an extended family consisting of aunts, uncles, parents, and assorted friends who congregated to talk about life in the manner of characters in a Chekhov play.[31]

Although neither Firestone nor Bengis could link her idealism about love to the possibility of remaining single, other women did use an ideal of egalitarian love as a reason to leave their marriages. Joyce O'Brien (a pseudonym for a woman who began attending women's liberation consciousness-raising groups in 1968), started a 1970s article with the sentence "Two years ago, married and with a young child, I fell in love with another man." In her article, titled "In Favor of True Love over Settling," O'Brien wrote about her decision to leave her husband, even though she knew her lover did not want a permanent relationship. Her mother, she learned, gave up love to settle for a marriage; O'Brien decided to give up her marriage in order to look for love. O'Brien, like many other women who divorced in the 1970s, was optimistic. But many of these women were surprised in the 1980s to find themselves still single in their late thirties. Susan Bakos, herself divorced, titled her best-selling 1985 book about their predicament *This Wasn't Supposed to Happen.*[32]

Feminists in the vanguard of changing norms in the 1970s did not connect their commitment to finding an idealized love—their belief that they did not have to settle—to an increase in the probability that they would remain single. Today, young women may be just as unaware of this connection. But any attachment to this cultural ideal also means that women who are well into midlife may continue to search for a soul mate, with harmful results, I believe, for their well-being. Psychologist Karen Lewis, who is single, articulates some of the personal costs of a culture that values the couple above all other intimate connections: "At no point do single women know for sure that they will never marry. The ambiguity always leaves room for hope: Maybe the right man will come along during the next week or next month, on the next vacation, at the next business meeting, during the next walk with the dog. And as long as there is hope, there is the pain of ambiguity."[33]

Because romantic love plays such a central role in contemporary culture, moving beyond the soul-mate ideal as the standard for personal happiness necessitates developing an alternative vision.

An Alternative View of Intimacy

Our modern Western ideal of intimacy goes beyond sharing physical space, beyond the familiarity of living and sleeping together, and it means more than being in a primary relationship as a wife or significant other.[34] Intimacy is different from the bodily contact involved in sexual exploration. Rather, intimacy now necessitates mutual disclosure, sharing your feelings, revealing your inner thoughts. To be intimate is to have a deep knowledge and understanding of, as well as empathy with, another person.[35] Such psychological intimacy is central to the soul-mate ideal, but how intimacy is linked to sexual expression is more problematic.

Today *a relationship* still means a sexual couple. When we ask someone if they are in a relationship, we do not mean do they have friends, family, kin, neighbors, or colleagues. Psychologist Celia Kitzinger found that in the lesbian community too "the question, 'Are you in a relationship with her?' means 'Do you have a sexual relationship with her?'—as though only 'sex' makes a relationship real or worth commenting upon."[36] But such a relationship does not necessarily meet our ideal of intimacy.

The main complaint of married or coupled women—according to the findings in my study, validated by hundreds of others—is that their partner (usually a male) is "not talking, not listening, not 'showing their emotions,' not caring, not taking an interest."[37] In extreme cases, this means that long-term spouses can be strangers to each other.[38] Conversely, social scientists find that women in good marriages see their spouse not as a soul mate but as their best friend. Friendship is seen as the key to a happy, lasting relationship.[39] Other studies show how married women in less than ideal marriages use female friends to compensate for the lack of emotional intimacy in their marriages.[40]

If friendship is the model for intimacy in marriage, or a compensation when the marriage is not very intimate, why can't friendship provide intimacy to those who are not coupled? Although friendship does not have the cultural cachet of romance or a soul mate, we do recognize intimacy as the essence of contemporary friendship and friendship as a major source of intimacy.[41] "What we seem to want from close friends is an opportunity to bond emotionally," writes Laura Pappano, "to share deep personal issues and have someone to listen and empathize with our daily traumas.... It is this desire for emotional connection that surfaces again and again in research on friendship."[42]

Many people experience their most successful and lasting intimacy with a friend, not with a soul mate, although once in a while the term *soul mate* is used as the ideal for a true friend.[43] A soul-mate attraction between two women friends, however, is often a fragile bond—fragile because "they're so dependent on the sense of the other as a second self," notes Sandy Sheehy. "Any significant difference carries the destructive power of a major disillusionment."[44] But in most cases, intimate friends are less merged than soul mates, with more boundaries and more room for the interplay of similarities and differences. It is easier to integrate autonomy and intimacy with a friend than with a soul mate.

Subsequent chapters give many examples of the importance of friendship and of networks of friends in the lives of single women. Psychologist Stephanie Dowrick expresses the psychological benefits of freeing up our ideal of intimacy so that it can incorporate more people.

> [K]nowing that you are not dependent on one crucial other to bring intimacy into your life can be a tremendous relief. It can diminish self-judgement and self-blame. It can allow life to be lived first-hand, rather than endured in a waiting pattern. . . . The world is filled with people, none of whom may be that special someone, but many of whom may share with you an enduring feeling that you matter, and that their being with you does, in some significant way, also matter. This can allow a life not shadowed by myths and longing for what might never happen, but shaped instead by less ambitious pleasure in what is.[45]

To recognize that their lives are full of intimacy, however, single women today *individually* have to reject the romantic ideal of finding a soul mate. This is not an easy process, as we will see in subsequent chapters. How do some single women come to reject the idea that they need to be coupled in order to have intimacy? What process do they go through to move beyond the point reached by Maria and Lanette toward an acceptance of the possibility that they may be single for the rest of their lives? What permits them to feel happy with this prospect?

Acknowledging the intimacy that we have with friends still leaves open the question of how single women will meet their sexual needs. Maintaining a satisfying sex life in middle age is a problem for all women, but single women have no cultural guidelines for sexual satisfaction outside a stable relationship or for how to live with celibacy.

CHAPTER 2

Sex and the Single Woman

> There are few narratives, stories, or myths to describe the
> variety of modes of sexual expression in singlehood.
> *The Sexual Organization of the City*

"Provocative title, but what you find will not be," said a friend when I told her about this chapter.[1] "You'll find sexually frustrated middle-aged women, angry because men their age attract younger women." But she was wrong—incorrect that one response would predominate and that I'd find that most midlife single women are sexually frustrated. I was surprised by the variety of responses I received to my question about the importance of sex in single women's lives. A forty-year-old woman said that sex was "overrated," whereas a woman in her late fifties said sex was "really important," something she needed in her life. Women for whom sex was a priority almost always found it. Love, not sex, I discovered, is the elusive entity.

My friend might better have said: "A provocative topic, but women don't talk to other women about sex; we talk to each other about relationships, and about sex, if at all, only to a sexual partner." Most of the women in my study spoke openly about relationships but did not give much detail about their sex lives. However, Myra Detweiler and Dorothy Sawyer, two women I portray later, talked more concretely about sexuality. Myra and Dorothy were willing to engage in sex without romantic expectations of permanence, but they were neither completely casual about sex nor interested in one-night stands. These single women could pursue sex without the illusion that they had found a soul mate, but they still sought relationships that involved sharing interests, activities, and friendship.

But many single women do not identify with Myra and Dorothy, for they are clearer and less conflicted about sex than most women—whether coupled or single—and willing to negotiate a sex life independent of their desires for intimacy and a partnership. I see their sexuality as a challenge to us—not as a model to be emulated, but as a probe to think about and define our own sexual desires.

The reluctance of women to talk about sex stems, I believe, from multiple sources, but an important one is our personal confusion about sexual desire and its connection to intimacy and partnership. How do we decide what we want physically? How do we decide if what we desire is morally acceptable and psychologically healthy? What if our physical desire is not satisfied in a relationship that provides the intimacy we crave? What if we are sexually attracted to someone who does not possess the qualities we desire in a marriage or cohabiting partner?

If women find it difficult to talk about their physical desires, they are even more confused by and reluctant to talk about a lack of desire. The sexual revolution of the mid- to late twentieth century recognized women's sexual energy as distinct from but equal to men's. This revolution, however, did not probe the wide individual variability in sexual desire and expression. Celibacy, which is traditionally valued by religious groups and accepted as natural in puritanical cultures, now came to be seen as unhealthy and shameful. Until very recently, neither feminists nor sexual libertarians viewed celibacy as part of the sexual spectrum, leaving it to mean only intentional, moral, or religious asexuality. As a result, few women embrace the term *celibate*. Few discuss it either as a situational condition that can change or as a state that can be experienced in sensual or positive ways.

As someone who has had an active sex life in her twenties and thirties but has been celibate for more than twenty years, I felt it incumbent to address the issue of celibacy—relevant for many women in my study but hard for them to discuss. One woman, Nancy Dean, had a particularly creative way to embody her sensuality without being sexually involved with a partner—an expression that opens new ways of thinking about celibacy.

My study, therefore, led me to focus on two types of sexual experience for single women—a celibate but still sensual life and sexual relationships without the need for permanence or deep intimacy. Neither conforms to the cultural norm linking women's sexuality with romantic love or to the empirical finding that the majority of women and men prefer sex in the context of love, attachment, or commitment.[2] But both celibacy and a plurality of sexual partners are more characteristic of single than married or coupled women.

The renowned 1990s survey *Sex in America* found that almost one-third of noncohabiting women between the ages of eighteen and sixty had no sexual partners during the previous twelve months —higher than any other group as measured by gender, age, marital/residential status, education, religion, race, and ethnicity.[3] More recent surveys of single, noncohabiting people over the age of forty found an even higher percentage of celibate women.[4] Surveys also reveal that the never married and divorced have more sex partners over their lifetime than do married people.[5] The researchers for *Sex in America* concluded that single people "have more partners, but they have less sex."[6]

Women's sexuality, I believe, is very individualized. Their unique sexuality has a biological component but is also shaped by how women incorporate cultural ideas about sex.[7] An individual's sexual choices result from a complex interaction of biology, cultural norms, and the social networks and institutions in which she participates.[8] During the second half of the twentieth century, cultural norms about sexuality and institutions (marriage) that previously had controlled sex were especially contested and in flux. The sexual revolution of the mid-twentieth century began with a more positive attitude toward premarital sex for young single women, a shift that set the stage for twenty-first-century alterations in our views about sex and mature single women.

Beyond *Sex and the Single Girl*

Sex and the Single Girl became a best seller in 1962. Helen Gurley Brown, the thirty-seven-year-old author (soon to become the long-term editor of *Cosmopolitan*), declared that "a sexy woman is a woman who enjoys sex." Not only did Brown seek to break down the sexual double standard between women and men, but she challenged the stereotype of the achieving single woman as unattractive and uptight. Brown proclaimed that "career girls are sexy." "A man likes to sleep with a brainy girl," she wrote.[9] In a breezy, forthright, and pragmatic style, *Sex and the Single Girl* advocated not just pre-marital sex with the one you were planning to marry but casual sex —a number of sexual affairs—for the working single woman. Frigidity and lack of orgasm, rather than promiscuity, were the evils that Brown sought to combat.

Some historians consider this book the epitome of the sexual revolution of the 1960s—one characterized foremost by the public legitimation of premarital sex for women, a cultural change facilitated by the introduction of the birth control pill in 1960 and consolidated by the 1973 Supreme Court decision in *Roe vs. Wade,* which legalized abortion.[10] This revolution, writes historian David Allyn, although not terminating the sexual exploitation of women, "paved the way for a new era of personal autonomy, sexual self-expression and freedom from fear. At long last, a woman could, like a man, maximize her opportunities for sexual satisfaction."[11]

But Brown's message was not the only one coming out of the 1960s. Her idea of sexual liberation was contrary to early second-wave feminist doctrines that emphasized egalitarian love, rather than sex alone. Sexual intercourse was a way to communicate love, sanctioned only within a monogamous relationship.[12] Monogamy, however, could be premarital and serial. As we have seen in chapter 1, this ideal of love evolved into the soul-mate norm of today. Brown said little about love, but her legitimation of casual sex for single women created an alternative norm that still exists and is embodied in the popular HBO TV series *Sex and the City.*

But what is the legacy of *Sex and the Single Girl* and its successor *Sex and the City* for single women over forty? I think the message is positive but limited. Brown helped legitimize single women's claim to individual fulfillment, rather than seeing family life as the only site for women's satisfaction. That one can be successful and sexual helps middle-aged single women defy the old notion of spinsterhood. *Brainy* and *sexy* are no longer incompatible attributes for a woman. Brown, however, put more emphasis on a single woman's use of sex appeal to further other goals (career or marriage) rather than as a source of pleasure in itself. A single woman's "body becomes her primary capital, her resources," notes Hilary Radner. "She must subject herself to consumer culture and the codes of femininity as defined by heterosexuality (she must be a *girl,* pretty, sexy, perky and subservient)."[13] This subservience is seen in the very term *girl*.

Sexual Relationships

Today, our culture is obsessed and saturated with sexuality. We are bombarded with images and discussion of sex outside marriage for those between fifteen and thirty-five, about extramarital sex, and even about sex after sixty-five. There is surprisingly little discussion, however, about the sexuality of those between forty and sixty-five who are not part of a sexually active couple. We hear a lot about sexually nonmonogamous single women in their thirties (for example, in *Sex and the City*) but very little about such women in their fifties. Books written about sex and the single middle-aged woman do not become best sellers and are not widely discussed. I was surprised, for example, when a friend told me that Helen Gurley Brown wrote a book in the 1990s about older women. I had never heard of *The Late Show,* which includes a long chapter on sexual issues for women over the age of fifty.[14]

In my study I found some women in their forties and fifties who pursued sexual relationships involving shared interests, activities, and friendship but without the necessity of permanence or deep intimacy. I look at the lives of two of these women, Myra Detweiler and Dorothy Sawyer, both of whom stated explicitly that sexuality was very important in their lives. Myra was in love relationships (a husband and later an affair with a married man) that did not meet her sexual and all of her emotional needs. A sexual friendship that lasted fifteen years helped her maintain her autonomy and develop a stronger sense of self. Dorothy, after two failed marriages—the second one was a love match—opened herself to sexual relationships without the expectation of marriage or deep love. Such sexual openness helped her accept with equanimity the end of a serious relationship and to come to terms with the prospect of being permanently single.

Sexual Expression as a Route to Autonomy and Personal Strength

I knew that Myra Detweiler still lived in the area, for I spotted her several times over the years at public events. When I called her in May 2003, I was surprised to hear her upbeat response. "I'd love to talk to you again," she replied. "There has been a big change in my life." The last time I had talked to Myra—six years earlier, in 1997 —she was recovering from a debilitating stroke that almost ended her career. At our first interview, in 1994, Myra had been divorced for five years, but she was still emotionally entangled with her ex-husband, a man ten years her senior with whom she cohabited for nine years, followed by nine years of marriage. When Myra was six, her alcoholic father left her, and she grew up in poverty with a single mother—sometimes on welfare. She had endured a hard life, one that accounted for, I concluded, at least some of her sadness.

So what was the source of her new buoyancy? I would not have guessed that Myra was celebrating her ability to leave two long-term sexual liaisons, since she had not mentioned these affairs in earlier interviews. At fifty-two, she was dating for the first time in almost thirty years. Myra, who considered herself "over the hill," loved the attention. With her slim figure, curly black hair, and rather plain face, she was attractive, but certainly not stunning. Yet through her community and volunteer work, and through friends, she found four men to date at the same time, turning away two others. She proudly told me that the men varied in age from forty-four to fifty-nine and were of different body types, races, nationalities, and occupations. For Myra, dating meant not being sexually involved, which for a while felt liberating to her, as she more carefully assessed not just each man's physical appeal but also his potential to sustain a healthy mutual relationship. After a few months, however, she settled on one man for an exclusive relationship that would include sex but not co-habitation or a long-term commitment.

But how had Myra arrived at this positive place despite a bad marriage, the difficulties of raising her teenage son after the divorce, physical illness, and much unhappiness? Recounting her childhood, Myra revealed the scars left by poverty and her father's abandonment. But she also disclosed her early resiliency, of which a positive sexuality was an integral part.

Of German origin, Myra grew up in the West. The family moved frequently to escape bill collectors. Her father had irregular employment, for "he was an alcoholic with sexual and gambling addictions," Myra explained. She remembered a lot of fighting and chaos. Her father was always leaving; then, after a couple of months, he would send for Myra and her mother to join him in a new place. She remembered a truck stop in the Idaho wilderness where her dad pumped gas and her mother worked in the gift shop. Always employed, her mother held on to the marriage until Myra was six. Then she planted herself in a central California town and refused to follow her husband. He never sent any child support, and Myra saw him only one more time.

Myra and her mother lived in subsidized housing on the edge of town without a car and with no bus service. Forty-eight years old, her mother walked across town to and from work as a maid. Eventually she bought a car, but they were still poor. Myra remembers children at her school laughing at her patched clothes and worn

shoes. Once, suffering from a toothache, she cried herself to sleep because there was no money for a dentist. But her mother did not
drink, smoke, or have a relationship with a man, and she was devoted
to Myra. "Once, my mother left work and drove all the way from
downtown on her half-hour lunch break to my elementary school
because my class was singing in the school assembly," Myra recalled.
"I thought I'd be the only kid who didn't have parents there. She
drove all that way in her uniform, watched me sing, and drove all the
way back, giving up her lunch. It was clear that she would do anything for me and that she loved me very much. That did sustain me."

To help make ends meet, Myra started babysitting, mowing
lawns, and delivering newspapers when she was twelve. Myra said
that her poverty left her feeling inferior, but as early as fourteen she
started to move up in the world. She loved school and soon was on
a college track in a special program for gifted students. Her mother,
with only a grade-school education, could not help Myra with her
homework but urged her to work hard. Although Myra wanted to go
to college and obtain better jobs than her mother's, she dreamed of
falling in love and marrying someone rich enough so that she would
"never have to live in fear of hunger and homelessness."

Myra started her first relationship at fourteen, which lasted until
she was twenty-one. Her boyfriend introduced her to the educated
upper middle class. His parents, the Andersons, were Oberlin graduates, the father a teacher and playwright and the mother an aspiring
novelist. They were sixties bohemians at the center of a community
of writers and artists. The Andersons took Myra into their family,
which included a brother and a sister; she would eat with them, go
camping, and enjoy the intellectual stimulation of their household.
They also helped her prepare for college, advising her as to what
high school classes to take, how to apply for scholarships, and so on.
They always included her mother on holidays and special occasions
despite the cultural differences. "They were charming to her, they
didn't put her down, or talk negatively about her," Myra remembered. Because of this, Myra's mother often let her spend the night
at the Andersons', not suspecting that she and her boyfriend slept to-

gether, or that when Myra was fifteen, Mrs. Anderson took her to get birth-control pills. Although she was sexually open, Myra passionately believed in monogamy.

The summer before they went off to the same state college, Myra and her boyfriend decided to live together. Myra knew her "straight-laced" mother would disapprove. So Myra moved out of the house while her mother was away for a few days visiting relatives. Despite the ensuing tension, Myra's mother remained proud of her educational accomplishments, and they retained their close relationship until her mother's death a few years later.

Myra broke up with her boyfriend during their senior year in college because she saw him as self-centered, unambitious, and lazy. She always worked to support the household, but he was often unemployed because he "didn't want to take a grunt job which he considered beneath him," Myra explained. After she left him, Myra immediately began a new relationship with another man, but one who "wasn't really sexually compatible." So after graduation, she moved to the Bay Area.

Myra's sexual precociousness never undermined her autonomy or her ambition, as it does for some young women. Born in 1950 and coming of age in the 1960s, Myra benefited from the change in cultural attitudes, and the introduction of the birth-control pill alleviated the fear of pregnancy. But the legacy of her poverty and of her father's absence led her into a deleterious relationship.

At a San Francisco dance club, Myra, then aged twenty-two, met Jack Dean, a thirty-two-year-old divorced man with two children aged four and eight. Myra was attracted to him for multiple reasons. "A very stable, hardworking, physically robust, protect-you kind of guy," Jack was also "an absolutely devoted father to his two young children," Myra explained. Because his wife had been unfaithful, Jack said he would always be faithful. "A man who won't have affairs," Myra exclaimed. "God, he is not like my father!"

Within a year, Myra moved in with Jack but found that life was less idyllic than she had envisioned. Jack's ex-wife made things difficult for them once she found out he was with Myra. Because of Jack's hefty alimony and child support payments, Myra and Jack had to live frugally. Myra always worked to pay for her half of their living expenses, but without more education, she often found herself in boring, low-paying jobs. Jack did not want to remarry, and Myra's place in his family was difficult and problematic. His parents resented her, as did his children. Although Jack was a good father, he was not emotionally open with Myra.

Eight years into the relationship, Myra found herself pregnant. Jack wanted her to have an abortion; Myra, now thirty, wanted to keep the baby, but remembering the struggles of her own mother, she could not face becoming a single, "unwed" mother. Myra did find the courage, however, to give Jack an ultimatum, and he reluctantly agreed to marry her. The following month, Jack and Myra got married in a small chapel in the wine country. Myra thought their marriage had a chance and that they could make it work.

Shortly after the baby was born, however, Jack started an affair, which he revealed to Myra. Devastated, Myra felt trapped. "I stayed because I did not have the money or the courage to leave," said Myra, "nor the wherewithal to support myself and my child without going on welfare. I could not relive some of my childhood; it was a bleak time for me." But Myra soon entered graduate school to become a marriage and family therapy counselor. This education led her to do some "heavy-duty therapy" on herself. "I learned how enmeshed my husband and I were," Myra explained. "We both had difficult childhoods and bonded very tightly; we probably had the deepest relationship each of us will ever have with anyone." Myra now saw the neurotic aspects of the relationship and began the "incredibly painful" and slow process of separating from Jack.

Myra's self-esteem was at an all-time low, and still she couldn't leave, but, fighting depression, she decided to have another relationship too. She still believed in monogamy and took this step out of desperation. She started an affair with a man who was even older than her husband, a man for whom she had a lot of affection, who was kind to her, and with whom she had good sex, but who ultimately was not a soul mate. This open marriage—with Jack involved with a much younger woman and Myra with an older man—lasted for six years. Myra did not think it was healthy, but it gave her some leverage. Jack, however, resenting her relationship, became verbally abusive.

With her graduate degree and a good, if not particularly lucrative, job, Myra finally moved out. As she expected, Jack was bitter and could afford a much better lawyer. Myra got little in the divorce settlement. But Jack, unlike her father, paid child support and did not abandon their son. They shared custody successfully.

After the divorce, Myra tried to cohabit with her boyfriend, Bart, in a communal household in the country. This was not a good arrangement for her ten-year-old son, however, for he was too far away from his father and Bart was not very good with kids. So Myra moved into a small condominium that was ten miles away from Jack, which she bought with the divorce settlement. She found a good position as a therapist in a county agency and began to build a small private practice.

Myra continued her sexual relationship and friendship with Bart, but neither of them had a commitment to monogamy. And Myra did not expect him to relate to her son. Bart lived in another town, coming to Myra's condo on weekends. For Myra, great sex was the most important component of the relationship.

About four years after the divorce, Myra fell in love with James, a married man she had known as a friend for some years. Myra found that her feelings were reciprocated and started what turned out to be a ten-year affair with a younger man with several small children. Myra thought she was the last person in the world to have such an affair. "He had a good marriage," Myra told me, "and he never misled me. We both felt it was an unfortunate miracle that we felt this way. I really do consider him my soul mate." Myra explained what she got out of the affair:

> Even though I don't want to romanticize it, that relationship was the healthiest I've ever had. Clearly, it also involved grief, pain, and longing for something that will not be. Yet, it was the first time someone really loved me for me, seeing my foibles, my shortcom-

ings, and seeing me make mistakes. He just continued to be loving in a consistent, caring, and mature way—to be more nurturing than any other man I've ever known. We were both astounded that our feelings for each other didn't seem to fade.

Although Myra and James saw each other about once a week, they did not have frequent sexual encounters. In one of the early interviews, Myra said that she had never been happy without a sexual relationship. "It is the way that people bond, "she said, "and a path to spirituality." But in a relationship with a soul mate, Myra, like others I discussed in chapter 1, did not make sex a priority.[15] Moreover, the ground rules were always that James's wife and children would be protected absolutely. "We got through it without destroying innocent lives," Myra said, "because one of us was always strong; when one wasn't, the other was." Myra never told anyone about the affair. Her sexual friendship with Bart, I believe, facilitated this contained love affair and prevented Myra from losing herself or becoming enmeshed as she had been with her husband.

Two years before my last interview with her, Myra ended the long sexual friendship with Bart, and a year later she terminated her affair with James, the married man. In both cases, Myra took the initiative and ended the relationships without hard feelings. Now that her son was grown, and with her improved physical and mental health, Myra decided to look for a relationship that did not have the limitations of either of these two. Her decision was facilitated by the work she did to establish a good community life. She became active in her church, in the Sierra Club, and in Amnesty International, as well as volunteering in a community garden and in an adult literacy program. Through these organizations, she made a lot of new friends. "I believe that my reaching out makes it more possible to meet someone, but also that my life is good if I don't meet anyone," Myra concluded. "To have a healthy relationship, you have to have an absence of fear of what will happen if it doesn't work." Hence her current ability to date. Myra isn't looking for a soul mate but wants a healthy intimacy and sexual pleasure. She'd like to cohabit again but knows she will be fine as a single person. "I'm proud of who I am; I like who I am," Myra concluded. "It would be really nice to have a partner. But I insist on someone who is going to be really supportive of me and capable of emotional intimacy."

Myra, unlike the celibate women in my study, initiated the topic of her sex drive and the effects of menopause on her. "I've changed a lot sexually; my sex drive plummeted when I went through menopause," Myra volunteered. "Before, I think I had a really high sex drive, probably unusual for a woman. Maybe I'm now average for my age. But to me it's alarming. I'm at the point of seeking medical advice."[16]

Myra's unconventional sex and love life did not interfere with her desire to be a good mother. Although she often felt guilty for taking time away from her son, she also felt that she needed some time for herself to be an effective parent. Myra and Jack cooperated in dealing with their son's difficult adolescence, his problems at school and experimentation with drugs and alcohol. "It forced his dad and me into a much closer relationship than we would have had otherwise," Myra observed. Jack and Myra are now friends, meeting each other for dinner and even for an evening out now and then. Although there was too much hurt for Myra to ever consider getting back together with Jack, he is now family for Myra and their twenty-year-old son. The son still lives with Myra but has a steady job and a girlfriend and is a caring adult.

However one feels about the morality and advisability of non-monogamy, affairs between a single person and a married one, and secrecy or openness about such practices, Myra's ability to have separate relationships—one with James primarily for intimacy, one with Bart for sex, and a third one with her ex-husband for family—facilitated her growth as a satisfied single woman. Regardless of whether she succeeds in her current search for a relationship combining sex and intimacy, Myra has constructed all the supports for a satisfying single life. From one of the unhappiest single women in my initial interviews, Myra grew into one of the most contented at the end of my study. Her ability to own, act on, and channel her sexual desires is, I believe, a key factor.

Sexual Relationships as an
Integral Part of Single Life

Dorothy Sawyer walked into the room looking extremely fit and younger than she had looked when I first met her eight years previously (she was now in her late fifties). When Dorothy was forty-nine, she dyed her hair and wore a lot of makeup; but now her attractive face and short haircut looked more natural, and her slim figure radiated self-confidence and security. In response to the question of what had changed in her life, Dorothy's first reply was that she had added a new sport—competitive sailboat racing—to the hiking and gym work she continued to enjoy. This emphasis on physical activity indicated the priority she gave to bodily pleasure—one that, in her case, led to an active sex life.

Dorothy has been divorced (for the second time) for thirteen years. During these years, she told me, she had averaged about one affair a year; she had had more sexual partners in midlife than any other woman in my study admitted. Since one of Dorothy's relationships lasted two years, and twice she was celibate for a year or more, some years she had more than one partner. Aside from a few mistakes —one man was mentally unbalanced, and once during the Christmas season she had sex with a man just because she was feeling blue —Dorothy never had sex with someone to whom she could not relate. Nor did she have affairs with married men. Dorothy did not define her sexual relationships as casual, but being in love, or feeling love, was not a criterion for starting a sexual coupling. Even though her life and values are different from my own, I came to admire Dorothy's ability to find available men and the equanimity with which she accepted the limitations and termination of these relationships.

Dorothy is not a radical or a bohemian. Raised in a conservative, upper-middle-class nuclear family in the South—her father was a dentist and her mother a homemaker—Dorothy, at the age of twenty-two and working as a stewardess after college, married the first man she slept with. The marriage lasted only five years. Dorothy explained: "I was not in love with that man, nor did I have a concept of what love was; I was very immature. Marriage was just something one did. A woman's goal was to catch a man, kind of like going fishing. You *caught* one who supposedly would take care of you in a good style. But neither of us had any ability to communicate."

Dorothy's second marriage—from the age of thirty-five to forty-five—was much more serious. She married a divorced man she loved; they had a lot in common and good communication. But physically and temperamentally, they did not mesh. He had severe sleep problems, was often depressed, and had a troubled relationship with his teenage son. He didn't have much money and moved into Dorothy's house. Soon he began to withdraw emotionally and sexually. "I felt very deprived physically, with him sleeping in the other bedroom because of his terrible sleep problems," Dorothy recalled. "I felt unloved. I suffered a lot because I did love him. But I was very lonely, and for a long time not assertive enough to speak out." After trying marriage counseling for five years, and even sex counseling, Dorothy asked him to leave. As in her first marriage, she took the initiative to end the relationship, even though she felt a huge sense of failure.

After the divorce, Dorothy flourished, feeling relief and a jolt of happiness. She continued "to work" on herself, doing more therapy, joining a women's group, and reading self-help books. During the first interview, when she had been divorced for almost five years, Dorothy reported that she felt she had made a lot of progress. "I'm a lot more assertive now and I communicate a lot better. I take more risks; I put my needs out there. I've reclaimed my power," she concluded.

Dorothy never wanted to have children, so this was not an issue for her. She remembers her mother continually complaining about how difficult it was to be a mother and what a terrible toll it took on her, despite having financial security, being a full-time homemaker, and having household help. "I think my not wanting kids is directly related to my mother's unhappiness in her role as a mother," Dorothy said. "I got the message of what a burden that would be, an impossible situation, and that one can't be happy if one has children."

In the interval between the two interviews, Dorothy, for reasons she would not discuss, broke off her relationship to her parents, declining to communicate with them or see them after they refused to go to a counseling session with her. Although she is close to her sister, and for many years has had a relationship with her sister's husband and their two grown children, Dorothy lacks two of the criteria I identify for becoming a satisfied single woman—a strong family connection and a relationship to the next generation. Certainly this lack partly explained Dorothy's desire in her forties "to find a really wonderful relationship with a man, a wonderful supportive relationship." She didn't care about remarriage, but she wanted to live with someone again if she could find a good relationship. "And I like sex, and so I miss not having that," Dorothy concluded.

But eight years later, not having found such a relationship, Dorothy was more sanguine about the prospect of remaining single. Finding a partner "is still my first choice," Dorothy said, "but it would have to be something much more than I've ever had before, someone who enhances my life. I've come to the realization that I may not find the right person, and I need to go on with my life and do the things I like to do. I'd much rather be myself than deal with a man with a mountain of garbage. I have a really good life. It would be nice to have someone around some of the time, but I've gotten set in my ways and I love my private time; I really need it." What was the quality of Dorothy's life? Had she really overcome the legacy of an unhappy childhood and unsupportive parents?

Dorothy owns her own home. Between the interviews, she sold an older house in the city that needed too much upkeep and bought a smaller, newer one in the suburbs. The commute to her job is about the same length and is prettier. The new house is closer to good hiking trails; she now has a dog and more of a neighborhood and community. "I'm happy out here," Dorothy concluded. "I call the house my 'old ladies' house,' because I can drive into the garage and it's all on one floor. I'm trying to pay it off so I'll have a place to live when I get old."

Working for many years with a research institute connected to the University of California, Dorothy started as a secretary and worked her way up to her current position as a program manager. Although her salary comes from the university, she has to raise grant money and is in charge of all the public promotion of the research—maintaining a Web site and editing books and pamphlets that publicize the research results. She likes the work and the small office, which has only ten people. Her only complaint is the relatively low salary she receives. Still, she is self-supporting and is proud that she has never depended financially on anybody, even when she was married. She wants to stay within the university system because of the benefits and pension and has yet to find a better-paying job. Although she works hard, she doesn't take her job home and has time for the outdoor life she loves.

Like most of the other satisfied single women in my study, Dorothy has a network of good friends. Her friends are single; some have never been married and others are divorced. Most are women, and a few are men with whom she was never involved sexually or romantically. Some of these friends have gotten to know each other, and Dorothy considers them her extended family. She always gets invitations for the holidays and often throws a big Christmas party. Her holidays with her friends are much more satisfying than those she used to spend with her parents or her second husband, who refused to celebrate holidays or even birthdays.

In addition to these good friends, Dorothy has casual relationships with colleagues at work, but she doesn't socialize with them. She has become part of a community of boat racers but doesn't socialize with them outside of sailing, and they are not connected to her friends or her work. "I find it interesting to have these totally different worlds; it works for me," Dorothy said.

Because she is so much more physically fit than most women (or even men) her age, Dorothy has had trouble finding friends with whom to travel. So she decided to go on vacations alone. She chose settings where she would meet other people—Club Med and a hiking group in Europe. On both trips she met interesting people; on the latter trip she met a married couple who later introduced her to the wife's divorced brother—someone with whom she now is involved even though he lives in the Midwest.

What distinguishes Dorothy from other satisfied single women, however, is her unconflicted sexual pursuit. "For a while I thought I shouldn't go to bed with anyone unless they were a serious candidate for marriage," Dorothy remembered. "But soon I said to hell with that; there may never be a serious candidate. I shifted into enjoying someone, having an affair for fun, and finding someone with whom to travel." After every affair, Dorothy has an AIDS test to protect her next lover. "I try to be very responsible," she said.

Dorothy meets men through her sports activities, through friends, in the neighborhood, through personal ads in newspapers, and through Match.com on the Internet. This open attitude makes it easy for her to find men—for example, the man she lived with for six months, the man she dated for two years and even got engaged to, and other men with whom she had less committed but sexual relationships.

Dorothy recounted having gotten involved with a retired man who lives in her neighborhood. He was attractive and liked to sail, and because he seemed well-off, she envisioned traveling with him. But most of all, she thought, it "would be convenient sex." After they went to bed a couple of times, he admitted that he was impotent and that taking Viagra hadn't worked. Dorothy was most upset by the fact that he hadn't told her in advance and couldn't talk about it. "I want to be with people who can tell me what's going on; I want to be able to 'problem solve' with somebody," Dorothy explained. She believes that a man with good self-esteem would be forthright.

Dorothy's comfort with her sexuality—and the strong sense of self that accompanies it—is evident in the equanimity with which she deals with relationships that don't work, whether she ends them or the man ends them. Dorothy was planning to marry a business-man she met while racing boats. Their physical compatibility in and out of bed attracted her, as did his affluence; but he was not an inti-mate soul mate. Dorothy recalled how she was in the process of sell-ing her house in the city, was planning to move thirty miles to live with him, and had been offered a new job nearby. She had long planned to sell her house, but she started noticing a lot of hesitation on his part, so she delayed quitting her job. When Dorothy confronted him with it, he admitted he wasn't ready. Dorothy didn't want to hang around. "I think I was saved from making a terrible mistake, even though it was difficult at the time," Dorothy could say now, several years after they broke up. "I don't think his inability to commit had much to do with me but came from his past; he had been in several terrible marriages."

At the time of our interview in 2003, Dorothy had been seeing the man from the Midwest for about four months, the one whose sister she had met on the European hiking tour. Len looked her up when he came to San Francisco to visit his grown son. Dorothy was immediately attracted to Len, who was two years younger, a super athlete (a cyclist rather than a boat racer), and very handsome. He had been divorced for six years and seemed to have no issues about commitment. He was personally open. But from the beginning, Dorothy had reservations about a more serious or long-term relationship. Len was a Republican and a Catholic, and Dorothy was a Buddhist and a Democrat who had voted for Ralph Nader. Could she couple with someone who had voted for George Bush? Len had been laid off from his high-tech job and spent two years retraining as a teacher. Dorothy thought this was admirable but was worried about his finding a job and about his financial stability. What did it mean that he had lived with his mother for the previous six years? He said it provided a home atmosphere for her and for his teenage children. For Dorothy, this meant that he did not own a house and she did.

After their first meeting, Dorothy and Len started a heavy e-mail correspondence and talked on the phone frequently. Before having sex, or even a second date, Len invited her to go with him on a European vacation he already had planned. Even though she loved to travel and the trip sounded attractive, Dorothy would not agree to go until they had had sex. Len couldn't take time off to come back to California, so Dorothy went to the Midwest for Easter. What would it be like at the age of fifty-seven to have their first sexual experience in his mother's house, she wondered. Len had said that his mother was "cool," but Dorothy first ascertained that he had his own space in the house and did not share a wall with his mother's bedroom. Dorothy, however, was still uncomfortable, so on the second day there she said to his eighty-two-year-old mother: "Your son seems very nice, but I don't know him very well. The reason I'm here is that he invited me to go to Europe with him; I'm trying to figure out if we are compatible or not. I don't want to buy a ticket to Europe for a thousand dollars, take three weeks off from work, and then have a disastrous surprise over there. Normally, I don't move this fast." The mother replied, "My dear, I think you are very wise." Dorothy was reassured when the sex was good.

When Len came to visit her in California, the sex was even better, and they had a lot of fun together. Dorothy talked about how she and Len have phone sex—the first time she had ever done so.

A few weeks after the European trip, Dorothy stopped by to return a book I had lent her. She said that the trip was mixed; she wanted to enjoy the present, and Len wanted to talk about a long-term commitment. He proposed to relocate to the Bay Area in six months, move in with her, and look for a job. This scenario reminded Dorothy of the situation with her second husband, one that she sees as a recipe for disaster. But even if he found his own place, Dorothy wouldn't be ready to make a commitment to him. When she told him so at the end of the trip, he reacted with intense disappointment, saying she had "fallen off the pedestal." Dorothy responded, "I should not have been there to begin with."

Dorothy and Myra are different from most of the other single women in my study because of their ability to separate their sexual desires from a desire for intimacy or a permanent partnership. Such an unromantic approach gives them confidence and the ability to make themselves vulnerable. Thus, they are more open to new partners, less nervous about whether he is *the one,* and less afraid of getting hurt. They are no more confident than anyone else about finding love or a permanent relationship, but they are in control of their sexual quest, and this helps them accept their single lives. Their ability to separate sex, love, and family makes these two single women more open to computer dating and placing or answering personal ads.

The majority of single women in my study did not want to engage in computer dating, but others besides Dorothy and Myra were open to it because they missed having sex. Paula Little, a fifty-nine-year-old woman who has been divorced since she was thirty-two, had many serial monogamous relationships until she was about fifty-four. In the last five years, she has not had a relationship. Even though she is happy and satisfied with her rich single life, she wants to have "just one more man" while she is still physically healthy. She wants this relationship to provide good sex and some spiritual intimacy, but Paula is open to many types of partnerships. "It could be a traveling friend, someone to date, or he could live with me," Paula explained about her decision to try an Internet dating service. Perhaps reading these stories will help her clarify her intentions and think about how she has dealt with sex and love in the past. Can she separate sex, intimacy, and family as Myra and Dorothy have done?

Other single women in my study—those who were not interested in pursuing a sexual life, as well as those who wanted sex only in a long-term love relationship—were not attracted to computer dating or the use of personal ads. The widespread availability of these dating aids meant that they could no longer convincingly claim they would never meet anyone, since most of them knew friends or colleagues who had found a partner through matchmaking services. But for Gail Palmer, a forty-eight-year-old divorced woman for whom "sex is not so much the issue as is companionship," Internet dating was too stressful. "It seems desperate," she said, "and I don't want to be desperate." She would rather meet someone through a friend, even though that rarely happens. Emily Jacobs, a forty-one-year-old bisexual (whom we will meet in chapter 6), agreed. "It is not a big deal to be celibate, but I miss the emotional connection," she explained. Emily did not include sex when answering my question about what she wanted in a relationship, and she prefers to meet a potential partner through friends or mutual interests, rejecting the "complete anonymity" of the Internet. However, celibate women like Emily do not find social support for their lack of interest in sex.

Destigmatizing Celibacy

Celibacy does not have a place in the broader legacy of the twentieth century's sexual revolution, which made sexuality central to individual identity, personal health, and a happy life. "Fifty years ago it took courage for a single woman to admit that she was enjoying an active sexual life," states British author Sally Cline. "Today it takes courage for her to admit that she is not."[17] Even lesbians who in previous eras were stigmatized as sick when they were sexual are now worried about "lesbian bed death."[18] African American writer Donna Marie Williams argues that today celibacy is stigmatized, even more so than homosexuality. "It is more acceptable for a gay man to admit he is gay than for a person practicing celibacy to come out of the closet," Williams concludes.[19]

The idea that life without sex is unhealthy became a social norm that was first applied to married people in the mid-twentieth century, and it soon became applicable to all adults. The idea of sex as a necessary element—not primarily for reproduction, but for physical and psychological health—incorporates Freud's notion of sex as a basic biological drive, a natural human impulse, something, in contemporary terms, for which we are hardwired. Sexual researcher and MD Lenore Tiefer, author of *Sex Is Not a Natural Act and Other Essays,* questions the widespread view that genital sex is necessary not just for health but for a positive gender identity.

> I worked in the urology department for many years [Tiefer explains], and guys would come in and say, "I'm impotent," and I'd say, "So how is that a problem for you?" And they'd look at me like I was nuts. They'd say, "What? I can't have sex!" And I'd say, "And why do you want to have sex?" in an extremely conversational tone of voice, making eye contact, all of that. And they would say to me, "What do you mean? Everybody has sex." They simply didn't have an answer for these questions. They couldn't answer them because the vocabulary is impoverished, profoundly impoverished. Sometimes somebody would be able to cough up a few

words and then say, "It means I'm normal." Not being able to have an orgasm is like the epitome of not being normal. It's the epitome of not being a man, of not being a woman.[20]

Tiefer would prescribe Viagra for those men with true desire or for those who wished to satisfy their partners, but not just to make the men feel manly.

In a culture that glorifies sex and views sex as necessary for one's psychological well-being, a woman (or a man) risks severe censure if she says that she doesn't like physical sex. Poet Sondra Zeidenstein, married for forty-six years, after some years of celibacy with her husband, found a way to have regular sex that satisfied both of them. At that point she had the courage to write a poem expressing her attitude toward sex.

> It has taken me/64 years to begin to know/that if I don't want/ hands on my breasts,/fingers grazing my nipples,/a browsing, swollen cock/knocking at my groin,/I have as much right/to not desire/as he has to desire/and the not desiring/is positive, worthy of self-respect,/and is not failure/to be his good woman.

Zeidenstein went on to ask, "Is this as amazing to the reader to read as it was for me to write? And as uncomfortable? Is it selfish? Uptight? Not spontaneous? It has seemed so to the part of me who always wanted to be the hot girl, the passionate woman. It also seems now—finally—just right. . . . It has taken me years to accept and then—even harder—to claim this need, without apology or self-blame."[21] Zeidenstein's decision to release the poem was facilitated, I believe, by her status as a married, sexually active woman. If a single, celibate woman published such a poem, she would immediately be branded a man hater or frigid, and certainly troubled and sex phobic.

Recently, a flurry of articles in the popular press presented evidence that a lot of hidden celibacy exists among married heterosexual and cohabiting lesbian couples.[22] But this is seen primarily as a cause of unhappiness, a sexual dysfunction and a problem to be fixed. Certainly it is a problem if one partner wants sex and the other doesn't, but should mutually agreed upon celibacy be a social concern?

Such critiques of the idea that sexuality is necessary for personal happiness and health, and empirical evidence that both short- and longer-term celibacy may be more widespread than previously acknowledged, raise questions about the nature of sexuality. Although some biological and social scientists who study sex still see sexual desire as either purely biological or primarily socially constructed, a synthetic consensus is emerging that the human sexual response depends on a complex interaction of both biology and culture.[23] In addition, cumulative evidence now attests to a gender difference in the strength of sexual motivation. A 2001 survey of many different studies found that on average men have more frequent and intense sexual desires than women as measured by spontaneous thoughts about sex, frequency and variety of sexual fantasies, desired frequency of intercourse, desired number of partners, masturbation, liking for a wider variety of sexual practices, and other measures. The authors, who are psychologists, conclude: "We did not find a single study, on any of nearly a dozen different measures, that found women had a stronger sex drive than men. We think that the combined quantity, quality, diversity and convergence of the evidence render the conclusion indisputable."[24]

This evidence suggests that it may be easier for women to be celibate. Indeed, that is what the authors conclude. They cite a study that found that "among men, fear of rejection was the main reason given for avoiding sex," while women "reported a lack of interest or enjoyment."[25] Supporting this conclusion, another psychologist found that for women "the state of celibacy does not have to be a soul-wrenching spiritual journey." Rather, "for some women it is more like a trip to the market."[26] We must remember, however, that such generalizations hide a wide span of individual differences about desire for sex and reasons for celibacy.

Despite this evidence, a negative cultural evaluation of celibacy continues. This explains why I was more comfortable asking about women's sex lives than about their experience with celibacy. Although sometimes it came up spontaneously, I never asked my subjects directly about celibacy. Even if I had asked, my guess is that most women would have rejected the term.[27] In the current cultural climate, no one would call herself celibate, and few would say that they chose or like celibacy. Much more acceptable is the view that one is temporarily abstinent while seeking a soul mate. A celibate but romantic woman is permissible.

Although celibacy is distinct from virginity and chastity, the difference has been clouded by the Catholic Church's policy of linking all three. When a scandal broke out in the 1990s exposing the fact that numerous priests had sexually abused children and teenagers, the word *celibacy* gained even more negative connotations. The scandal reinforced the cultural view of celibacy as an unhealthy state. Priests' celibacy was seen as an unattainable ideal that masked sexual repression and immaturity and led to the sexual exploitation of the powerless. This view holds some truth, but we need to distinguish enforced celibacy from celibacy that is personally chosen as the best option at a particular time. Based on the case study that follows and on my reading, I propose an alternative view of celibacy.

Celibacy Can Be Sensuous and Passionate

Not until recently have writers attempted to revive celibacy as a viable and joyous option, especially for middle-aged women. *Sensual Celibacy* by Donna Marie Williams and *Women, Passion & Celibacy* by Sally Cline are especially important. They enumerate a number of advantages to a celibate life.

The absence of a sexual partner, they argue, frees women to focus on self-actualization, creativity, and personal power.[28] "Being celibate certainly gives you plenty of time to figure out your own stuff," remarked one of my subjects. Lesbian researcher and therapist Jo-Ann Loulan writes about her own experience of celibacy—one that applies to heterosexual women as well: "Without the concerns that accompany sexual relationships—whether our expectations are the same, whether we are sexually compatible, whether the relationship is going to work, whether the relationship makes sense to my friends —I am free to focus on myself."[29] She is also free to focus on caring for others—friends, extended family, neighbors, and the wider community. Thus, the autonomy fostered by celibacy is compatible with either an individual or a more communal ethic.[30]

In addition, Cline argues, celibacy frees women from boring and unfulfilling sex, simplifies life, and allows more time for other interests, especially satisfying work. Celibacy encourages spiritual growth and a focus on developing intimacy with a wider network of friends and family; it also provides some women an escape from interpersonal violence.[31] Single women who accept their celibacy do not wait for a soul mate, for a relationship, or for sex. Heterosexual single women over the age of fifty, including those who want to be partnered but recognize the odds against it,[32] may prefer to find sensuality and passion in their celibate lives, rather than take the path forged by Myra and Dorothy. Williams and Cline independently introduce the idea of sensual celibacy, a condition where other pleasures— touching, hugging, music, dancing, delicious foods, and stimulating cultural events—can replace genital sexuality.[33]

Sensual celibacy is not the same as masturbation. Although neither Cline nor Williams is opposed to masturbation, their notion of the sensual doesn't focus on genital sex or orgasm. Their position is validated by sex surveys that find sexually active women are more likely to masturbate than those who are celibate.[34] "As much as possible," Williams states, "I infuse sensuality into every aspect of my life, from the clothes I wear and the sheets I sleep in, to the pictures I hang on my walls. Even my prayers are romantic and passionate. Day by day, I am learning to experience life through all my senses."[35] Williams realized that sex had been her only playful activity; the rest of her life consisted of work. As such, she had been totally dependent on men to have fun. Now she opens herself to a wide range of ways to play.[36] Cline, in a similar vein, argues that women can be powerfully moved by any number of objects and activities—art, travel, dance, politics, spirituality, their family, intimate friendships, and God.[37] I found a wonderful example of such nonsexual sensuous passion in a woman who participated in my study.

A Sensuous Passion for Flamenco Dancing

Nancy Dean, forty-nine, ever single, and childless, invited me one Sunday afternoon to experience the new passion in her life—flamenco dancing. She was to dance in a small performance for family and friends. Finally, I found the place—a one-story oblong building, squat and dull, hidden in a suburban strip mall next to the chiropractor's office, with an inconspicuous sign—Flamenco Dance Studio[38] —announcing its mission. Inside, mirrors on two walls magnify the small space, but the dull linoleum on the floor denotes better days. Yet when the guitarist starts to play and the dancers' heels hit the floor in a staccato rhythm, this ordinary American room is transformed into an adobe café in the southern Spanish city of Seville.

Nancy comes here twice a week to forget the cares of her intense work life and to abandon herself to flamenco dance. She takes both her work and her dance seriously. In her position as a partner in a large investment firm, Nancy is respected for her open but no-nonsense approach to business and for her commitment to working with women clients. Nancy, blond and slim, dresses conservatively, wears no makeup, and talks in quiet, modulated tones. She is known for her even temper and her ability to treat those on all sides of an issue with respect.

But on the dance floor a different woman emerged. Wearing a long black dress that fitted tightly over her hips and with a flowing skirt emerging below her knees, Nancy had accented the black dress with red accessories—bright scarlet lipstick, large magenta hoop earrings, and an oversize rose pinned in her hair. She began her solo dance by holding her body erect and, with eyes flashing, swayed her hips to the music. Drumming her two-inch heels in a complex rhythmic pattern, Nancy swung one arm in an elegant movement to toss her skirt, then lifted both arms above her head, wrists flexing in delicate arches as her fingers gracefully traced patterns in the air.

"How," I asked Nancy after the performance, "did you discover flamenco?" She replied that when she was ten years old, her older sister went on a trip to Spain with her high school class and brought Nancy back a bottle of Spanish perfume called Maja. On the front of the bottle was a picture of a woman in a flamenco costume. "The smell of the perfume was very exotic to a white, middle-class California girl," Nancy said. Periodically, as a young adult, Nancy would see flamenco in a movie and in several PBS specials. "My heart leaped," she said. But she never did anything about it, until in her midforties she saw an ad for a class in Spanish dance in a local community education program. The folk dance taught there was "flamencoized," rather than pure flamenco, but Nancy loved the class and took it three or four times for about a year and a half. Each time, she learned a bit more of the intricate routine. A student in the class told her about the more advanced and classical training in the Flamenco Dance Studio. She has been studying there now for almost five years.

I first talked to Nancy about being single nine years earlier, when she was forty. Then, as now, Nancy stated clearly that she never made a conscious choice not to marry. Her life was far from settled; she had finished her MBA but did not yet have a secure position. She had recently left a relationship with a man she loved but who was verbally abusive. "I should have left after two months, rather than two years," she said. But more than any other woman I interviewed, Nancy asserted her satisfaction with living alone.

> I've lived alone for about sixteen years now, since I was twenty-three or twenty-four, and I really love it. One of the major sources of joy I have in my life is that I can take care of myself. That I can do this enhances my own sense of self, my sense of character, my sense of strength. I like my privacy. I like coming in and throwing stuff down, or coming in and putting it away, if that's what I want

to do. It would be difficult for me to give up this independence, even as I yearn sometimes for an emotional connection and a commitment to a partner.

Five years earlier, in her midthirties, Nancy suffered from chronic fatigue syndrome and caught pneumonia several times. She was ill off and on for about two years. Even though she felt very vulnerable during this ordeal, she was proud of her ability to call on friends and to survive on her own. She became increasingly secure in her single life.

The youngest of five children in a family of teachers, Nancy grew up in California's Central Valley. Her mother married and divorced twice, having three children by her first husband, and Nancy and her sister by her second. Nancy's mother and father divorced when she was fourteen; her mother never remarried, and her father's second marriage did not last. Even before the divorce, her family life was far from ideal. "There was a lot of silence in my house," Nancy explains. "A lot of attitudes and emotions were not expressed. I was not even told my parents were getting divorced. One morning I came down and he was packing up his things."

After the divorce, Nancy felt even more alone, with no one "paying much attention" to her. Her mother moved to New York, and Nancy and her sister lived with their father and his new wife. Nancy never got along with her stepmother. Three weeks before she graduated from high school, her father kicked her out of the house. She lived with friends during the summer and then left for college. Her parents paid for her education, but she never again felt she had a family home. Her mother died when Nancy was in her early thirties, and she is still estranged from her father.

Unlike some single women whose unhappy childhood lead them to invest heavily in finding a relationship (see chapter 4), Nancy became self-reliant. Not only did she enjoy living alone, but she liked to travel by herself. In 1994 she proudly took her first solo trip to Europe. By 2003, she regularly took vacations unaccompanied. She loved making her own itinerary and going at her own pace. As a solo traveler she met many other tourists, often sightseeing for the day, or even for a week, with a couple or another single woman or man.

During her forties, Nancy created many of the structures that would support a satisfying single life. She obtained a permanent position in a field she loves. She bought a house only a few blocks away from her brother and his family and reconnected with her two sisters, who also live nearby. Now the four siblings and their significant others spend holidays together. Nancy is thrilled at this re-creation of family, as she is with the close relationships she is building with her niece and nephew. In addition, Nancy has formed a network of friends and built several communities—one around her workplace and another anchored in flamenco. Her two communities are beginning to overlap. At the dance performance, I was introduced to a number of her colleagues, including the vice president of the company. When I asked Nancy about their attendance, she replied that she talked about her dancing in casual conversations with colleagues, and they asked to be invited to a performance. At first, she didn't want to have them there since she considered flamenco part of her private life, a place she went to to get away from work. But now she is glad that she got over that feeling. The melding of her communities, I conclude, along with the integration of work and her personal life, indicates a deeper acceptance of herself.

But it is dancing, not work, family, friends, or community, that makes Nancy's face light up and her voice sing. Dancing evokes a joy that was absent nine years ago. In an interview a few weeks after I saw her dance, I asked Nancy if for her flamenco is a mode of sexual communication. "I don't know if I would use the word *sexual*," she replied, "but it definitely expresses sensuality, passion, desire, and emotions, all of which keep me a sexual being. Sex with a partner is great," she continued, "but this is another way of expressing the same energy." Nancy appreciates that flamenco is so emotional and that she can express anything from "earthly joy to railing against fate and everything in between." Although Nancy said that she has celibate periods, she would not label herself celibate. Still, the sensuality and passion she conveys in flamenco enhance a single life lived without a permanent lover.

Expressing emotions through dance seems perfect for a woman who grew up in a family that did not talk about their feelings. A dance that emphasizes solo and group dancing, rather than a coupled pair, symbolically supports single life. Although men dance flamenco too, they rarely pair up with a woman, and if they do, they do not partner her as in classical ballet or in Latin dances like the tango. Flamenco encourages dancing by mature and older women and does not subordinate women to men. It is characterized as an introvert's dance.

> The emotional power of flamenco comes from within the per- former who abandons himself [sic] to his art, who breathes life into it. Flamenco is a profoundly intimate art, which is what differen- tiates baile flamenco from classical ballet. The movements of the two are exactly the opposite. Ballet takes to the air, seeks to be light, almost weightless in its movements and to hover by using spectacular gymnastics, while flamenco dancing is concentrated downward toward the ground.... The dance roots itself in the earth, as though drawn there by some powerful magnet.[39]

Nancy's flamenco teacher gave her the nickname Chispa, which means "spark" in Spanish, or someone who sets fire to the dance. Flamenco, indeed, is the spark in Nancy's life. She moves her body to express strong feelings of sensuality and passion, and sometimes pain and anger too. Nancy integrates this sensual dance into her single life in a manner that both mirrors and enhances her self-esteem, personal strength, and autonomy. Instead of seeking a soul mate, Nancy has discovered a soulful tradition, one rooted in an ethnicity and folk experience very different from her own, but one that speaks deeply to her.

Yet in a culture that emphasizes genital sexuality and stigmatizes the celibate as abnormal, prudish, frigid, puritanical, and chaste, one can easily denigrate Nancy's sexuality. Those who feed on popular psychology might say that she is afraid of relationships and has a fear of commitment. They might declare that flamenco dancing expresses anger at her parents' neglect of her and at a past lover's abuse. What if their analysis holds some truth? Does this invalidate the satisfaction Nancy experiences? Would years of therapy or constant computer dating be *better* for her? Can we say that she will be *really* happy only if she finds an intimate sexual partner? Or can we applaud her for incorporating a rich sensuality into a successful and satisfying life?

Other celibate women in my study incorporated sensuality into their lives in less spectacular ways. Single mothers enjoy the sensuality of children, and pets provide bodily contact for other single women. Some women find sensual pleasure in gardening or nature. Some women are not very sensual, but others miss it and have not found ways to be sensual outside a sexual relationship. Gail Palmer, a forty-eight-year-old single parent whom we will meet in chapter 7, said that she masturbated regularly for physical release, but she misses the holding and touching associated with sex.

That celibacy works for many single women is attested to in sex surveys. *Sex in America* reports that "evidence argues against the theory that a woman without a partner is a sexually thwarted creature. Instead, we find women—and men—who have no partners think less about sex and report having what often are very happy and fulfilling lives without it."[40] A 1999 AARP survey of the sexual attitudes and practices of Americans forty-five and older found that they "cited close ties with friends and family as very important to their quality of life—more important than a satisfying sexual relationship."[41]

■ ■ ■

Nancy Dean, Myra Detweiler, and Dorothy Sawyer negotiated their sexuality based on a realistic appraisal of the improbability of reaching the soul-mate ideal. Separating sensuality/sexuality from psychological intimacy or a permanent relationship, they found diverse and separate ways to meet their needs for sexuality, intimacy, and family. They were quite forceful in taking charge of their sexuality. Other women in my study—like those in the larger society—were more confused, unsure, and conflicted about their sexual lives.

In their range of sexual responses, and in their sexual satisfactions and dissatisfactions, single women may be not much different from their married counterparts. Sexually dissatisfied single women, however, are more publicly visible than coupled women and thus more vulnerable to being labeled victims to be pitied. But single women have more social space and cultural support to find a solution, since for them both celibacy and promiscuity are more acceptable than they are for married women.

Why are Myra and Dorothy such sexual beings, and so accepting of their sexual needs? Why is Nancy able to integrate creatively the sensuous practice of flamenco into her celibacy? Sexual science and the sociology and psychology of sex have as yet no explanation for such individual differences, nor are they able to discern the distinctive pathways through which biology and socialization intertwine. Although unable to explain, we can celebrate and affirm such sexual and sensual vitality and variety.

CHAPTER 3

Crafting Singular Lives

> There are decisions we can make more consciously,
> strategies we can employ more usefully, consequences
> we can understand more fully.
> PEGGY ORENSTEIN, *Flux*

Becoming a new single woman at midlife—that is, accepting and being happy with one's singleness—is a long and often conflicted process. We do not choose to be single, but we have made a number of choices that have led us here.

In our twenties, some of us chose to emphasize careers, politics, or unconventional adventures. For us, it was important to find satisfying work or to experiment with life, thereby developing a strong personal identity. We assumed that a life partner would just turn up in our early to midthirties. A few of us preferred not to have conventional weddings and were attracted to alternatives to the nuclear family. By the time we were in our thirties or forties, some of us opted to have a child as single mothers, assuming that we would more easily find a partner when we were not pressured by a biological clock. Others firmly resolved not to have children. Then there were those of us who chose to leave abusive relationships and marriages or ones that smothered us psychologically. Rather than looking for another coupled relationship, we focused on developing careers, raising our kids, and looking for alternative sources of support. Some of us were abandoned by a partner we adored, making us feel vulnerable and mistrustful, but we struggled past this. Many of us experienced more than one of these scenarios. But none of us imagined we would be single in our forties, fifties, or sixties. We certainly didn't envision that as single women we would *not be alone* and would be leading full and satisfying lives. We wrestled with and moved beyond the cultural message—which many of us deeply internalized—that happiness depends on being coupled.

Many of us held on to the ideal of a soul mate throughout our thirties, forties, and into our fifties, but we did not spend most of our time looking. Rather, we built lives for ourselves. Many of the social supports we wove together are similar to those created by coupled women. But as single women, we achieved them with help from friends and relatives rather than a mate, a situation that is accorded less cultural recognition. Often we were unaware that we were creating the infrastructure for a viable single life, so we were surprised to find ourselves so satisfied in our fifties as we let go of the idea of finding a partner.

In the following pages I trace the choices an ever-single woman, two divorced women, and I made and the supports we created for ourselves. The four of us represent the diversity of women in my study who became new single women. Three of us are white; one is African American. Three of us are parents, and of the three, one is a lesbian parent. The nonparent made a firm decision not to have children. One woman hardly has any family, and another has a large family. Three of us grew up middle class, and one is from a working-class background. Two of us had mothers who were full-time homemakers; the other two had mothers who worked outside the home as well as in it.

The choices the four of us made and the supports we created for ourselves are reflected in the lives of many other women in the study, including those whose stories I tell in subsequent chapters.

Life Choices Supporting Long-Term Singleness

Our choices are historically specific and made within a particular cultural context. All of our individual choices were made possible, and were partly shaped, by the rise of new social possibilities for women after 1965, especially those created by the women's movement and by innovative cultural justifications for new lifestyles. These changes coexisted with more traditional ideals of marriage and family life.[1] In the future, single life may be facilitated by different, or a broader range of, choices. Moreover, these are all middle-class choices, presupposing at least modest economic security and access to higher education and white-collar occupations. None of our choices, however, necessarily meant that we had to remain single or become new single women. All of them can be combined with a coupled life. But women who make these life choices are less likely to expend a lot of energy on finding a partner, and they are less likely to compromise themselves in order to be coupled.

Choosing to Be Unconventional

Choosing to be unconventional may be most relevant for women who came of age in the 1950s and early 1960s when the nuclear family dominated personal life in a way it does not today, as well as for those women who chose to divorce in the 1970s and early 1980s before it became a common occurrence. Gillian Herald and I are ever-single women who chose not to marry but to live alternative lifestyles. Wynona La Blanc and Julia Cohen[2] divorced in 1980 in a manner that was unconventional in their social circles.

Choosing Not to Marry

Gillian is a short, attractive, and very energetic community college teacher of history and interdisciplinary studies who was fifty-four when I first interviewed her in 1994. She loves teaching, owns her own home, and is financially secure. As I heard her story and followed it for eight years, I saw both similarities to and differences from my own life history.

We were born in the same year, 1940, in the Midwest. Gillian is an only child from a stable middle-class Catholic family; I am the oldest of three in a similar family. Our mothers were Protestants who converted to Catholicism and became full-time homemakers. Our fathers were professionals: mine a professor at the Agriculture College of Cornell University in upstate New York, hers a lawyer in an industrialized farm town in Ohio. Our parents defined their marriage as good and believed in staying married until they died. Gillian said that her mother's second marriage, after she was widowed in her fifties, was even better. But from our teenage years on, we both rejected our mother's lives. We did not want to become housewives who, as we perceived, lost their individuality by dedicating all their energies to family life. We were not alone; in fact, we were part of a generation of highly educated, middle-class young women coming of age in the late 1950s and early 1960s who did not want to replicate the lives of our mothers.[3]

When I was seventeen, I told my mother that I would never have a wedding. I didn't mean that I would remain single, and certainly not a spinster, but I did not want her life. My mom was an excellent cook and seamstress. She made clothes for her three children, gardened, canned, and played bridge with her friends. But she was always negative. She constantly criticized my father for not being home, nagged me to get my nose out of a book, and condemned my unruly long hair and unfeminine style. She even put herself down, saying she wasn't smart like other housewives in our university town. My father, by contrast, loved his work, and when he was home, his laughter and warmth made him much more fun than my mother. His life seemed preferable to me. I wanted a career too, although I knew no woman whose life I could emulate. This void perhaps explains why, well into my thirties, I had a recurring nightmare: I was sucked back into suburbia, unable to resist the temptations of love and children. I was pulled against my will into a life that would make me miserable.

Gillian, as a teenager, didn't really think about the future but knew only that she had no desire to live her mother's "narrow, traditional life." Gillian wanted to escape the Midwest to a more exciting life in a big city on the East or West Coast. Although her parents pushed her into a Catholic college in a nearby town, Gillian turned down a marriage proposal in her senior year and set out for graduate school in Boston. For Gillian graduate study was not a path to a career but a way to facilitate her entry into an urbane, more bohemian life. The Beat and bohemian culture that developed in large cities in the 1950s, the sexual revolution, and the general upheaval of the 1960s provided Gillian the support for exploring an alternative lifestyle.

I did want a career. But I got the message very clearly that for a woman a career and marriage did not mix. My college boyfriend and I broke up in 1961 while I was in my last year at Cornell and he was away in his first year of medical school. He *knew* that I wanted to continue in school and have a career, and that I would be miserable at his university because it didn't have a good enough graduate school. He *knew* that as a career woman I would be a lousy mother. I tearfully protested that I didn't know what I wanted. This was not surprising, since none of my undergraduate professors was a woman, and I still did not know any career women. But as soon as we separated, I applied to graduate schools. Would I have married him if he had been less traditional and more accommodating? Would it have worked? I'll never know.

In the spring of 1962, I received a phone call from the University of Chicago. The man on the line said that the university was considering offering me a fellowship, but he wanted to know if I had any plans to get married. I could truthfully say no, and I got the fellowship. But the message was clear, and this time it came from an authority.

Such cultural messages complicate the issue of choice. I accepted both my boyfriend's and the professor's proclamations that marriage and career are incompatible. I held on to this idea even when the culture began to change. In 1963, during my second graduate year, Betty Friedan published the best-selling book *The Feminine Mystique,* in which she advocated that women combine marriage, motherhood, and a career. I didn't really believe that was possible. What spoke to me was her rejection of the full-time housewife model and her stress on the importance of finding fulfilling work outside the home. I was happy that the new feminism legitimated careers for women, but I wanted to look for other ways to combine my career with a nontraditional personal life. *Single* meant asexual spinster, and that was a turnoff. The existence of alternative cultural models helped me as they had Gillian.

Bohemia had always attracted me. But I was only eighteen when I realized it would be a lot harder for me than for Jack Kerouac to "go on the road." By the 1960s, however, French feminist Simone de Beauvoir had provided an appealing alternative. She refused to marry or cohabit but had a great love relationship and intellectual partnership with the philosopher Jean-Paul Sartre. Drawing on her example, I and other second-wave feminists became early advocates of a philosophy that is now widespread: a soul mate in an egalitarian partnership. It was with disillusionment that I later learned from biographies, especially Deirdre Bair's *Simone de Beauvoir,* how unequal, conflicted, and unsatisfying de Beauvoir's relationship with Sartre was. I, too, was thwarted in several attempts to form unconventional relationships with intellectual "soul mates." Cohabiting with one in my early thirties was a huge disappointment. But it is only in writing this book that I have come to terms with both the attractions and the inadequacies of this ideal.

My alienation from my mother's life, an alternative vision on how to couple, and my career ambitions led me away from conventional marriage. At the age of thirty, with a PhD in hand, I rejected the lawyer who would have been a good husband because I didn't want to follow him to the Midwest and become a politician's wife. Although we shared many interests and values, he was neither a soul mate nor a great love. Moreover, I still had nightmares about being sucked back into suburban domesticity.

Gillian's life in her late twenties and early thirties was more adventuresome and less structured by career goals than mine. After finishing her MA in Boston in 1965, Gillian hopped in her car and moved to Los Angeles. There, Gillian had two ten-year cohabitations—one from the age of twenty-five to thirty-five and the other from thirty-nine to forty-nine. Gillian married the first man with whom she cohabited, but only to get him a green card. She did not present herself as divorced. Marriage was never, and is not now, her goal, for to her marriage meant a loss of freedom and living her mother's narrow, traditional life. Neither of the men with whom she cohabited was a "soul mate," but in both relationships Gillian enjoyed a lot of autonomy, especially in the second one, where she and her partner had separate households. She loved the balance of having her space and privacy during the week and companionship on the weekend. Although much in these two relationships was "really good," the relationships were also problematic, and Gillian chose to end both.

I cohabited for only two years but lived in an alternative family in a communal household for eight years. From the age of thirty-seven to forty-five, I owned a duplex with a slightly younger feminist sociologist and her partner (and later husband). We bought the house together in the late 1970s with the explicit goal of living communally, though without sexual experimentation. We each had our separate space, but we ate communally; thus we successfully created a household that was the center of a network of friends and political activity. In the middle of this eight-year relationship, I adopted a baby and my sociologist housemate gave birth to one; both babies were boys, nine months apart.

When making my decision to enter a collective household and to become a single mother, I did not consider the possibility that I might remain permanently single. An objective outsider might have observed: "Your last serious relationship was with a divorced man living in Berkeley temporarily as a researcher; he had a good job in a distant city, a child in college, and no desire to parent again. That didn't work out. How can you imagine that you will find someone in his midthirties or older who will be able to, or want to, insert himself into a communal household with a single mother in a demanding occupation?" But I was not being objective. At that point I still believed I could find a partner—if not a soul mate, then at least someone who was capable of an equitable relationship.

Parenting in this context, however, left me little emotional space to look for a partner. This was true especially since the communal household did not work well after we had children. Once my housemates had a child, they became more coupled and did not want or need to share child care. Moreover, we had different ideas about child rearing, a topic we had never thought to explore. Despite therapy together and separately, our household broke up in a hostile "divorce" that also split our community and separated my son, aged four, from his younger "brother." The household had lasted a year longer than my longest romantic relationship, and this rupture was much more traumatic than any breakup I'd had with a man.

Thus, I, at age forty-five, and Gillian, at age forty-nine, found that our attempts to create alternatives to a conventional marriage had failed. We both were able to buy a house but found ourselves living alone. Neither of us could yet envision a fully realized life as permanently single women.

Choosing to Divorce

Wynona La Blanc is a stylish forty-nine-year-old. An African American lawyer, Wynona wears big hats and lots of jewelry. She swings her hips, but she takes care of business. Like Gillian and me, Wynona came from a stable Catholic family, but hers was working class. Wynona grew up in San Francisco with several siblings and parents whose fifty-seven-year marriage ended only with her father's death. Wynona's mother (who is illiterate) always worked as a house cleaner. Wynona was married at eighteen, right out of high school, to a thirty-five-year-old distant cousin and a friend of the family who, with her father, worked in construction. She had her first child at nineteen and had four children in all—two sons and a set of twin daughters. Wynona and her husband lived off and on in San Francisco and in a rural part of the greater Bay Area. In both places they had a large network of extended family. Wynona always worked; when the children were small, she worked as a typist out of her home between 11:00 p.m. and 3:00 a.m. Later, she was a secretary and administrative assistant, and in her early thirties she started taking college courses part-time. By this time, the family was living on a farm in the country. Wynona was in charge of the chickens, a few cows, and the garden, as well as all the cooking, cleaning, and child guidance.

Wynona left her husband when she was thirty-five; at that time her children ranged in age from eleven to seventeen. She was still a secretary and had not yet earned her BA. Her husband was verbally and physically abusive to her and the children. Because she had been too ashamed to talk about the abuse, her mother did not speak to her for a year after she left her husband. Both his large and her smaller extended family condemned her and cut off communication. They all said that a woman does not leave her husband. Wynona recalls her divorce and her situation afterward: now *family,* for her, meant just she and the children.

> After the divorce, we pulled together as a family. The children knew that when they came home, there weren't going to be fights, there wasn't going to be yelling, and they knew that when I said we were going to do things, we would do it. It was just like a pressure that was alleviated from them. Despite the stigma from the outside, our family life improved. They'll tell you that 100 percent. It improved for our survival. We would never have survived if I had stayed married. By survival I mean that I'd probably be either dead or I would have had a nervous breakdown, and my children would not be particularly healthy. There is not a doubt in my mind that I'd do it all over again. I'd do it a little differently, but I'd do it over.

I probed Wynona on why she was able to make the break. She laughed when I asked her about feminism. She hadn't heard of it in 1980, although later, through her college education, she became a committed feminist. At the time of her divorce, she knew no single black women. Everyone in her large extended family was Catholic and married. Later, four of her cousins divorced, including two who had shunned her. Her father, although at times alcoholic, had never hit her mother; so Wynona knew that physical abuse did not have to be part of family life. Probably the factors that most facilitated her ability to leave her husband were her employment and a certain economic naïveté. Wynona had not squirreled away any money before she left, and she did not anticipate her ex-husband's cutting off all financial support for the teenage children.

The first few years were tough. Three of the children went to work after school and pooled their salaries from fast food restaurants with her meager secretarial salary. She and another divorced woman at work traded tips on how to avoid foreclosure on their homes when they couldn't meet the mortgage payments on time. She was frequently scared. But gradually, with the children's economic help and a better-paying administrative assistant position, she got back on her feet and continued her education.

■ ■ ■

Julia Cohen looks the opposite of Wynona. She is a thin, wiry, and effervescent foundation funding officer who is Jewish and a bit macho. She too divorced in 1980, the same year as Wynona, but at thirty-two, she was three years younger. When Julia divorced, her daughter was four and her stepson, ten. Then, a few years later, at the age of thirty-five, she came out as a lesbian. Julia's divorce, unlike Wynona's, was supported by her family and friends, but her coming out as a lesbian was distinctly unconventional.

Julia grew up in a stable nuclear family in a middle-class suburb on Long Island, with a younger sister and brother. Her father was a middle-level business executive, and her mother, a grade-school teacher. Both were secular Jews and Roosevelt Democrats. Julia was influenced not only by a working mother but by two grandmothers who had worked all their lives in small family businesses. Yet when she was filling out college applications, her mother persuaded Julia to put down "home economics" as a possible major. Although her sister and brother were quite conventional—marrying at ages twenty and twenty-one respectively—Julia was a rebel. She moved to California and went to the University of California in Santa Cruz and then to Berkeley for graduate school. Julia was politically active both as an undergraduate and in graduate school. She was an early member of

Students for a Democratic Society (SDS) and later a member of other left-wing and antiwar groups.

She met her husband in 1973 in a political group at Berkeley when they were both graduate students. Bill had a three-year-old son and was separated from the boy's mother. "One of the things that I was really attracted to was the fact that he had a kid, because I really like children," Julia said. "I loved it that we had an instant family." Julia and Bill cohabited, but she eventually gave in to her parents' pressure to get married after she got pregnant. They received their doctorates in the same year, and both got teaching jobs at different colleges in Boston. They were living the feminist dream of an egalitarian marriage. But in their first year there, Bill had a psychotic breakdown and was diagnosed with a mental illness. They moved back to California to be close to family and friends. Julia took a less stressful job, the one she still has.

Bill and Julia remained together until 1980, when she left him. These are years that she does not want to remember or talk about. Julia does say that Bill refused to let her see his son for some years after the divorce and that he cohabited with another woman, with whom he had another child. Bill died unexpectedly in a car crash in 1989, when their daughter was eleven, his son was seventeen, and the young child five. Fortunately, the son had come back to live with Julia, and she helped all three children remain close to each other.

Julia's coming out in 1984 was unusual in that it was "not a big deal." "I had a sexual relationship with a woman while I was still married," she said. "I met a woman, got involved, and that was it. So it was not a really traumatic or dramatic event in my life." Julia's parents had a hard time with her lesbianism, but her sister, brother, and all of her friends (almost all of whom were heterosexual) were very supportive. Julia was unconventional, not just in coming out but also in the kind of lesbian she became. For all the years her daughter was at home, Julia did not cohabit, and she did not become part of a lesbian community. Rather, she retained her strong network of heterosexual friends and for about six years had only short affairs.

Some years after their divorces, both Wynona and Julia formed other primary relationships, but these were much less conventional than their marriages. Eight years after her divorce, Wynona met an international businessman who was also African American and several years younger. He was a romantic who wooed her, but he was away a lot, for he worked mainly overseas. Wynona loved both the romance and the autonomy the relationship offered. In addition, he was wonderful with her children. They were together for five years and married for two and a half. He died of a massive heart attack in Africa at the age of forty-five. This shock was followed by the news that he had more than $100,000 in business debt, for which she was responsible. Providence intervened. She broke her foot after tripping on an uneven pavement outside a local restaurant. She sued and won; the settlement was large enough to pay off most of the debt. Her first husband died in the same year.

After some years of casual affairs, Julia too found another committed relationship—also one with a good deal of autonomy—with Elizabeth, who lived and worked four hours away. Although they never lived together, as Julia said, "It was a wonderful, wonderful relationship." It lasted more than eight years. But when her daughter, Jessie, moved east to go to college, Julia became dissatisfied with her relationship with Elizabeth. She longed for a partner who lived closer and was more sexual. She wanted passion and companionship with the same person. So Julia initiated a change in their relationship, and they went from being lovers to being friends. They are still very close. Julia said: "We are good friends, and she is family. My daughter and my son really love her a lot."

By our late forties and early fifties, Gillian, Wynona, Julia, and I realized that unconventional relationships had not worked for us. But the choices that the four of us made as we continued our single lives from our thirties into our forties and fifties created structures of support for singleness. Our earlier unconventionality helped us accept long-term singleness, but we now built stable lives that were quite conventional except for the fact that we were not coupled. Our experiences, and those of long-term single women portrayed in other chapters, suggest six supports that are necessary (but not necessarily sufficient) to build a satisfying life as a single woman.

Crafting Supports for a Satisfying Single Life

The six supports are (1) fulfilling work, (2) connections to the next generation, (3) a home, (4) intimate relationships with a network of friends and extended family, (5) a community, and (6) acceptance of our sexuality whether we have an active sex life or are celibate.

Pursuing Fulfilling Work

When recruiting middle-class single women to interview, I sought out women who did not have high-powered, high-paying careers. Although work was important to all the women in my study, very few were in elite institutions or positions, and few were workaholics.

For all four of us, the process of finding meaningful work—work that would give us economic security, but also an identity and sense of purpose—was of central concern. All of us pursued advanced degrees and professional occupations at a time when no other woman in our families had done so. By middle age, however, all of us made compromises to integrate work with other life choices and goals. All of us chose to settle in one geographic location and often to stay with one institution, rather than move to pursue greater career opportunities.

I made the decision to become a professor in the early 1960s in my first year of graduate school, but the realization of my goal was not easy. My years as a graduate student at the University of Chicago from 1962 to 1966, first in education and then in sociology, were filled with contradictions. I loved my studies and worked hard. The gray gothic buildings, the intellectual stimulation in small seminars, the emphasis on interdisciplinary exchange, the elite atmosphere that downplayed the importance of grades and requirements, and the adequate fellowships granted to almost all graduate students made me feel that I had finally found the right world. Unconsciously, I tried to become one of the boys, verbally competing with the male students to win the male professors' attention. But I also dressed in a feminine, though unprovocative, style—skirts, stockings, pumps.

One December, after I had finished all my classes and passed my exams for advancement to a PhD program, I made elaborate Christmas cookies (as my mother always did) and took plates to my professors (all male) and to the secretaries (all female). They were amazed, since none of them viewed me as domestic.

I had no real friends. My one woman friend in the department dropped out after her master's, and I never felt comfortable with the several women who married fellow students. I and the other *boys* felt they weren't really serious. Years later, one of them, still married, told me how intimidated and inadequate I made her feel. But at the time I was oblivious. I knew a few women students in other departments, but we didn't talk about personal issues. Nor did I have a mentor with whom I could identify. I didn't like the two women professors with whom I'd taken a class. I felt they were cold, and their work (as part of a husband-wife team) didn't interest me. In retrospect, I'm sure I picked up the subtle male disdain for them. During my second and third years in graduate school, Hannah Arendt, the famous political philosopher whom I admired, lived across the street from me. From my window, I'd watch her walk in and out of her building, and I went to some of her lectures. But I was too intimidated by her erudition and Germanic manner to approach her.

Although I never considered deviating from this career path, my isolation from other women took its toll; I often felt lonely and confused. This, and my desire to be taken seriously as an intellectual, led me into two secret relationships with married professors, one in a professional school at the University of Chicago, and the other in a university across the country. I thus entered a pattern that was common among aspiring career women. Although I was a willing participant, these relationships did not bring me happiness.

In 1966 I was hired as a full-time lecturer in sociology at Columbia University to teach in the (nonelite) School of General Studies for adult learners. Because a visiting professor didn't show up, I was asked to teach one course in the elite Columbia College. I had not finished my PhD dissertation and had never taught; at the age of twenty-six I was thrust into an extremely elite and *sexist*—a word I learned only a few years later—institution where I was an anomaly. The next two years were probably the loneliest and most difficult of my life.

Before I left for New York, several of my professors and peers warned me to watch out because professors in the Sociology Department at Columbia had a reputation for seducing their female graduate students. Since I was the first young woman ever hired there who was not a spouse or a student of these men, they thought I would surely be seen as "fresh meat."

I was so intimidated that I never went to see any of these professors in their offices, even when they invited me. And I seldom ran into them, since my office was in the basement of the School of General Studies and theirs were in the more prestigious graduate school or in Columbia College. I did see them at the department faculty meeting, held once a month over lunch in the Men's Faculty Club, but neither they nor I knew what to say to each other. I could only fume silently when the chair, more than once, commented at the start of the meeting how nice it was, for the first time in their history, to have "three lovely ladies" at these lunch meetings. The club had graciously made an exception to let us attend.

The other two women barely spoke to me or to each other. One woman, only a few years older than I, was an assistant professor and a graduate of the department; everyone knew that she was the mistress (later second wife) of their most famous professor. I never knew whether she shunned me because we had little in common intellectually, because she viewed me as competition, or because she, too, wanted to be one of the boys, untainted by association with another lowly woman. The other woman was older, probably in her forties, a recent PhD who was given a course or two to teach, but her real worth lay in the academic journal she edited for one of the other "stars" in the department. It was clear to me that none of us was taken seriously.

I, who had never had trouble speaking out in class or in meetings, fell silent and became tongue-tied during these horrible lunches. My only solace was walking across campus after lunch with three other junior faculty who, like me, were "outsiders" because they had not gotten their PhD at Columbia. These men complained that they, too, felt invisible, and we all derided the sham democracy of the meeting when the real decisions were made by three or four of the stars, who met informally. After two years at Columbia, I was let go because, I was told, I had not finished my dissertation. But one of the men, who also had not finished his, was retained. Nor was I unaware of the irony of being fired as a full-time instructor at prestigious Columbia and rehired as a part-time lecturer at Barnard, the women's college across the street.

When the students rebelled at Columbia in the spring of 1968, I joined fully in spirit, although I didn't become part of the political action. I remember one scene where the hierarchy described earlier was reversed. Some of the sociology graduate students were among students who occupied Fairweather Hall, where the most senior sociology professors had their offices. The professors were pacing in front of the building, anxious about the research materials in their barricaded offices. The graduate students invited a few of us *outsider* junior faculty to come in. We told the senior faculty that we would check on their offices. Later, the sociology faculty met to discuss the rebellion. For the first time, I spoke up, defending the students, and was actually happy when a senior member started shouting at me. I now had a voice. The first article I ever published was on the student rebellion at Columbia.

A year later, in the spring of 1969, I attended the founding meeting of Columbia University Women's Liberation. I can't remember why this name was decided upon when most of the faculty and students attending were from Barnard. Perhaps it was an attempt to break out of that female ghetto and/or to use the more prestigious label of Columbia.

In 1972, in my early thirties, I moved to the Bay Area, partly to explore a relationship with a man, but also because I felt it had the right mix of urban and outdoor life for me. It seemed more open as an environment, politically and intellectually, than New York City. After a year, I gave up my tenure-track (but untenured) job at

Queens College of the City University of New York for a lectureship at San Jose State. Although my relationship didn't work out, I decided to stay in northern California if I could get a stable academic position. In 1975 I got an assistant professorship at Sonoma State University, where I pursued a modest but fulfilling career in teaching and building the Women's Studies Department. This decision disappointed several colleagues, who felt I should take my career more seriously and apply for a position at a more elite university. But I wanted to stop moving around. I wanted friends, a community, a home. It was a decision I've never regretted.

■ ■ ■

Gillian also ended up in a teaching career, but through a more circuitous process. When she moved to Los Angeles in the mid-1960s, she went there for the lifestyle, not to pursue a career. But after a year as a secretary in a large LA legal firm, she was bored. She applied to UCLA's PhD program in history. She was accepted and started her studies in 1966. Although she was a good student, she felt invisible and never was encouraged to apply for a fellowship or a teaching assistantship. During her entire graduate education, she had only one woman professor, was assigned only one book written by a woman, and had very little mentoring.

Her inheritance (from her father) paid most of her educational costs. But to earn her living expenses and to avoid going back to secretarial work, she applied for community college teaching positions. She got one, and then another, and although they involved a commute, she found out that she loved teaching. The lecture style with which she was familiar didn't work there, and so she experimented with more participatory teaching and found it very satisfying. In 1970 she got a full-time temporary job at a community college and, with her hippie boyfriend in tow, moved to be near her job. Although teaching absorbed her time, she finally finished her degree in 1978. She did not, however, obtain a permanent position at the college for many years. These years were very difficult for her, as her job was never secure. But finally, with the support of colleagues, and based on her superb teaching record, she won a permanent job. She is still there, still loves teaching, and her department and the campus provide more of a community for her than mine does for me.

■ ■ ■

Wynona's trajectory from a working-class black family through a marriage at eighteen and four children, to years of working as a secretary, and finally to a professional position is impressive. During the years after her divorce, from the time she was thirty-seven until she turned forty-seven, and despite the economic difficulties she faced, Wynona finished her BA, went on to earn an MBA, and then obtained her law degree. She became a lawyer in a large firm where she was once a secretary. Soon, however, she moved to a smaller firm where she would have more control over her work and her hours. She became a partner in this firm with three other woman lawyers and specialized in family and divorce law. Although she loves her work and takes it seriously, Wynona puts her family first. She turned down opportunities that would involve much longer hours, a lot of travel, or relocation.

After the death of her second husband, and as she moved into her fifties and had fewer family responsibilities, Wynona began to focus more on her work. Although still enjoying her legal cases, she has now started attending academic conferences on minorities, women, and the law. At our last interview in 2002, she told me she was about to leave for her first conference in Europe.

■ ■ ■

Julia, about eight years younger than Gillian and me, and three years younger than Wynona, has had the most direct, and least conflicted, route toward an advanced degree and a job. But she compromised the most in regard to her career plans after her husband's illness and death. Yet she, too, found a meaningful career. Julia used her PhD in political science to find employment as a funding officer in a private foundation that endows projects for teenagers from poor families. She loves her work. It permits her to put into practice some of the progressive values she developed through her social activism in the 1960s and 1970s. From the beginning, however, the job gave her the time and space to focus on raising her daughter and to pursue a home life. Yet domesticity would never have been enough for her. Julia plans to retire in five years, when she is sixty, but she is already preparing for an alternative career that she can practice part-time. She is taking courses to become certified as a personal coach and already volunteers with an agency in Oakland that provides career and personal counseling for disadvantaged young women.

Finding a meaningful and sustainable work life provides economic autonomy and psychological identity but is not a single woman's whole life. The new single woman integrates her work with other aspects of her life. She may be less free to move for career opportunities than a coupled woman. Ambitious single women who relocate often to advance their careers sacrifice the stable homes, friendship networks, and community life necessary to sustain a good single life. In chapter 5 I explore how satisfying work fosters autonomy in single women, and how such autonomy promotes an acceptance of single life.

Forging Connections to the Next Generation

Making a distinct choice about parenting without a partner is a major step toward becoming a new single woman. Clearly, single life is more difficult for women who want children only within a good cohabiting partnership, as it is for those who are ambivalent about this issue. The four of us made deliberate choices about parenting. We were not ambivalent, and we did not drift.[4] Gillian chose to be childless and to find alternative ways to relate to the next generation. I chose to become a single parent. Wynona and Julia chose to put the welfare of their children before the marriage. Both became effective single parents. Wynona, Julia, and I sought help in parenting, but *not* from our extended families, former husbands, or new partners. Wynona pulled her four teenagers together into an effective family unit; Julia and I got support from a close network of friends.

Gillian, throughout her twenties and thirties, "just didn't think about" having children. But in 1980, at the age of forty, she got pregnant after a casual relationship, despite having used birth control. She admitted to herself that she had never wanted children, so she chose to have an abortion. Gillian emphasizes that it was *not* a hard decision. She was happy to be able to get a legal abortion, unlike a friend who ten years earlier (before the Supreme Court's decision legalizing abortion) had to go abroad to get one. She felt fortunate too that her mother never pressured her to have children and accepted that she would never have grandchildren. An only child, Gillian wishes she had siblings; she would have loved to be an aunt.

Throughout the years that I followed her life (from the age of fifty-four to sixty-two), Gillian gradually formed a familial bond with two young women. A good friend of hers with terminal cancer asked Gillian to be the trustee for her two daughters, then in their twenties. Gillian was "terrified about taking it on." She realized, however, that she could never replace their mother, who had died, and didn't have to try. Over the course of eight years, as the young women moved into their thirties, Gillian, who at first had just watched over their economic affairs, became "really deeply connected" to them. One of these "daughters" is now divorced, and the other is a lesbian whose partner has just had a baby. Gillian often spends her holidays with all of them.

I had always wanted to be a mother, but not until my thirties. When I was thirty-seven, now with a tenure-track university position, I seriously began to explore the option of having a child without a partner. Because I had formed a communal household, I did not really face up to being a single mother. Unconsciously, I had absorbed the liberal feminist ideal that women could have it all—career, a partner, and motherhood. I combined that with countercultural ideals about alternatives to the nuclear family. I would parent not alone but in a communal setting.

I also sensed, without fully articulating it, that having a child would build bridges back to my family—parents and siblings who did not share my politics and interests and although proud of my success, didn't really understand my life. Grandchildren were what my parents valued, and children were the center of my brother's and sister's lives. Thus, a potpourri of new and traditional cultural values propelled me toward becoming a mother at the age of forty. Although being the single parent of an adopted biracial boy was much more difficult than I imagined, I have never regretted my decision. After the breakup of my communal household, I started sharing child care with another friend, a single mother who had given birth three weeks before I adopted my five-day-old son. Although our relationship had its ups and downs, we are still friends, and our sons became "brothers," a relationship that lasted into their twenties. I discuss my experiences as a single mother in chapter 7.

Wynona's main motivation for divorcing her husband was to save her teenage children. While she was married, everyone thought of them as an outstanding family who dressed well and went to church. The children were so well behaved, everyone said. In fact, Wynona said, "the children were a mess." Before the divorce Wynona's oldest son was always high on drugs and alcohol, and the younger one had shut off all communication. One of her daughters was "eating herself to oblivion," and the other one talked about suicide. After the divorce, the children were in much better shape, though everyone saw them as being at great risk.

Because they were African American kids with a single mother, it was assumed that Wynona's daughters would get pregnant in high school and her sons would become gang members and drug dealers. None of this happened. They all finished high school and eventually went to, and graduated from, college; today all have good jobs. Three of her children are married and have children. One daughter, in her midtwenties, decided to become a single mother.

The deaths of Wynona's first and second husband in the same year precipitated a great family crisis. Again, Wynona and her children pulled together. The children, now in their twenties and early thirties, were in such shock and pain after the death of both their beloved stepfather and their unforgiving father that Wynona used her credit card to take them on a cruise. It took her two and a half years to pay off the debt, but their time together at sea was therapeutic.

Following this, the children were ready to return some of the support Wynona had always given them. Her older son and his wife moved into her house so that she would not be alone. They stayed for three years, and when they left, her youngest son moved back home for a short time. In 1999 Wynona's unmarried daughter moved in with her after she decided to have a child on her own. Wynona accepted her but made it clear that she could not be counted on for child care. Her daughter pays her share of the household expenses, does all the cooking, and relies on her sister, grandmother, and babysitters. Wynona loves the arrangement. She has lots of autonomy but is never alone or lonely.

Wynona's children help her in other ways too. They insisted she buy a better car and install a beeper while commuting to law school. When Wynona broke her foot while still in school, all the children pitched in to take care of her and help her cope. After her father's death, Wynona bought a house for her mother a mile from her own. Wynona has always had a love/hate relationship with her mother, so her daughters and sons take most of the responsibility for helping their grandmother.

Family remains the center of Wynona's life. By 2003, she had six grandchildren and one stepgrandchild. All of her children and grandchildren now live within a radius of thirty miles of her and each other. They are all good friends and see each other often.

■ ■ ■

Julia's divorce, like Wynona's, left her a single parent with a hostile ex-husband who could not be counted on for either financial or emotional support. Whereas Wynona could pull her four teenagers together as a family unit, Julia's daughter, Jessie, was only four at the time of her divorce, and her parents and siblings lived far away. Julia had a full-time job that took her out of town several days a week (although with no overnights). But rather than seek a lesbian partner to move in with her as a coparent, Julia brought together a group of friends to nurture both her daughter and herself—friends she had made primarily during the political movements of the 1970s and in her neighborhood.

Every Tuesday night Julia and Jessie had dinner with a married couple, Emily and Joe, and their daughter, who was three years older than Jessie. Julia knew Emily and Joe from their political work together. One week, dinner would be at their house and the next at hers. These dinners lasted for ten years, and the adults still have a close relationship with each other's daughters. On her early mornings, Julia would drop Jessie off at Emily and Joe's at 6:45. They would give Jessie breakfast and take her to school. Jessie loved her after-school programs, and if Julia couldn't make it home in time to pick her up, Doris, her next-door neighbor, would collect Jessie and give her dinner. Doris, a single woman with no children, played another important role in their lives: "Doris made sure that Jessie bought me birthday and Mother's Day and Hanukkah presents," Julia explained. "I think it is important for kids to give as well as receive, and when you are a single parent you need someone else to help."

It was this alternative family that Julia turned to when she heard that her ex-husband, Bill, had died in an auto accident. She called Emily to come over and be with her when she told Jessie. Elizabeth, her long-distance partner, dropped everything, came down, and moved in for a while. Doris cut short a European trip to be with them. Such support from friends helped Julia parent Jessie through the tough teenage years, making it possible for her to get into an elite eastern college and later an Ivy League graduate school.

Connections to the next generation can be made through one's children and grandchildren, nieces and nephews, younger protégées, or volunteer work with the young. Chapter 6, on childless single women, provides other examples supplementing Gillian's story of how single women form relationships to the next generation outside a family setting.

Creating a Home

Fifty-seven percent of single women own their own home.[5] The figure is probably higher for single women over the age of forty. During the course of my study, a number of women bought a house or condominium, some with help for the down payment from parents or a sibling. For the minority who still rented in their forties or fifties, owning a home, and getting beyond the insecurity of renting, was a primary goal. Younger single women, however, can be at home without owning. Decorating an apartment can be a way of creating a living space for oneself. In an online discussion group sponsored by the *Utne Reader* called Single and Loving It, young single adults talked about the purchase of furniture as a sign of settling down. One woman wrote, "I'm just about to turn 28 and I just bought my first bed last year. But man there's nothing like it. It sure beats the hell out of a futon. The coolest thing is that I bought the bed for me, not to be with someone else."[6]

The experience of the four of us (and of others in my study) demonstrates that one does not have to be coupled to enjoy a satisfying domestic life. All four of us own our homes and pursue lives rich in domesticity.

Gillian has the largest and most beautiful house of any of the women in my study.[7] She lives in an urban setting, in a tasteful, modern house with a river view. Gillian bought the house after her mother died, using part of her inheritance. Originally, she thought that the house was too costly and too big for one person. So she rented part of the house to a colleague and friend who was fifteen years younger. It worked, but after a couple of years, Gillian decided to try to live by herself. She thought she would be lonely and that this would spur her to find a relationship. Instead, she found she loved living by herself with her big dog, Oscar. Because her life is so busy and her mind "very full," Gillian finds that she needs "an enormous amount of space and quiet just to sort out what's going on in there." The house is divided in such a way that individual rooms seem cozy. Since the house is all on one floor, Gillian sees it as adaptable to her needs as she ages. Visiting Gillian at her home modified my earlier opinion that she had tendencies to be a workaholic. She admits as much, but now I could see how domesticity moderates her work commitments. She proudly escorted me through her beautiful garden filled with native plants. Gillian then served me a gourmet lunch, leftovers from what she had cooked for a dinner party the night before.

When my communal household broke up, I feared that I would be lonely and isolated living by myself with my son. But like Gillian, I loved owning my own home. A friend who was a real estate agent helped me find a small house that I could afford because it had two rental units, which would help pay the mortgage and property taxes. Gradually, I had repairs and improvements made to the house, gaining confidence in my ability to find and hire reliable, and sometimes even creative, women and men. After my son left home, I was amazed to find that he was doing a lot of renovations on the house where he now lives. Recently, he called to ask me a question about the kitchen floor that he was tiling. He reminded me that he had watched and helped the man who tiled our kitchen and bathroom. I had no memory of the latter and could not answer his question, but I'm pleased to call on him regularly for repairs to my house. I always liked cooking, and although no gourmet, I'm a good home-style cook. I never explicitly taught my son to cook, nor expected him to prepare food, but I'm gratified that he and his girlfriend cook together, spending a lot of time trying new dishes and sometimes cooking for me.

My son moved out of the house at the age of nineteen, but a young woman ten years older, the daughter of my oldest friend, moved into his room while she finished her degree at Berkeley. It was a relief and a pleasure to live with an autonomous adult who shared more of my interests and lifestyle than a teenage boy. Her moving in delayed the transition to living by myself, something I had not done for twenty-three years. Sasha moved out two years ago, and for the first time in my life I have a guest room. May Sarton, in her *Journal of Solitude,* remarked: "Not enough has been said of the value of a life lived alone in that it is lived in a house with an open door, with room for the stranger, for the new friend to be taken in and cherished."[8] I enjoy the quiet (except for my noisy dog), keeping the house the way I like, having friends over often, and maintaining a room for friends and family from out of town.

For many years during her marriage, Wynona lived on a farm. Not only did she work for wages, care for the children, do all the housework and cooking, but she had a garden, chickens, and sometimes a pig. She canned and preserved food from the garden. Often she was exhausted. After the divorce, Wynona was happy to sell the farm and move into a smaller, suburban tract house. In her cozy, attractively decorated house, Wynona is happy to leave all the cooking to her daughter and her mother. She now enjoys the domesticity provided by her family.

Julia, in contrast, is probably the most domestic woman I interviewed. She loves cooking, gardening, and housekeeping. When her daughter was growing up, she cooked "gourmet vegetarian meals six nights a week." As we will see, her love of children and domesticity led Julia to a disastrous relationship after her daughter went away to college. Now in her midfifties, Julia lives by herself in a house she has remodeled. She said: "I love having a bigger house. I love to cook and entertain, and I love having my own bathroom. I love the quiet. I'm not eager to have anyone move in." Julia doesn't know if she will ever live with a partner again, but she is clear about where she will be. "I'm not moving out of my house," Julia proclaimed. Like other women I interviewed, Julia fantasizes about having a partner live next door or down the block.

Single women need a home, but few of the women I interviewed lived by themselves for their whole lives, and when they did, they had close connections to friendship networks, extended family, communities, and neighborhoods. In chapter 8 I explore additional examples of women who have created new kinds of homes— women who live with relatives, with friends, or in alternative living situations.

Developing Intimate Relationships with a
Network of Friends and Extended Family

To become a new single woman, one needs more than a home, ful-filling work, and a resolution about whether to have children. A new single woman—whether she is a single mother or childless—needs a network of friends, or family and friends, that provides compan-ionship and intimacy and that she can rely on in times of trouble. Because friendship is not an exclusive relationship, and because American culture stresses equity and mutuality as important qualities in a friendship, friends are more supportive of women's autonomy than most family and romantic relationships. Single women over the age of forty are especially good at forming and maintaining friend-ships and often create large networks of friends.

Julia's friendship network, which now includes her ex-lover Elizabeth, provides intimacy as well as care and support. It is with her friends, not her family, that Julia shares her feelings and inner thoughts and to whom she looks for empathy and caring. My friend-ship network, like Julia's, emerged out of my participation in the New Left and feminist movements of the 1970s. Most of my friends are women, mainly single women, with only a few couples and men. My long residence in one community encouraged the formation of friendships. In addition, the communal household facilitated a net-work of friends. But only after the household broke up did I recog-nize the rich network of friends I had built and how important they were to me for intimacy, emotional support and companionship, and practical help. A friend let me use her house as collateral so I could get a bridge loan to buy a new house before the complicated sale of the communal house was completed. In addition to the single mother who became my primary support, other friends, both moth-ers and the childless, were always there to lend an ear and give advice about parenting. I made new friends too—friends I met through my son, through work, and through other friends. Women new to town looked me up, based on the recommendation of their friends who knew me. After a while, women who were widowed, newly divorced, or facing divorce sought to become my friend, seeing me as someone who seemed happy with her single life. I was surprised to find myself with so many friends and—despite conflicts with a few of them—to find my relationships with them so satisfying.

As for Gillian, her workplace became the primary source of her large network of friends. When I first interviewed her in 1994, friends provided the daily substance of her life and companionship for holidays and travel. When she had a serious automobile accident, a number of friends provided all the care she needed. She helped to care for a divorced friend who was ill with cancer until her death. A daughter of a friend lived with her for a while, as did a younger colleague. But initially Gillian did not have enough self-awareness to recognize her rich friendship network. This is not surprising, since we live in a culture that sees family as the center of life, where alternatives to the nuclear family often fail and the importance of adult friendship is culturally invisible. Eight years later, however, Gillian had changed her perspective.

In 1994 Gillian talked of going into therapy to ease the grief over her mother's death and then staying on for self-exploration, with emphasis on how she could find a more successful relationship. In 2002 Gillian recognized that therapy had helped her "become aware of her own and other people's interiors," and she said that this increased her capacity for deep and successful friendships. Gillian now speaks at length and with joy about her wide network of friends. A number of her friends are former students who are ten to fifteen years younger. Most are women, but she also has close male friends. Several friends, male and female, have gotten married at her house. Many of her friends are now coupled (including some lesbian couples), and Gillian has comfortable relationships with them. One married couple comes over every Monday night after their therapy. They come to decompress as they all eat burritos together and watch *Antiques Roadshow.* Other friends have stayed at her house at difficult points in their lives—after a divorce or other traumas or when recovering from an illness.

For many years, her work, education, and family responsibilities left Wynona little time to cultivate friendships. Being black and living in Sonoma County, the county that is the least diverse in the Bay Area and has the lowest percentage of African Americans (1.3), further impeded her ability to find women friends. Her grown children remain her best friends, but Wynona has gradually created a friendship network of single women for support, travel, and recreation. Her two best friends are Hispanic women whom she met at work. In 2002 she had just returned from a trip to Las Vegas to celebrate the birthday of a cousin, a divorced woman who is now a good friend.

A friendship network has distinct meanings for different single women, as these examples attest. Wynona's and my friendship networks revolve around single women, whereas Julia and Gillian have more married couples as friends. Wynona and Gillian have many younger friends—Wynona's grown children and Gillian's former students. All of our friendship networks originated in, and then helped sustain, a community—a political community for Julia and me and the workplace as a community for Gillian and Wynona.

Sustaining a Community

The new single woman has a community created and maintained primarily through her friendship networks. Researchers find that four types of ties—between friends, kin, coworkers, and neighbors —create the networks that sustain a personal community, and of these, friends provide the largest number of bonds.[9] Friends made in a specific organization or setting (at school, college, work, church, the gym) are linked together to become the basis of community today. Political scientist Robert Putnam, in *Bowling Alone: The Collapse and Revival of American Community,* found that single people, rather than fitting the cultural image of being alone and selfish, were more involved outside their families than married people. "Holding other demographic features constant," he wrote, "marriage and children are *negatively* correlated with membership in sports, political and cultural groups.... Married people attend fewer club meetings than demographically matched single people.... Interest in politics is actually slightly higher among single and childless adults than among married people and parents."[10]

Neighborhood can also be a source of community, as it is for Julia. Julia has close neighborhood ties that provide a distinct kind of daily sharing. She lives in a central city block of mainly one-story wooden houses and small apartment buildings. Although the block is quiet, it is near two busy thoroughfares. Belying the stereotype of an anonymous city existence, renters and homeowners on the block form a community. Most have lived there a long time, but newcomers are incorporated into the group. They hold neighborhood potlucks, exchange meals, and help each other out. This neighborhood sustained Julia when she was a single mother and still does so now that she is living by herself. She said: "My neighbors are my friends. For example, recently when I was having my house remodeled, I did my laundry at my neighbor's across the street. One neighbor would hard-boil eggs for me. Others invited me to dinner. It is really a community."

Accepting Our Sexuality

Julia, Gillian, and I have had sex outside of marriage and sometimes outside a committed relationship. Although I did not ask her explicitly, Wynona talked only about sex with her two husbands. Part of accepting our singleness as we moved into our late forties, and then our fifties, was coming to terms with the role sexuality would play in our lives. To supplement the discussion in the last chapter, and to reinforce the point about the diversity of our sexual desires, I now describe how Gillian and Julia talked about their sexuality.

In the late 1990s, a student introduced Gillian to her widowed father, Sam, a man ten years older than Gillian. She found him attractive, enjoyed his company, and appreciated his support of and interest in her work. She admired his professional achievements and his close involvement with his children and grandchildren. He was a good man, and they had the same political values. For Gillian, "he was appropriate in all kinds of ways."

Although she was not in love with him, Gillian eventually agreed to become his lover. "I was curious," she said, "because it had been about ten years since I had sex, and I had not had any great sexual longing. I feared I would not function. But when we decided to have sex, I was pleasantly surprised. I was in full working order; there was nothing wrong with the body. It was just fine." But Gillian did not stay in the sexual relationship. She realized that she really wanted sex only in a love relationship with a "life partner," someone who could engage her "mentally and emotionally." Gillian preferred celibacy to sex without love. But she and Sam have remained friends, and because the relationship has deepened over time, a love and sex relationship may reemerge.

Similarly, Wynona and I accepted celibacy in our fifties because of good sexual relations in the past, our dislike of casual sex, the full lives we lived, and our unwillingness to compromise to be with a partner. Julia, however, does not want celibacy. She sees herself as a very sexual person but has found it hard to be so as a lesbian. Julia explains: "Sexuality for me doesn't have a lot of the baggage that other women seem to associate with it. I am not opposed to casual sex. But the segments of the lesbian community that accept this tend to be younger."

As we have seen, Julia broke up with Elizabeth because she wanted more sexual passion in her life. Even though she is not opposed to casual sex, Julia preferred to combine "passion and companionship" in a cohabiting, familial setting. She wanted to replicate as a lesbian what she had in the early, idealistic days of her marriage. We examine in the next section why this didn't work for her. A year before our last interview in the spring of 2003, Julia was set up by a friend, who knew that neither Julia nor the other woman was interested in a "relationship" and that both wanted to have fun in and out of bed. They did have fun and began a relationship.

From Support Structures to
a Changed Consciousness

Although the structures that single women often unconsciously create are necessary to become a new single woman, achieving them does not mean that a single woman automatically will accept her singleness and be happy with it. Only after the four of us experienced personal disillusionments and disruptions between our midforties and late fifties did we begin to accept our single life and recognize its satisfactions.

For Wynona, the death of her second husband was a turning point. In 1994, several years after his death, Wynona, then forty-nine, was one of the few women in my first interviews who was not looking for another partner. She said:

> I have a rather full life right now with my children and grandchildren, all of whom live nearby. I would like to have a relationship, but I think that's just because of the monogamous upbringing that I had, and I don't know when I will find time. And then my expectations have changed. It's not that I want a man just for the sake of having a man around. If he's going to be a nuisance, I don't want him. I don't want to have to start making a lot of concessions. I don't want to have to start operating on his schedule. I want intellectual stimulation as well as other stimulations. I don't know that it's going to be possible to find all that in one individual. Now for the first time in my life, all I have to really worry about is me.

I read this statement back to Wynona in early 2003, more than eight years later. She was still single and still felt the same way. The structural supports she had created—especially the home she owned, her fulfilling work as a lawyer, and her strong family network supplemented by friendships—laid the basis for her satisfactory single life.

For me, it was the breakup of my communal household that became a turning point. I was surprised to find that I liked living in my own house with my son. I had settled into a satisfying life as a single mother in a supportive network of friends and a loose community, with renewed connections to my parents, siblings, nieces, and nephews, and with a fulfilling career in teaching and building a women's studies program. Three years after establishing my own household, I decided to look up the old boyfriend who would have been the good husband. Had I made a mistake in rejecting him while I pursued a soul mate?

I was going to the Midwest both for a celebration of my parents' fiftieth wedding anniversary and for a reunion with the large Trimberger extended family. Since I would be passing through his city, I called in advance and arranged to meet him. While my two aunts who are nuns took my seven-year-old son to a natural history museum, I met Larry[11] for coffee. He had married another lawyer, who became his partner in a law firm, and together they had raised her children from a previous marriage. For years Larry had served in the state legislature, reelected many times as a Democrat in a Republican district. He had created the life he had envisioned in his early thirties. He would have been a good husband. But I realized I had made the right choice. As I told him about my very different life, I became aware that I really liked it. I had created a life as a single woman, which suited me. I was a homeowner and a homemaker, living in a university town but in a very different context from my mother's. Adopting a baby when I was forty and single and raising a biracial boy while pursuing a full-time career did not mean replicating my mother's life. I was a professor, like my father, but a professor of women's studies. Bohemia had merged with and transformed suburbia. For the first time, I had a vision that this was a life I might live on a permanent basis.

Gillian, finding what seemed to be a suitable partner in her late fifties and then realizing that was not what she wanted, came to a new acceptance of her single life. In 1994 Gillian wanted a "good, in-depth, one-on-one relationship." She blamed herself for not putting enough energy into finding a partner. "I hope I will find a long-term, loving relationship," she said. "But the immediate thing is, I don't have one, and I'm not doing a lot about it. I'm just sitting still. I probably shouldn't be doing that at the age of fifty-four." In 2002, after deciding to break up with Sam, Gillian, who by then was sixty-two, felt very differently. She was still living by herself, but she was much "calmer, more settled, happier." Although she was open to a sexual/love relationship if one came along, she no longer was actively looking for a partner or bemoaning the lack of one. She did *not* think something was wrong with her for remaining single. Her single life was "just fine." Thus, Gillian's life did not change much over eight years, but her perspective altered significantly.

It was not until well into her fifties that Julia gave up the dream of an ideal couple. For her this meant lesbian partners who raise children together. In 1995, at the time of our first interview, Julia had just met Pat, a much younger woman with a five-year-old son. They had been dating for only eight weeks. Pat seemed to meet her desire for passion and companionship, and Julia marveled that for the first time she had a girlfriend "who lives ten minutes away, in the same town, in the same area code."

But Julia had reservations about the future. "I don't know if I want to live with someone," she said. "I'm pretty set in my ways, I have a housemate, because I have a daughter in private college, but it's clearly my house, and you do things my way. When you have a partner living in your house, you have to negotiate. I don't want that. Living together, dealing with dirty socks, I don't think so." Reading her transcript eight years later, Julia wished she had listened to her own reservations.

Instead, Julia rented out her house and moved in with Pat and her son. She went from one extreme—her relationship with Elizabeth, in which each led a separate life—to merging her life with Pat's. In retrospect, Julia realized that she had envisioned a traditional coupled relationship: "She had a child. I thought it would be great to raise a child with a partner. I split with my husband when my daughter was four. Here was the opportunity to be a lesbian couple raising a child in a nuclear family. I thought: 'Oh, I've never done that. It would be really cool to try.' But it wasn't. It worked for a while, but ultimately it didn't work."

Although the concept of a soul mate did not seem attractive to Julia, she couldn't believe that as a lesbian feminist she had bought into the cultural ideal of a nuclear family. Julia turned fifty while still involved with Pat. "It was bizarre to be celebrating my fiftieth birthday with a six-year-old bringing me presents. I found myself dealing with PTA and school lunches. I thought, 'This is not how I envisioned fifty.' Now when I celebrate my birthday, I do it with adults and it feels better." Julia lived with Pat for four of their five-year relationship, but when Julia moved back into her own house, Pat was very bitter and broke off any contact. Unlike the close relationship she maintains with Elizabeth (now with a new partner), Julia has no relationship with Pat. Julia still sees the son (now eleven), but only because his other mother likes her and lets Julia spend time with him during the periods he is at her house.

When I asked Julia where she would be in ten years, she said that she would definitely be living in the same house. She would never move out again to live with a partner.

■ ■ ■

The supports necessary for a single life—a home, meaningful work that is not one's whole life, a satisfactory sex life or a level of comfort with celibacy, a connection to the next generation, a network of friends and/or extended family, and a community—also support couples and married people. When we embark on adulthood, few of us really know where we will end up. Given that, it is important for single women in their twenties, thirties, and forties more consciously to pursue these goals. Whether they hope to couple or not, this is the route to a richer life and one with more options later on. Conversely, to focus primarily on finding a partner while other parts of life are neglected is a recipe for unhappiness. As new single women become culturally visible and accepted, it may no longer be necessary for young women to make unconventional choices on the road to singleness. Becoming a long-term single woman, whether divorced or ever single, will be seen as one of several conventional paths to a good life.

CHAPTER 4

"Nobody's Wife, Nobody's Mother, Nobody's Lover"

Obstacles to Building a Satisfying Single Life

Today, all long-term single women go through a process of struggle and change to craft and accept their lives. But not all single women make this transition, or they do so only with great difficulty. Even women who make many of the same choices in their twenties and thirties as those depicted in the last chapter, and establish some of the supports for a long-term single life, may regress in their fifties. They may put most of their energy into finding or keeping a partner while neglecting other relationships with extended family, friends, colleagues, and communities.

Rachel Brown and Beth Gilman, unlike other women portrayed in this book, became more unhappy during the time that I followed their lives. Both have been single most of their lives; Rachel has no children and Beth is a single mother, with two out-of-wedlock children from different fathers. In analyzing their lives, and the sources of their malaise, I was aided by the autobiographical writings of an Irishwoman, Nuala O'Faolain, a columnist for the *Irish Times* and a TV personality in Dublin. In the late 1990s, I read *Are You Somebody?: The Accidental Memoir of a Dublin Woman.* Published in Ireland in 1996, the book became a best seller there and was reprinted by an American publisher in 1998.[1] At the time, I was bothered by O'Faolain's despair about her single life, as reflected in the self-pitying quote that became the title of this chapter. Upon re-reading it, I saw many parallels between O'Faolain's life and that of Rachel and Beth.

An Unconventional Life and a Conventional Desire to Partner

Rachel, Beth, and Nuala O'Faolain were born in the 1940s, and all embraced the lifestyle and political changes of the 1960s and 1970s. If anything, they were more unconventional in their twenties and thirties than those of us portrayed in chapter 2. Yet they too wanted to find a soul mate.

Rachel Brown is an intense, funny, articulate, extroverted, and friendly woman. I immediately liked her. This fifty-one-year-old never-married woman had created many of the structures that support a viable single life but was unhappy with her inability to find a love relationship. In that, she was not very different from many other women I interviewed.

Rachel grew up in Cleveland with two brothers in what she labels a lower-middle-class Jewish family. Starting at the age of seventeen (in about 1960), Rachel considered herself a Beatnik, attending both civil rights demonstrations and radical poetry readings. She also became interested in art history. Rachel stayed in Cleveland during her college years. But in the mid-1960s, as a college graduate and still a virgin, she escaped to New York City. There she pursued both her master's degree in theater arts and a bohemian lifestyle. Rachel became friends with a large group of young women and men who were creating a countercultural lifestyle, one that included many sexual affairs. Some of the women introduced her to radical feminism. Rachel absorbed the changing and often contradictory messages of feminist groups as they shifted from defenders to critics of the sexual revolution, and from critics to renovators of marriage and the family.

At first Rachel enjoyed promiscuity. She "realized how much power one has when you sleep with anyone you want." But she also was hurt when several boyfriends she particularly liked slept with other women. Rachel, returning to the United States in the late 1960s after a year in Argentina (as part of her master's program), was surprised to find out what had happened to her old friends: "We had said to each other, 'Well, this is really fun, and this is the way that we are going to run our lives. We're never getting married. We're going to show that things can be different.' But I turned around one day and everybody was married. I said, 'Hey, what happened to the way we were going to do it?' " Rachel too now wanted to find one person to settle down with. But in retrospect she realized, "I had extremely high standards because I knew that I didn't want to end up divorced like my mother. When I got married, I wanted it to be forever."

In New York City and later in San Francisco (where she moved in the 1970s), Rachel taught in both high school and a community college. In the mid-1980s, Rachel left teaching to become codirector of a well-established and well-financed museum in a wealthy suburban community. But her personal life didn't improve. She thought maybe she would have more romantic success with women, so for a time she convinced herself that she was a lesbian. But after experimenting with women for five years with no greater success, Rachel admitted that she was definitely heterosexual.

When I first interviewed Rachel in 1995, she had owned her own house for eight years and loved her work. Her parents were dead, but her two brothers, one of whom was married with children, lived nearby. It was important for her to spend Thanksgiving with family, but she had to struggle with her married brother because his wife liked to go away for the holiday. He had finally agreed that they would always have Thanksgiving together including her other brother, who was single.

Rachel would have liked to have kids, but she had an abortion when she was thirty because she did not think she was strong enough to have a child on her own. By her late forties, she felt psychologically ready to have a child, but by then she "was too tired." However, she had begun to create a familylike relationship with a young adult. She had invited the nineteen-year-old son of an Argentinian friend to live with her for a year while he went to school in the United States. She was looking forward to "instant parenthood." She was also establishing a relationship with her sixteen-year-old niece and ten-year-old nephew. In addition, Rachel had a network of friends, especially a group of gay men, some of whom she had met in the museum and others as a volunteer with an AIDS prevention organization.

Despite having created many of the structures to support a viable single life, Rachel was quite unhappy. She felt that the sexual freedom she had enjoyed so much in her twenties and early thirties had led primarily to hurt in her forties. For the previous ten years she had only short affairs and no real relationships. She had been in therapy for five years and had many insights about how her parents' "terrible marriage" and her mother's dependence on and criticism of her had affected her. Through therapy, she had come to see that "I am not as horrible as I thought I was, and I've actually started to believe that somebody could love me." But she also retained many negative self-evaluations. She called herself "retarded in relationships," with a "lack of ability to commit." Another woman in the group interview commented on how Rachel characterized most of her past attempts at relationships as "failures."

Eight years later, I located Rachel at the same address and heard that she was still single. Before continuing her story, let us meet Beth Gilman.

Beth, a soft-spoken, pretty woman, projects a calm demeanor that belies the unconventional life she has struggled through. She is almost the same age as Rachel but has a very different life history. I first interviewed Beth when she was fifty and had a fifteen-year-old son and twenty-five-year-old daughter. The two children had different fathers; she had not married either man, although she had a brief marriage when she was eighteen.

Beth married after her freshman year in college because she was pregnant. On the day of her wedding, however, she miscarried. Beth and her husband dropped out of school and moved to Denver to live with his parents. The glow quickly faded, and the marriage lasted less than a year. Beth worked in Denver for a while, but she soon left for

Arizona to be near her large family and to finish college there. In her junior year, in the mid-1960s, Beth studied in France and then traveled in Europe. She came back politicized and soon considered herself a revolutionary. Beth was a founding member of Students for a Democratic Society (SDS) at her campus, and with a group of her political allies she moved into a collective household. These became her core friends for many years, and she is still close to some of them.

Beth combined her radical politics with a more conventional notion of coupling—an ideal that did not fit her experience. She said of these years: "I had very romantic notions of this great revolutionary man I would meet one day, and he would be the perfect mate. Well, my daughter's dad, when I got pregnant, abandoned me. . . . Abortion was really not an option back then: it wasn't available, and it was not something I even considered."

Beth was twenty-five and pregnant. She had graduated with a BA in social work, trained after college as a paralegal, and worked for a legal services program. She lived in a communal household where several other women had children. Beth's mother was shocked that she was pregnant outside of marriage and wanted her to put the baby up for adoption. Beth gave birth in 1968 surrounded by housemates and friends and felt she had a family. She also expected that she would find another relationship. She defied her mother and kept the baby girl, Emily. Later, Beth's mother fell in love with the baby and formed a close relationship with Emily.

When the communal household disbanded in 1975, Beth decided to move to California. She settled in Santa Cruz, where her best friend, another single mother, had relocated. They shared child care. Beth got a secretarial job at the university and learned Spanish, but soon she decided to move to a suburban area closer to San Francisco, where she also had friends and more job opportunities. She started as a secretary in a large social work agency, but her fluency in Spanish, her legal aid background, and her excellent organizational skills permitted her to advance to the program-planning and administrative position she holds today.

In the late 1970s, Beth got involved with prison support work.

There she met a black political prisoner of some fame, who was acquitted after an eighteen-month jury trial. She fell in love and they moved in together. Perhaps he was the great revolutionary man she had dreamed about. Neither believed in marriage, but Beth thought she had found her soul mate. Soon she was pregnant, but this time she did not expect to be a single mother. She knew that she might continue to be the primary breadwinner of the family, but she expected her partner to be a good father and to provide more than half of the child care. They were together for about four years, but Beth became increasingly disillusioned. Her partner didn't work, went back to hanging out on the street, developed a bad drug problem, and became abusive. "I was not going to have my son growing up around this kind of a role model," Beth explained, "a male who ordered me and my daughter around and was disrespectful of women." So she told him he had to leave.

Beth was now in her late thirties and the single mother of a fourteen-year-old daughter and a four-year-old son without a supportive network of friends to help her. Beth could talk to her woman friends about her problems as a single mother, but neither her single friends nor her coupled ones were involved with her children. Emily hated her high school and was becoming rebellious. So Beth called Emily's father, who had never taken care of her and only occasionally sent money. He was still in Arizona, now was making a good income, and lived in a stable relationship. He agreed to let Emily try to live with him and go to high school in Tucson. It helped that Beth's mother, sister, and other extended family members lived nearby and that Emily liked all of them. Beth was relieved when Emily bonded with her father and did well in the new high school. She graduated from high school there and stayed for college.

When I first interviewed her in 1994, Beth, after many years of not being in a relationship, had been seeing a man for about six months. Beth thought she had finally found her soul mate. Although she did not envision getting married, Beth, who was fifty, yearned for a permanent partner and wanted to cohabit. Beth had many friends, but she said that most of the active social life in her

circle revolved around couples. Too often she felt lonely and isolated. It was only during an individual interview nine years later that
I learned more about this relationship and how it too had disappointed her.

■ ■ ■

Nuala O'Faolain, who was a few years older than Rachel and Beth
and had grown up in a more conservative society, also led an unconventional life in her twenties and thirties. Although Nuala was more
professionally successful than Rachel or Beth and later became famous, I see many parallels in their lives as single women.

With the aid of scholarships and some financial help from family
friends, Nuala pursued studies in English literature at University
College, Dublin (UCD). In the early 1960s, she did a year of graduate study at the University of Hull in England. Nuala then won the
most prestigious scholarship in Ireland, which she could use anywhere in the world. She chose to go to Oxford for two years. With
her Oxford degree, O'Faolain became a lecturer in the English Department at UCD. But after several years, she returned to England to
be with a man. She got a job with the BBC making TV programs in
the humanities for the new Open University. She loved the challenge
and the travel and soon went to another unit of the BBC as a producer for a new public access program called *Open Door.*

But despite her interesting and creative work history, in her
twenties and thirties Nuala had no sense of developing a career. She
wrote in her memoir: "My aim in life was something to do with loving and being loved. That was going to work out, somehow. In the
meantime, and on the side, I did the job."[2] Nuala also held very contradictory ideas about personal life. As a young woman, she had two
long-term serious relationships, and she envisioned marrying both
men. Nuala wrote that she was looking for a man to love and have
babies with, yet she didn't want to be a woman in the home. The two
Irish women she most admired were famous writers who were single
(one was Maura Laverty, at the time one of Ireland's best-known

women writers). But she viewed them as isolated and lonely—not women she would want to emulate.[3]

Nuala's most serious (ten-year) relationship was with Rob, an English writer. They had a stormy relationship, and both had many casual affairs with others. Although she was living a sexually permissive life with cultural approval in her circle in the late 1960s and the 1970s, Nuala yearned for a perfect marriage. At one point, Rob offered to marry her, but Nuala backed out, partly in response to opposition from her Catholic family and partly because of her idealism about the man she would marry. O'Faolain admits that she was very idealistic about love, that she wanted a hero to look up to.

In her late thirties, depressed about her relationship with Rob and concerned that she was becoming an alcoholic, Nuala decided (in 1977) to break with him and return to Ireland. There she created a well-received TV talk show and later became a respected columnist for the *Irish Times*. But her ideas about personal life matured more slowly. She began to realize that in her daily life "idealism was something quite destructive. It manifested itself as a nostalgia for, or a hankering after, something better and other—something more overwhelming—than even the best thing that actually happened."[4]

Nuala felt lucky that in all those years she never got pregnant. When at the age of thirty-nine she unexpectedly did and then miscarried early, she didn't know how she felt. At the age of fifty, she wrote in her memoir: "I still don't know."[5] But she admitted that she was not reconciled to her childlessness: "I would have been a very bad mother, during most of my life. But I'd be a good mother, now. Too late. Sometimes I have to look away from small children—hopping where they stand as their mothers try to put on their little jumpers, or talking to themselves pressed against the window in the seat in front of me in the bus. They are too beautiful to bear."[6]

Back in Dublin, Nuala, like Rachel, became involved with a woman—Nell McCaffrey, another Irish writer and feminist activist. However, unlike Rachel's attempts to have relationships with women, Nuala's attachment to Nell flourished. They bought a house and lived together for fifteen years. For the first time in her life, Nuala felt she had a home; she did not drink as much as before and felt much healthier. Nuala never uses the word *lesbian* or *bisexual,* but she does call the relationship a loving partnership; she was very hurt and felt lost when it ended in her midfifties.

Failing at Relationships

The women portrayed in previous chapters certainly had many unsuccessful relationships. Many felt hurt and suffered from a sense of failure, self-blame, or victimization when their marriages or relationships ended. But they put most of their energy into building a life for themselves and, for some, for their children. As I followed their lives, the women did not focus on their failures. Over time they gave up the idea that finding a new partner was essential to their happiness. But Rachel, Beth, and Nuala were fixated on their failure at romance and still expressed an intense desire to be coupled, often neglecting other relationships.

In June 2003 I arrived at Rachel's home to reinterview her, eight years after I first met her. Aged fifty-nine, Rachel was still attractive and dressed in an age-appropriate hip style. She was still funny and vivacious. She lived in the most unconventional community in a rich suburban county. She showed me around her attractive house, which had great views and was furnished in an artistic but casual style.

Rachel's dissatisfaction, however, was evident from her first comments about the house. She talked about the expensive foundation and structural work it needed and how she was tired of living so far from the city. She said she was thinking of selling it because she needed a change. She thought she might use the equity from the house to travel and maybe settle in Mexico, Bali, or somewhere exotic. Rachel was a single woman who did not feel at home.

Rachel soon revealed that during the previous eight years she had expended a lot of energy on finding a partner and again felt she had failed. During that time, Rachel had two significant relationships, one that lasted six months and the other more than a year. The shorter one was more meaningful to her. Rachel met Mel, who had been single for most of his life, at a theater party when she was fifty-four and he fifty-eight. Unlike her previous affairs, the relationship was not very sexual because of Mel's ambivalence or dysfunction. But for Rachel, there "was a tremendous connection intellectually and personality wise—a lot of laughing, a lot of understanding, and a lot of tenderness." When Mel broke off the relationship, Rachel was heartbroken. She said: "It took me a long time to get over it. I was wailing."

Whereas other women might have blamed Mel, Rachel felt "afraid to let someone know her." She went back to therapy and started taking several relationship workshops, which she found very helpful. One she especially liked was called Life Works and was led by the author of a book entitled *Finding the Man You Want*. Based on advice by workshop leaders, she forced herself to do Internet dating. Through Match.com, she met a man who lived four hours away. "When we first met," she explained, "we said we weren't a match, but we slept together anyway. Sex was great and kept us together. I became very attached to him, and then he broke up with me. That ended two or three years ago. I was hurt by him, but not as much as by the other man."

Rachel persists in computer dating, although with no success in the last few years. She might do well to consider journalist Lee Reilly's analysis of the vast gap between the goal of computer dating (or personal ads) and the nature of the process:

> The goal—intimacy—is about the whole person; her context, her work, her friends, her family, the life she has constructed, her interests, the way she listens, the way she shares, how much she has to offer, and how much she wants to take. The process—services such as video-dating and personal ads—removes her from her context and draws attention only to what she has to show—her face, her figure, her ability to say something pithy in two minutes on tape or forty-five minutes over coffee.[7]

While Rachel focused ever more energy on finding a romantic relationship, the other relationships in her life deteriorated since our first interview. Her network of gay male friends disappeared, but she had three new friends, she told me, one of whom was a man she had met through Match.com. "When we met, neither of us was attracted to the other, so we became best friends. We still are friends. I guess the connection was around the pain. He had also been hurt many times."

But this man lived an hour away, and perhaps because they connected mainly around a negative emotion, Rachel was now "feeling the need to separate" from him. She had two new woman friends, but one lived four hours away and the other in New York City. Thus, Rachel had no friends who lived nearby, no network of friends whom she saw on a regular basis. Rachel called herself a hermit and admitted she needed more friends. But she had no concrete plans on how to find them.

Rachel's relationship to family and to the next generation also had worsened since the first interview. Her parenting of the Argentinian youth had not worked out. Rachel said: "Now he works in Silicon Valley and makes more money than I do. He doesn't call me. I had a falling out with his father when he came to visit. I think the son didn't tell his family how much I helped him because he was embarrassed. I felt slighted by them because they did not thank me for everything I had done. I had really sacrificed a lot for him."

Her relationships with her brothers, both of whom still live nearby, also are conflicted. She sees her older brother only twice a year, on their respective birthdays. Rachel dislikes his noncohabiting partner, with whom he has been for six years. Rachel sees her other brother, his wife, and her niece and nephew more often. She always spends Passover, Thanksgiving, and other holidays with them. The previous Thanksgiving, while Rachel was spending three months in LA as a guest curator, her brother and his family came down for the holiday. Rachel said: "It turned out to be a big fiasco." Rachel got angry with her niece, now in her twenties, and her teenage nephew "when they brought sand into the house and were very messy." Her brother defended his kids and lit into her with what Rachel called "a character assassination." They have since tried to patch things up, but seven months later there are still "uneven edges." Rachel now feels that it is better to see them less often and that she had become too dependent on them. She feels that the incident in LA damaged her relationship with her niece and nephew, which was never particularly close. Thus, Rachel has weak family ties and has not created satisfying relationships with the next generation.

Nor has Rachel come to an acceptance of her childlessness. Although she no longer yearns for a child, she sees herself at a disadvantage compared with people with children. She said: "I see people my age who now have kids who are getting married and having children. Their lives seem a lot fuller than mine. Their teenage years did not look that good, but being a grandparent seems attractive. It looks like an automatic community."

Even more disastrous to her life as a single woman is a simmering conflict with her codirector at the museum, a conflict that recently erupted into open warfare. Rachel described at length the conflict with her colleague, a man who had been hired seven years earlier. Rachel admitted that he is very talented and has done incredible things, but she never liked him. As she talked, it became clear that she felt threatened by him, something she almost admitted. Recently, they clashed over who would produce a particular exhibit about women. Rachel felt it was her right to do it, so she appealed to the chairman of the board of directors, who met with the two of them. During the meeting, Rachel "lost it" and started yelling obscenities at her colleague. He walked out. After reflection and therapy, Rachel wrote a letter of apology to him and to the chairman. Subsequently, her colleague dropped his threat of a lawsuit. But even if her contract is renewed next year, Rachel doesn't know how she can continue to work there.

Rachel is now contemplating retiring from an institution that she loved and that provided an identity and a community for her. She is thinking about looking for another career. Maybe she could become a travel writer, she thought, or finally finish that screenplay she had been working on for years. Neither of these options seems very compelling to her.

Rachel now feels very isolated and depressed. Regardless of what happens at the museum, it is no longer a community base for her and she has no other real community. The only solution she can think of is to find a permanent partnership with a man. But psychologists would dispute whether this would lead to happiness for her. A longitudinal study of twenty-four-thousand individuals over the age of fifteen found that marriage led to only a temporary increase in subjective well-being. After a few years people are no happier than in the years before marriage. Richard Lucas and his colleagues conclude that "on average, people do not experience long-term changes in satisfaction following marriage."[8]

■ ■ ■

A few weeks after I interviewed Rachel, I reconnected with Beth Gilman. I asked her for details of the relationship she had been so hopeful about nine years earlier. Beth recalled her attraction to Jose, a charming and charismatic political leader who was ten years younger than she. Beth had a wonderful time with him, and she was drawn into the kind of activist community she loves. They were together four years. Beth would have liked to live together, but Jose refused. "We lived near each other," Beth explained. "Jose always wanted to have his own little spot. He had been in relationships before where he lived in the woman's house, and when it ended he was without a home. So he didn't want to get into that situation again." In addition, Beth knew that Jose would not want to move in with a troubled teenager.

Her son, John, was a "teenager from hell." He dropped out of high school and started abusing alcohol and some drugs. Beth obtained medication for his depression and demanded that he work and help around the house. They lived together for three miserable years, the same years that Beth was involved with Jose.

In the fourth year of their relationship, Beth found out that Jose was lying to her, probably had been for a long time, and that he was involved with other women. Crushed, she broke up with him. She knew that he had never been coupled for long and now admitted that he was probably a commitment-phobe. Talking to me about the relationship more than four years later, Beth admitted that she had not completely healed. She was not looking for another man, but she seemed to accept her singleness out of disillusionment, rather than for positive reasons. In addition, her focus on being coupled as the route to happiness inhibited her from creating structures that would support single life.

Beth never bought a house. Her desire to find a "revolutionary man" led her to dismiss any wish to become a *bourgeois homeowner.* But just before she broke up with Jose, her long-term rental building was sold, and she was forced to move to another town some distance away. The move and the breakup, together, were extremely disruptive. In addition, Beth's friendship network had deteriorated.

During the years she was with Jose, three good friends—a couple and a single woman—moved away, and other friendships faded, as Beth had little time for them. With her focus on Jose and doing social things with other couples, Beth did not make the effort to find new friends. Although she still communicates with, and occasionally sees, the friends who moved out of the area, Beth now admits she needs new local connections. She needs people to go to movies and concerts with and just to hang out—activities she did exclusively with Jose. She also needs friends who want to travel.

But for several years, Beth's depression over the end of the relationship prevented her from reaching out. Her long tenure and supervisory role at work limits her ability to make new friends there. "But what about your rich political community?" I asked. "Isn't that a natural source of friends, now that you have gotten over your depression?" Beth responded: "During the period I was with Jose, a political community was an integral part of our relationship. I was very active in lots of local political activities. But when we broke up, I terminated everything because he is everywhere. If I go to any political event, he is always there. It was too hard. I didn't want to expose myself to people asking, 'Where is Jose?'"

I must have looked surprised because Beth said defensively: "I needed to withdraw for a while, and it has been good for me, but I don't see my withdrawal from politics as permanent. Maybe I need to work on forgiveness, since it has been four years. I don't long for him anymore, but I haven't gotten over that rejection and the feeling of being lied to by someone I trusted more than anyone. It was really a betrayal."[9]

Thus, Beth, like Rachel, feels she has failed at relationships. Although she has a family life and satisfying work, at the time she broke up with Jose, Beth did not have a home, an adequate friendship network, or a supportive community—important supports for a single life.

■ ■ ■

Nuala O'Faolain wrote *Are You Somebody?* a few years after she and Nell ended their fifteen-year relationship. Because she was partnered for a longer period than either Rachel or Beth, her despair about being single in her fifties was greater. Like them, Nuala sees herself as a failure at relationships. She longs to find a new partner, a soul mate, which now is a man. Nuala wrote:

> Millions and millions of people besides me have thought that another person is what you need to complete yourself and to offer completion—that together you can unlock the best of the world and the best of yourself.... The time and culture I grew up in proposed to me that somewhere in the creation there was another person—my other half—walking toward me. The person would catch sight of me. But a woman past the age where she might be contemplated as a sexual partner is hardly seen.... Who wants to know about them? If no companion depends on them? If they're nobody's mother? Nobody's wife? Nobody's lover?[10]

Nuala ends the memoir with another set of bleak lines: "That's how the life I have described here has been.... Each thing is itself, discrete: near each other, and made from the same material, but never flowing into each other. . . . There has been no steady accumulation; it has all been in moments. But in front of me there is a vista: empty, but inexpressibly spacious. Between those two—landscape of stone and wide blue air—is where I am."[11]

In the afterword to the U.S. edition of the memoir, published two years later, Nuala recorded her surprise at writing a best seller, at finding that "What I had thought was merely personal had turned out to have meaning for other people."[12] She had received thousands of letters from people telling her their own troubles and expressing admiration and love for her. Yet she expressed regret that not one of her former lovers sent her a note, and no one tried to ask her out.

> I'd called the book *Are You Somebody?* But I had wanted for a long time to call it *Personal Ad.* It did confess. Especially it confessed— evasively, far too prettily—to sexual yearnings I could not assuage. Once responses began to flood in, I began to hope even for that. Maybe someone who'd read it would come for me and change everything? But nothing happened. I'd go out, and there would be praise and affection and even drama. . . . And I would come home to my quiet room. I'd say to the cat and the dog, "Any Princes or Princesses Charming come down the chimney while I was out? No? Thought as much."[13]

Finally, one man did make an advance, but he never showed up for the date they had made. O'Faolain concluded by confessing: "There's nothing I wouldn't stop at in pursuit of even a parody of love."[14]

Family of Origin and Single Life

Contemplating the sources of these three women's unhappiness with single life, I began to look at their families of origin in comparison with women who had crafted a satisfying single life. Those of us portrayed in chapter 2 were not especially close to our mothers, and none of us chose to replicate our mother's life. But all of us came from stable families and had a relatively happy childhood. I knew this was not true for Rachel and Nuala, but I realized I didn't know enough about Beth's childhood. I knew only that her parents divorced when she was very young and that her mother and grandmother helped with her perturbed teenagers. I interviewed her for a third time and learned that she too had a troubled childhood, not because of divorce per se, but because of her mother's remarriage to a man who was an abusive stepfather.

While my case studies are too few to generalize with confidence, I can hypothesize that dysfunctional parenting and an unhappy childhood impede, but certainly do not destroy, a woman's ability to develop a strong sense of self and to craft the social structures that support a satisfactory single life. Ironically, having parents with a bad relationship seems to lead women to internalizing more completely the cultural message that one must be coupled to be happy. This was true of Myra Detweiler and Dorothy Sawyer, the sexually assertive women we met in chapter 2, and perhaps of the flamenco dancer, Nancy Dean, too, all of whom had an unhappy childhood. Through their sexual and sensual agency, however, these three women increased their self-esteem and autonomy, which helped them to create the structures that supported their lives as long-term single women. Can Rachel, Beth, and Nuala overcome their unhappy childhoods?

One of the first things Rachel said in the group interview was that her parents "were completely mismatched. They had a terrible marriage that lasted twenty-three years," she said. "They wanted completely different things. He loved fishing and hunting, and she couldn't stand being outside. Although neither of them had a college education, she loved to read. My mother was from an Orthodox Jewish family; my father's family believed in assimilating into American culture." Rachel portrayed her mother, Ruth, as an unhappy, neurotic housewife, completely incompatible with Hank, her dashing husband who owned an appliance store in the ghetto. As a teenager, Rachel sympathized with her father, but she now knows that he car-ried on many affairs, some of them lasting a number of years. As an adult, Rachel learned that she had a half sister, a mixed-race African American.

Ruth's unhappiness led her to emotionally abuse Rachel. Ruth often reiterated the story about Rachel's difficult birth. Ruth said that she was in so much pain that she asked the nurse to give her poison. Later, whenever she got angry at Rachel, she liked to say, "I wish that nurse had given it to me." Ruth often denigrated Rachel but also demanded her emotional support. When Rachel was a teenager, for example, Ruth found a picture of Hank's girlfriend. Rachel's mother showed her the picture of "the tramp," seeking to enlist her sympathy and to undermine Rachel's attachment to her father. In retrospect, Rachel says: "They both were without communication skills, utterly at a loss in knowing how to get what they wanted." She felt that she had to "play some role in taking care of both of them."

In the 1950s neither her mother nor her father could contemplate the possibility of divorce. Finally, in the early 1960s, after their youngest son had his Bar Mitzvah, Hank left. Now that his son was a man, his job was done. Rachel was left with the responsibility for her mother. She recalls the day her father packed his things. Ruth, only five feet tall, always staged dramatic scenes, but this day she topped them all. Ruth ran around the house screaming, carrying a large kitchen knife, saying she was going to kill herself. Rachel was both disdainful and scared. She took the knife away, but her mother then ran down to the basement. Rachel heard a loud whining sound and realized that Ruth had turned on Hank's table saw. Rachel rolled her eyes and waited for a couple of minutes. "Let me see if she can actually go through with this," she thought. When she went down, Ruth was standing there, almost in a trance, staring at the blade. Rachel turned off the saw. "At this moment, at seventeen, I hated my mother," Rachel concluded.

Although Ruth did not try suicide again, she did have a nervous breakdown. Rachel, who had yearned to escape by going away to college, reluctantly agreed to go to the local university and live at home to provide support for her mother. It took Ruth twelve years to grant the divorce, but Rachel escaped in four.

Rachel continued with what she called the soap opera: Her father's "other woman" soon developed bone cancer. "He had to take care of her and exercise every muscle in her body until she died," Rachel said. "My mother said, 'I didn't wish it on her.' I'm sure that she did, but she was uncomfortable with having any kind of power." Finally Ruth recovered, got her own apartment, which she liked, and made plans to travel. But she died suddenly at the age of fifty-nine. Hank died soon after.

■ ■ ■

Beth's story is different—more WASP, less dramatic, but almost as damaging. Beth was born in the East, but her parents divorced when she was only two. Her mother moved back to Arizona to be near her siblings. Beth never saw her father again. Soon her mother remarried and, when Beth was seven, had another daughter. Beth, unlike Rachel, considers that her mother and grandmother were excellent parents, but she had a terrible relationship with her stepfather. "My mom must have been in her early thirties when they married, and he was the same [age]," Beth recounted.

> I liked him a lot at first, and tried to get his attention, but he was always very cold to me. He had never been around children. I tried and tried to get him to like me, but he was always severe and critical, never loving or accepting. He was not physically, but very emotionally, abusive. I grew to hate him, and came to view him with fear and loathing. Although I begged her to leave, my mom stayed with him because she did not want to go through another shameful divorce. After my sister graduated, long after I had left home, my mom separated from him.

Beth feels that this family dynamic had a big impact on her. She had "a huge core of sadness" because of her stepfather's hostility. Her relationship with her mother was undermined too. "She "didn't protect me from his abuse," Beth said.

Fortunately, Beth had a good relationship with both her mother's mother and her stepfather's parents. His parents were warm and loving grandparents, and she became close to them. They said they could never understand why their son was so mean to her. But this grandmother died when Beth was still very young, and she now had a more distant relationship to her grandfather. Nor did her maternal grandmother, despite being a strong and loving woman, provide a good image of marriage. Beth described her grandmother:

> She was an incredibly strong, loving woman and was the glue that kept the family together. Her family had come across the prairie in covered wagons and lived in a sod house in South Dakota. But my grandmother married a doctor and became very middle class, one of the better-off families in town during the Depression. She had four children and was a very respectable lady. As a married woman, she went to a teacher training college, which was unusual in her day. She became a kindergarten teacher and just loved children. She divorced during the war. Her husband was having an affair with his nurse, and it was a huge scandal in her little town. She was incredibly humiliated and never allowed his name to be spoken in her presence. So she moved East to help Mom out with me. They moved to Arizona and lived together until my mom remarried.

Beth left home immediately after high school graduation and chose to go to a small college in the Midwest, partly because she wanted to try to reconnect with her father, who now lived in Chicago. A few months into her freshman year, she made plans to drive to Chicago with her boyfriend to see him. "I was eighteen by then," Beth said, "and I really, really wanted to meet him, especially because of my awful stepfather. I really wanted to see where I had come from. He was a Protestant minister who never remarried or had other children." She learned from her mother that her father was an alcoholic and had tried to commit suicide when they were together. But

Beth was impressed that he had been able to keep his position in the church.

A few weeks before she planned to go to Chicago, she heard that her father had died—from alcoholism, she assumed. She decided to go to Chicago anyway to meet his mother, who was very old. Beth recalled the experience: "She sat with me for several days, showing me pictures in her photo albums and talking about him. She was the sweetest lady, originally from Scandinavia. I cried and cried and cried. I also met a couple of cousins who were watching out for her. But then I never saw any of them again. We never contacted each other. But it was [a] catharsis around my dad, I guess."

About four years ago, Beth's mother told her that her father had committed suicide. Certainly, the absence of her birth father, the abuse by her stepfather, and the negative example of her maternal grandfather did not provide good models of men or marriage for Beth. An ideal revolutionary man was much preferable.

■ ■ ■

Nuala grew up in Dublin in the 1940s and 1950s in an unusual combination of riches and poverty. Both of her parents were college educated, and her father was famous—the first journalist in Dublin to write a daily social column about the receptions, parties, and events that happened around town every night. While he went out dressed in a tuxedo and was picked up by a chauffeur, her mother, with nine children, stayed at home, often living in misery with little money and few luxuries. But the real impoverishment that Nuala (the second child) faced was emotional. Nuala and all the children knew that their father was a womanizer, with one mistress after another and several other children. Her mother hated being a housewife, neglected the children, and became an alcoholic. Nuala felt she was saved when her father scraped together money to send her off to a Catholic boarding school at the age of fourteen.

This legacy of an unhappy family life was complex because Nuala's father never deserted them entirely. "Just when you thought it was safe to hate him," Nuala recalled, "he'd make some loving and sensitive gesture."[15] This was especially seductive, because her mother was emotionally absent. Although her mother retained her "great passion" for her husband, retelling in drunken revelry their wonderful life together as newlyweds, none of the children "had mattered very much to her,"[16] Nuala concluded. She asked: "How did my mother and my father not care more for the small children around them? How did they not pick them up, not comfort them? How did my father strap his defenseless sons with his army belt?"[17]

In her twenties and thirties, Nuala played out aspects of both her mother's and her father's life. Like her mother, she was, on the road to alcoholism and addiction to sleep medication; she was also involved in a ten-year relationship with a man who was always with other women. She, like her father, became a journalist, a career that gave her a lot of recognition and pleasure, but one that she never valued as much as the personal life that seemed to elude her. Nuala concluded: "It is not a coincidence . . . that I started getting healthy when death took him [her father], and a few years later my mother."[18]

Moving Beyond a Negative Family Legacy to Become a New Single Woman

Women like Nuala, Beth, and Rachel, who grew up with few role models of happy women, whether coupled or single, and who were emotionally abused as children, seem to hold on longer to an idealized notion of a great relationship as necessary to their well-being. They have trouble building a satisfying coupled or single life. But both Beth and Nuala are changing, and Rachel may be able to as well.

Beth is no longer looking for a soul mate, "a perfect person out there for me." She now says: "I was very idealistic—about the revolution and about relationships. Of course I didn't have a realistic model of a good relationship in my parents. I never had anything to aspire to other than the ideal that was in my imagination." Such a realization indicates that Beth is open to new conceptions of a satisfying life.

Beth's change was facilitated by her strong family ties, especially those to her children and grandchildren. At the age of fifty, Beth was an isolated single mother, one of the unhappiest single mothers I interviewed. But by age fifty-nine, she basked in her children's success and their close ties to each other and to her.

Beth proudly recounted her daughter Emily's journey: During Emily's high school and college years in Arizona, she faithfully spent vacations and summers in California with Beth and her brother, helping when he became a troubled teenager. After she graduated from college, Emily served for several years in Americorp and then returned to the Bay Area for graduate school. With her master's degree, she got a good job in San Francisco. Beth is very proud of Emily, who is thirty-three and single. Beth said of Emily:

> She is very political and a strong feminist. She is an environmentalist. She is much stronger than I was. Women's liberation didn't even exist when I was young, and I sort of stumbled onto my political beliefs. But Emily always hated the color pink and never curled her hair or shaved her legs, despite criticism from other girls. She was always her own person. She has had some long-term, meaningful relationships, but she hasn't felt like settling down. She may be concerned about whether she will ever have children, but she won't talk about it. She is very private. But I know she does not want to be a single mother. Having a child without a partner is not an option for her.

Beth's positive feelings about Emily's singleness indicated a change in how she views her own state.

The change in Beth's son, John, and in her relationship to him is even more dramatic. When John was twenty-one, he fell in love with a woman who had just graduated from high school. They had their first child when John was twenty-two and his girlfriend was twenty. As soon as she got pregnant, they moved in together and he got a good job. They got married in 2003 and have another child on the way. Beth loves her two-year-old grandson. She sets time aside every weekend to take care of him. Emily adores the baby too and drives the hour's distance regularly to be with them and see the baby. She wants him to know her as "the auntie."

Two years ago, at the age of fifty-seven, Beth bought a house for the first time. As a renter, she had to move often, uprooting herself from a house, neighborhood, and community that she valued. The little house she rented in a good neighborhood—a house she loved—was put up for sale. The owner gave her the first option to buy. Beth thought it was above her ability to pay, but Emily urged Beth's mother to help her out. Beth was proud that she had always supported herself and never asked her mother for anything. But with pressure from her daughter, she accepted her mother's offer of the down payment and bought the house. She loves her home and spends long hours in the garden.

Beth realizes, however, that a home and family life are not enough. I recounted earlier how she can now articulate her need to reconnect with a political community and to make new friends. This is where she plans to put her energy, not into looking for a relationship. For the first time, Beth is happy with her single life.

■ ■ ■

When I read Nuala O'Faolain's 2003 continuation of her memoir, *Almost There: The Onward Journey of a Dublin Woman*, I was surprised to find that she too had changed.[19] In the new book, O'Faolain critiques the ending of *Are You Somebody?* seven years before: "I see how vague a vision that was, and how little there was in it to sustain me. Time had no presence there. And where are other people? What good are stone and air to me now, in the real world?"

In the intervening years, Nuala, unlike Rachel, but like most of my other subjects, had built the supports for a single life and gradually changed her consciousness to accept her singleness.[20] Nuala found that "happiness—or if not happiness, a robust vision of how to manage its absence and live well—had crept up on me."[21] She could now see that "it has been shouted at us for so long that we're second-rate if we're not in a pair with someone else, that we've come to deeply believe it."[22]

With this changed consciousness, O'Faolain wrote an auto-biographical novel, *My Dream of You* (2001). This is the story of a middle-aged, single Irishwoman who is able to reject her married English lover's proposal that she live in a place where he could visit her twice a week—that in essence she become a permanent mistress. O'Faolain is clear that alterations in her own thinking permitted her alter ego in the novel to make such a decision: "I don't think I myself, most of my life, would have been able to turn down such an offer," she wrote. "I wouldn't have weighed what the loss of family and friends and community and work would mean. I would have be-lieved, rightly or wrongly, that I could live perfectly happily on books and the natural world and the company of animals, as long as somebody drove toward me as a light with purpose as Kathleen's lover swore to her he would." But Nuala now sees that "it became not in character for Kathleen to live for love alone. She had become too widely life-loving to ruin her own life, even for honest passion perfectly expressed."[23]

Real changes that Nuala made in her life preceded changes in her thinking. She bought a cottage in the west of Ireland and feels at home there living by herself. But she also recounts how she came to a new understanding of the importance of friendship. After the breakup of her fifteen-year relationship with Nell, she moved in with a male friend and reestablished friendships with a number of male, and a few female, friends. Before, she had seen friendship as only "the most commonplace relationship of all, one I gave hardly any value to compared to love."[24] She now found that "friendship, and the small sources of well-being in daily life, . . . are nurturing the way being loved is."[25]

In addition, Nuala describes reconnecting with her seven living siblings and their children and grandchildren. She invited four of her siblings and their spouses to go on a trip to Italy with her to celebrate her sixtieth birthday. She was surprised, she wrote, "because we are the remnants of a family who never went on a family holiday nor even a family outing, not even once, and for whom every shared meal was perilous."[26] These family vacations now are a yearly event.

In her early sixties, Nuala found a new relationship. During the year or so in which she was writing the novel, she lived in New York. There, through Match.com, she met, and started an affair with, a divorced American lawyer. They spent part of the summer together in a country cottage with his eight-year-old daughter. But Nuala found herself dissatisfied with the relationship. The lawyer was very committed to his work and spent long hours at it. In addition, Nuala found it difficult to share him with his daughter, especially since she was not used to being around children. In the new memoir, she expresses her dissatisfaction:

> Do these parents know anyone besides other parents? Do the kids dictate every single thing about adult life? I mean, after all the play dates and the watching videos of *Beauty and the Beast* and making them macaroni and cheese and reading them stories and brushing their teeth and helping them find the toilet paper—what's there left for the parents? Maybe that's fine by parents, but why the hell would it be fine by an outsider, who had nothing whatsoever to do with the decision to have her, who's interested in having a relationship with a grown man? [27]

Nuala, however, now had a new perspective to evaluate the positive and negative aspects of the relationship. She no longer felt a failure: "The expectation that I would retrieve my independent self at some point helped when I began discovering our problems."[28] She realized that both their lives stand on "big, solid, weight-bearing structures that it took long years to put in place."[29] In addition, Nuala perceived that Ireland is both home and community. She concluded that she could not give up Ireland to live permanently in America: "I have no relationship with America except the one with him, and no place in it except the half of his bed. Whereas I have something

thicker than blood, more intimate than love with Ireland. . . . I want
to live where I know the politicians and where the woman beside
me on a bus was at school with my aunt and where people take the
trouble to try to talk well and where I can hear my own language, my
own music, jokes I understand."[30]

At the end of the memoir, O'Faolain has not given up on the relationship, but I sense that it will be sustained only if both she and her
lover find some way to forge an unconventional pairing, something
between being single and being coupled (see chapter 8).

Nuala offers an explanation of why she has been able to change.
She believes that writing her memoir was a key element: "Surely the
self has begun to move toward health when it takes itself seriously
enough to tell its story. . . . The attempt to describe your experience
to an audience pushes you forward into an understanding of it."[31]

In a similar way, participating in this research helped Beth, me,
and many of the women I interviewed begin to view our lives differently. It helped us to see the disconnect between our full lives and
what the culture tells us. We came to see many positive aspects of our
lives and to accept that singleness suits us. If Nuala and Beth, despite
the psychological damage they suffered in childhood, can shift,
maybe Rachel and other women who grew up in negative family
settings can change too. Perhaps Rachel, seeing her story in print and
reading this analysis, can still turn her life around to find some joy in
single life.

CHAPTER 5

Becoming a Whole Person

Autonomy and Long-Term Singleness

While living by myself and writing this book, I started listening to novels on tape in the kitchen and when driving around town doing errands. I listen to have company and as a way to take my mind off my work. Once in a while, however, I hear something that crystallizes my thinking about some aspect of single women's lives. This happened with Jonathan Franzen's *The Corrections,* the best-selling 2001 novel about the generational disaffection of those growing up in American middle-class suburbs. The novel as a whole did not seem particularly related to my concerns, but one character in the story, Denise, the sister of the male protagonist, said something that sparked my interest. Bored as a student at Swarthmore, Denise drops out and takes a job at a fancy restaurant where she finds her life's work; she falls in love with the life of a chef. "She loved the crazy hours, the intensity of the work, the beauty of the product," Franzen writes. "She loved the deep stillness that underlay the din. A good crew was like an elective family in which everyone in the little hot world of the kitchen stood on equal footing, and every cook had weirdnesses concealed in her past or in his character, and even in the midst of the most sweaty togetherness each family member enjoyed *privacy* and *autonomy*: she loved this."[1]

Denise's sentiments indicate how fulfilling work can foster autonomy in women—autonomy that does not arise out of isolation or individualism but is promoted by supportive relationships, in this case the "elective family" of the kitchen crew. Such *relational autonomy* is especially important for women.[2]

Like an autonomous man, such a woman enjoys a high degree of self-determination and self-definition and feels that she is a whole person. Her work is especially important to her self-esteem and promotes her self-fulfillment.[3] All these *self* words are significant. But unlike the classic Western term *self-made man,* those with relational autonomy achieve self-actualization through supportive relationships. While she may value solitude ("privacy," in the Franzen quote), the woman whose autonomy is relational is not lonely or isolated. She is not a loner.[4] Living according to standards that are "one's own" does not mean being on one's own; it may include a mutual concern for and the care of others. Work that is economically sustaining and personally fulfilling is necessary for autonomy, but it is not sufficient. An autonomous woman needs a life beyond work.

In a Western culture that values self-definition and individual expression, autonomous women—whether single or coupled—are likely to feel good about their lives. My study and others find this to be true too for women who come from working-class and ethnic cultures.[5] But to retain a strong sense of self—to remain autonomous —is harder for coupled women than it is for single ones, for we live in a culture that encourages women to couple with someone who is older, stronger, taller, richer, and smarter. Philosopher Marilyn Friedman finds impediments to women's autonomy even in egalitarian couples: "To the extent that a lover is engaged in joint undertakings which are guided by the joint commitments and identity of the couple..., she is *not* being guided by the commitments and identity that define her as an individual."[6] The coupled women who achieve autonomy while maintaining a satisfying relationship attain the cultural ideal. But this is not an easily obtainable outcome. In contrast, single women, especially those without children, have more social space to pursue autonomy, often by focusing on fulfilling work.

We have seen that most women do not choose a single life; they do not have a life plan for remaining single. Rather, the self-actualizing choices they make over a lifetime gradually lead them toward a sense of being a whole person with a unique identity.[7] Thus, autonomy is not a precondition but rather an outcome of the long drama of crafting a satisfying single life. Women of many personality types—whether divorced or ever single—become more autonomous through this process.

The self-determination necessary to become an autonomous woman takes place in a social context, however, one in which we don't have total control and where men often have more power. The process of shaping a life for oneself is likely to be more difficult for those women who face ethnic, racial, and class, as well as gender, barriers.[8]

I examine the lives of three childless single women who solidified their autonomy by pursuing meaningful work and struggling to create satisfying lives. Elena Morales, a Chicana in her thirties from a working-class family, grappled to define what she wants as a middle-class professional; Anne Rosetti, a creative entrepreneur in her forties, struggled to create a personal life; and Mary Bishop, an ex-nun in her fifties, provided insights into how an autonomous single woman faces a life-threatening illness.

For all three women, divorce (from a man or the church) was a significant marker in their process of becoming autonomous. The real divorces of two of the women had consequences that were similar to a life-changing choice of a never-married woman.[9] All used a personal crisis as an opportunity to develop new competencies and to expand their self-definitions.[10] Contemplating the evolution of their lives enables us to examine how a single life fosters autonomy and to appraise the benefits and costs of the autonomous life.

The Long Road from Working-class Childhood to Autonomous Professional

I met Elena Morales when she was thirty-one, single, and just beginning her research for a PhD dissertation. With smooth brown skin and thick shiny dark hair cut in an attractive bob, Elena was a feminine woman who laughed easily. Her glasses enhanced her serious and intense manner. Elena articulated the conflicts she faced in reconciling her work with a personal life. We met again when Elena was thirty-eight. I discovered that Elena's work history had been full of conflicts and created more discord in her personal life than she would have predicted seven years previously.

Elena grew up in a small town in California's Central Valley, where her parents made a transition from farm labor to other working-class jobs. Her father became the janitor in a garment factory, and her mother earned a high school diploma and then worked in a child-care center. Born when her mother was thirty-three and her brothers were thirteen and sixteen, Elena's childhood was often like that of an only child.

Elena noted that her parents "always had a little home library; we always got newspapers, and my mother always took us to the public library." Although her mother might have been unusual in this respect, her stress on the importance of education and her role model as a strong woman are found in many working-class Chicana families.[11] She told Elena she could be anything she wanted to be. From the time she visited San Francisco at the age of seven, Elena's goal was to get out of her small town. Education, she knew, would be her route. By high school, Elena was in college prep classes, and her mother insisted she focus on her homework rather than doing domestic chores, since there were no small children at home asking for her help. But Elena soon experienced conflict between her educational aspirations and the more conventional sexual values that her parents also instilled.

After high school graduation, Elena elected to go to the nearby community college to be near her sweetheart from high school, a Mexican American boy who did not earn the same high grades. After only a few months of college, Elena told her mother she thought she was pregnant. She wasn't, but since she was having sex, her mother insisted she get married. So Elena married at the age of eighteen. Now she was even more determined not to get pregnant, to pursue her education, and to get out of town. She coached her husband, and both were accepted at a prestigious California university. Elena flourished and was admitted to a summer program in the East for prospective graduate students from minority backgrounds. Meanwhile, she was trying to help her husband to ensure that both would succeed. But when she returned from two months in the East, she found that her husband wanted to get out of the marriage. The divorce, while stressful, was also a relief. Now twenty-one years old, she had her life before her.

As a married woman, Elena had considered only graduate schools in California. But after the divorce, she applied all over the country. She was accepted into a master's program in public policy at an Ivy League university. In her mid- to late twenties, with her MA, Elena worked as a policy analyst in Washington, D.C., and then in Los Angeles. She was happy to return to California to be near family and live in a culture and an environment that were her home. Passed over for a job she thought she deserved, Elena, on an impulse, applied for a PhD program at the University of California, where she could focus on her interest in health policy.

In the ten years between the end of her marriage and our first meeting, Elena almost always found herself in a relationship—one for six years with a Mexican American man and another for four years with an African American. She talked about her problems with Latino men and with men who are not from her background. "Most Latino men can't deal with the fact that I have a career goal," she said, "much less that I'm not going to sit around making tortillas for dinner. But on the other hand with a non-Latino man, there are things I would have to explain that a Latino would just know." The black man, in contrast to her Chicano boyfriend, was very independent, and they were less coupled than she had been in the past. From this relationship, Elena "learned that a relationship doesn't have to fall apart because you keep very separate identities." At the same time, she couldn't accept this kind of distance. So she ended the relationship.

In her confusion about why she hadn't found a successful relationship, Elena, in her early thirties, turned to self-help books. But there her ethnic and class background often led her to feel alienated by these books. "I read things that sort of make sense," Elena explained, "but there is this whole set of values I carry around with me that is different. For example, to put marriage in a market framework is just so foreign. Where I come from, marriage is about love and romance."

Facing similar conflicts between her personal values and those of the world of work, Elena found it hard to express her own voice in the realm of academic research. She explained that her identity never rested on achievement alone but always focused on relationships, the social ties to a partner, family, friends, and community. But in the professional world, she realized work was not just something one does but a lot of who one is. Now that she was a PhD student,[12] Elena found it frightening. Even though she had always wanted to go to college and have a career, she had never seen herself primarily as a career woman. She loved her work, but finishing her PhD took a huge amount of time, energy, and concentration. As a result, relationships with family and lovers became secondary. "To have to put on hold some of the other things like finding Mr. Right is to me a very scary and at times depressing thought," Elena explained.

With her friends, however, Elena discovered a sounding board to help her work out these conflicts.[13] For several years, Elena roomed with Lanette, the black woman we met in chapter 1. As I mentioned, Lanette was extroverted and quite autonomous. Elena enumerated the benefits of her friendship with Lanette:

> I have changed a lot since living with her. I was always a very private person and didn't really reveal a whole lot, especially about relationships with men. Then I started living with Lanette. She wonders why people call her with their problems, but I think it's because she asks questions in very nonthreatening ways. She can tell when someone really needs to talk about something. So I learned how to open up. That has spilled over into my other friendships. Now I've bonded even more with some of my other good friends. I can sit on the phone for an hour and talk about how I feel and how I'm doing.

Elena experienced what philosophers and psychologists have observed: Friendships, unlike most relationships with a partner or family member, encourage alternative perspectives for viewing ourselves, "a plurality of standpoints from which to assess our choices, values and principles."[14] Political theorist Martha Ackelsberg concludes that "families seem to demand one's fitting into prescribed roles. By contrast, friends seem to support us to become the person I am."[15] Thus, friendships can help women develop a separate sense of self and promote autonomy. "Friends become for us a mirror of the self," notes social psychologist Lillian Rubin, "and what we see there, whether it pleasures or pains us, helps to affirm those parts of self we like and respect and to change those whose reflection brings us discomfort."[16] Rubin goes on to observe how having a number of different friends permits us to develop a more complex and differentiated self: "One friend taps our intellectual capacities more deeply than others, another connects most profoundly to our emotional side. One calls upon our nurturant, care taking qualities, another permits our dependency needs to surface. One friend touches our fun-loving side, another our more serious part."[17]

Elena found that her friends do not judge her, and she, in turn, tries to understand their situation. Elena attempted "to imagine what it would be like to be in their shoes." This, she felt, is "part and parcel of being a good friend." Friendships also provided her with practical aid in social mobility: "I have borrowed money from my friends," Elena admitted, "only because my parents were never in a position to help me in that way." But in becoming an autonomous woman, Elena had to separate herself from her community of origin in ways that women from middle-class backgrounds often do not.

In 1995 Elena still had conventional desires about her private life. "I still would like to remarry, which sounds weird to me, because the divorce was such a long time ago," she said. "I would like to have children, whether it's by adoption or having my own." Like her friend Lanette, Elena did not want to be a single mother, both because having two parents was important for her while growing up and because "it's just too much work." Unlike Lanette, who could not conceive of any circumstances in which she would become a single mother, Elena acknowledged that she might feel differently in five years. She might be willing to become a single mother rather than not be a mother at all.

I reconnected with Elena in 2002, when she was thirty-eight. I found that the conflicts she had described continued after she completed her PhD. Stressed by workplace dynamics in her first two professional positions, Elena felt that her work difficulties were a major factor undermining a serious relationship.[18]

As her first job after the doctorate, Elena secured a research position in a state health department, which she found was filled with petty politics and backstabbing. She was so stressed that she often had trouble eating and sleeping, and Elena felt eager to return to a research institute based at a university. When she received an offer from a research center connected to the University of New Mexico, she decided to take it, even though it would mean a commuting relationship with her cohabiting partner.

Just as she was finishing her dissertation, Elena had met Jaime, a Mexican American man who was her age and was pursuing a master's degree in archaeology. He was also a full-time artist specializing in sculpture. Elena responded to the new interests he opened for her, meeting people who were different from those she knew in her circles. She loved being in this environment. Jaime too was committed to social justice, but he had a distinct, artistic way of expressing it. His romantic pursuit clinched the attraction. Jaime initially showered her with flowers and small gifts, things to which she was not accustomed. Elena loved the attention.

Elena and Jaime moved in together. Now coupled, Elena lost contact with many of her old friends. In 1995, Elena told me how the year before friends from up and down the state had come to her father's funeral, even though most of them had never met him. Five years later, many friends had moved away to pursue career opportunities or, like Elena, were busy with their own lives. Now that she was partnered, Elena expected that Jaime would be her main emotional support. She leaned on him to help her deal with the stress at her job.

She discussed with Jaime whether she should take the position in New Mexico. He said that she should do anything she could to stop the pain she was experiencing at her current job. Elena thought that he supported her move for her own well-being. He probably did, but later he admitted that he needed relief from her problems. He was about to start a graduate program that was one hundred miles away, so Elena reasoned that their relationship would change at any rate. In retrospect, she found moving to another state, which involved air travel to see Jaime, more disruptive than she imagined. But it was not the main impediment to the relationship.

Unfortunately, Elena's new job was not much better than the old one. Rather than finding the scientific community she had hoped to be a part of, one that was oriented toward improving people's health, she found that most of her colleagues were after power and recognition. For Elena, neither of these goals was a motivator. Instead, she valued "modesty, humility, and service." She wanted to connect her research to social justice issues and to be a mentor to other researchers from minority backgrounds. She found herself unable to put any of these values into practice in the New Mexico research center.

Elena moved to Albuquerque without knowing a soul there and found it impossible to make friends in the competitive environment of her workplace.[19] For the first time in her life she was truly lonely. She couldn't name her condition at the time because she had never experienced such personal pain. Elena had always relished spending time alone. Because her brothers were older, and because her mother was very strict about whom she could play with, Elena, from early childhood, spent a lot of time alone. "So it wasn't living alone in Albuquerque that bothered me," Elena explains, "but if I felt like calling someone, there wasn't anyone close by."

Elena's loneliness stemmed not just from social isolation but from a lack of personal validation.[20] In New Mexico she was surrounded by colleagues with very different values and goals from her own, and without any of the reality tests offered by daily interaction with family members or old friends. Elena experienced what Louise Bernikow in *Alone in America* defines as the root cause of loneliness—"not being known, not fitting, not being right."[21] Elena, like others who are lonely, felt deserted by her own self.[22] Even though loneliness can also be felt by those who are in unhappy families or in uncommunicative marriages, for those who, like Elena, have put so much effort into professional development, loneliness in the workplace can be devastating.

Since she no longer had friends she could call, Elena turned to making long daily phone calls to Jaime. In retrospect, she sees that "unconsciously I expected a huge amount from him." She admits that she overwhelmed him with her unhappiness. A year later, when he withdrew from the relationship, Jaime said to her: "First you had all these issues with your job in California, and then when you moved to New Mexico, you found that your colleagues there, too, were not supportive and you did not have allies. They stressed you out, and then you would call me and unload everything. You should be able to do that, but I can't take it anymore."

Three years later, Elena still didn't know how much emotional support she should expect from a male partner. She interrogated herself: If their roles were reversed, would she feel the same way as Jaime did? Or was he following primarily his own needs and would have ended the relationship anyway? Early in their relationship, he had said that he did not want to get married again (he too was divorced). Did he have commitment fears? Why did he break up with her only after he moved to Santa Fe (a few hours' drive from her) to work with a professor there? Why did he leave only after they started to talk seriously about having children? Why did he refuse to go into therapy with her? Would things have been different if she had been able to phone a few friends routinely to discuss her problems at work?

Elena acknowledged that her unhappiness at work and her emotional dependence had damaged their relationship. But Elena never once said that she wished she had followed a more traditional path, choosing work that was less demanding and with more roots in her ethnic heritage or class background. Rather, losing Jaime prompted her to face her dissatisfaction at work and to make new choices.

I heard the story about Jaime when I reconnected with Elena after she returned to live and work in northern California. Jaime remained in New Mexico, and Elena still missed him. "I still think of him as someone who came very close to being the ideal partner I envision," she said. But Elena did not stay in a job and city she disliked with the hope that if she remained geographically close, Jaime might return. Rather, she moved on with her life, involving herself in activities I identified in chapter 2, thus creating the basis for a viable single life without excluding the possibility of coupling.

In 2002 Elena talked about her satisfaction with her new job and about her happiness in reconnecting with family and old friends. She now works in a smaller, less prestigious, and less well funded but more policy-oriented research center, one where her colleagues share her values. Supervising a number of student interns from minority backgrounds, Elena tries to combine high standards and rigor with nurturance. Trying to help the students combine good scholarship with social justice concerns, to combine values from their backgrounds with professional goals, she hopes to provide a bridge for her students that she did not have—a bridge that will integrate their new work worlds with those of their families and communities of origin. Her colleagues now support and applaud her efforts.

Elena was pulled back to California, too, by the desire to be closer to her mother and two brothers. Although her mother is seventy-one and still lives in the same town, she approves of Elena's life, and they are good friends. Elena explains to me how her mother has become more autonomous. "I don't know if you have had experience dealing with Latinas," she said, "but we have a real hard time being direct. We avoid conflict, many times at all cost. But you can't really function that way for very long. With age, my mother has become a lot more direct and has set limits on what family members can demand of her."

The solitude Elena now relishes in living by herself is very different from the loneliness she experienced in New Mexico.[23] She is saving to buy a house or condominium and considering becoming a single mother, probably through adoption. Elena feels ready to think about this option. "I feel a lot more established—not financially—but just in terms of who I am and what I want," Elena said. Tentatively broaching the subject with her mother, Elena found her mother very supportive. Elena's two older brothers do not have children, so this would be her mother's only chance to have grandchildren. Elena discovered, in addition, that her mom had a lot of younger female friends who are divorced or haven't found a partner, and they are considering having children on their own.

Elena asks to be included in family events with her many married friends and colleagues who have children. "They think I'm strange," she recounted, "because I like to show up, play with their kids, and hang out with them; most of their other single friends won't do that." Her friends were surprised that a woman without children would want to go to a three-hour Christmas program at their children's school. Even though the kids, who were five and six years old, were falling asleep on stage, Elena loved the performance.

But Elena is not quite ready to start the adoption process. Although she still hopes to find a partner and give birth, she does not obsess about finding someone and does not make a special effort to find dates. Elena's sister-in-law suggested that she let go of some of her romantic ideals and focus on finding a man who would be a good father. Elena, however, doesn't believe that such a relationship can be sustained without a sexual attraction and a romantic connection. She would rather be a single mother than compromise her desires just to have a father for her child.

Although Elena feels sad when she thinks about going through life without a child, she explicitly said that she does not feel bad about the prospect of being permanently single. Elena vows she will not repeat the "extreme drama and crisis" of her past serious relationships. Once she got over the heartbreak of her breakup with Jaime, she realized, her health improved tremendously. Elena feels lucky that her family does not pressure her to be coupled. Unlike friends who dread going home for the holidays because their whole family is constantly questioning them about when they are going to get married, she never has to face that.

Thus, at the young age of thirty-eight, Elena is poised either to become a new single woman or to build a more satisfying coupled life. She has meaningful work and anticipates buying her own house and raising a child. She has a supportive network of family and friends and connects to ethnic communities through her work. Elena did not bring up sexuality, and I did not feel comfortable asking her about it.[24] Given that she is still in her thirties, she probably has not resolved this issue.

In addition to having established the preconditions for a viable single life, Elena feels good about her autonomy. Like other successful Chicanas, her individual achievement is built on family and community support and reflects positively on them.[25] Some might say that the price for romantic intimacy has been high. But Elena takes pride in now knowing "who I am and what I want." Not yet ready to abandon her romantic dreams, Elena's family and friends provide a basis for the broader definition of intimacy that I explored in chapter 1.

The Entrepreneurial Road to Autonomy

I met Anne Rosetti—blond, blue-eyed, and pleasingly plump—when she was forty-six; she was referred to me by her sister, who had received one of my letters asking for subjects for my study. A successful woman, articulate and decisive but also warm and funny, Anne had been divorced for ten years. Of all the women I interviewed, Anne had the most interesting and varied career path, working her way from successful restaurateur to film and TV producer, high-placed political staffer, and communications director for a large corporation. But she struggled for years to combine her career success with a satisfying personal life.

At thirty-five, after fifteen years of marriage, Anne discovered that her husband was having an affair with a family friend, the sister of his oldest friend. Anne did not "fight for her man" but chose to divorce instead. Given the adultery she faced, Anne, to be true to herself, felt she had to leave the marriage. She said, "I just wasn't willing to suck it up and be a humble, forgiving wife. I would have had to make a decision to sacrifice a certain part of myself to stay. It was like somebody gave me a saw and said cut off your arm. I couldn't do it." How could Anne make such a clear decision, and how it did affect her life?

Born in Alaska into an upper-middle-class Catholic family, Anne, the third of ten children, grew up in the West—in New Mexico, Washington, and California. The family moved often so that her father, an executive in the U.S. government, could advance his career. Anne thinks her parents had a faithful and compatible marriage, but she saw her mother's health and vitality ruined by constant pregnancies, births, and child care. Her mother almost died during her last pregnancy, when she was forty-three.

Anne's mother was bedridden, her father's job necessitated constant travel, and her older brother and sister had already left home. So Anne, during her senior year in high school, took over much of the care for the baby and her younger siblings. "The baby," Anne remembered, "was allergic to everything; he was allergic to walnuts, and we lived in Walnut Creek. His skin was breaking out, and he was always squalling." Anne was barely able to get through her senior year and described herself as "a basket case." "By the time I moved out," Anne said, "the last thing I wanted to do was take care of kids. There was nothing glamorous about pregnancy, babies, or toddlers. Even though I loved my brothers and sisters, I didn't want to fold another diaper for as long as I lived. I didn't want to have children." In addition, Anne recognized that the experience of almost losing her mother and her shortened childhood had a profound psychological effect on her, leading to what Anne termed "something akin to post-traumatic stress syndrome." For years, contemplating the role of housewife or mother brought on acute anxiety. This trauma opened Anne to the possibility of a life that was different from her mother's.

In 1963, when she was fifteen, Anne picked up *The Feminine Mystique* at the local library, having never heard of Betty Friedan. Anne said that she didn't really have the sophistication to understand everything that Friedan had written about, but nevertheless the book made a big impact on her. Friedan critiqued the oppressive life of a full-time homemaker and advocated that women combine a satisfying career with marriage. Anne envisioned a professional career that engaged her passionately and that "you devote the same kind of time and energy that our fathers had devoted to their professions." Without thinking much about it, Anne assumed she could combine a traditional Catholic marriage—but one without children—with such a career, an assumption fostered by *The Feminine Mystique.*

Before discovering this book, Anne's only alternative role model to her housewife mother was the nuns. For Anne, nuns "were the only free women I knew, the only women who had gone to college and were active in the world." Perhaps it is not incidental that so many Catholic women turned up in my study, and that Anne, I, and others saw nuns as fulfilled single women. But in the marriage-obsessed U.S. culture from 1945 through the late 1960s, personal examples of contented single women (including influential teachers) could not override the cultural denigration of spinsters.[26]

Anne entered the University of California at Berkeley in 1968, during a time of turbulent protest on the campus. Radical politics formed a backdrop to Anne's life but at the time did not involve her. Anne wed after her freshman year, marrying John Rosetti, the first man she slept with, an Italian Catholic high school teacher seven years her senior. Asked what attracted her, she said: "Well, sex had a lot to do with it. He was really gorgeous, and he was a wonderful lover. He also had that 'the entire world loves me' grace of an only child of Italian parents. When I fell in love with John, it was just like 'blitzo.' It just obliterated everything."

Anne was married at age twenty in a traditional Catholic ceremony with her uncle serving as the priest. Because the uncle was influential in the church hierarchy, he got the pope to send a plaque blessing the marriage. Despite this traditional setting, Anne was relieved that John said he was not interested in having children and that he supported her work. "I told him that I was really serious about working and having a career," she said. "He thought it was wonderful. What I didn't understand was that he was thinking of his mom, who would always take part-time, low-level jobs in order to buy the extras in the household. But then she came home and made the ravioli and scrubbed the floors."

During the second year of their marriage, Anne, to pay for her college tuition, obtained a job that turned into an exciting career for her. She started keeping books at a little restaurant that had been open for only a month. Soon the restaurant became famous as it led the way in creating the new California cuisine, a style of cooking in which fresh, organic ingredients and subtle spices in interesting sauces—without the heavy cream and butter of French cooking— are used. Anne quickly convinced the owner that she should become the business manager, something no one at the restaurant had thought about.

Today the restaurant is in an old, but refurbished, brown shingle house, discreetly set back from the street. It is easy to miss as you stroll along Shattuck Avenue in the gourmet ghetto of North Berkeley. Once in the door, however, you enter a world of quiet elegance defined by the wood-paneled and polished oak floors of the downstairs dining room. Upstairs in the café, a different mood prevails, one of chic, noisy bustle. The restaurant began in the early 1970s in the same house, but back then it was a run-down, one-story bungalow. Anne described it as a "tenement."

Anne worked out of a broken-down cottage in the back, where she shared space with vegetables, a wine cellar, and a big refrigerator. The wiring was so bad that in the winter she had to choose between a light and a heater. She wore her husband's long underwear to work so that she could see the calculator. Anne worked very hard. "We were developing a reputation," she said, "but it was not all the glamorous stuff that people think. A lot of nights I'd wake up terrified that I wouldn't make payroll."

As the restaurant prospered, Anne became a partner. She remembered her happiness: "I was doing what I always dreamed I would do. I was being successful and having something that was creative, something that I could feel confident about and that other people appreciated." But this prominence had an unexpected impact on her husband.

Later in therapy, trying to understand his affair that broke up their marriage, Anne concluded: "We got to the point where people would introduce John as the person who was married to Anne, the restaurateur. I didn't have a clue how much of an impact this would have on a man, so I had no concept of even showing any sensitivity to it. He was in his midforties and was sort of topped out in his career or at least in his expectations for himself. I was not paying attention by then at all. I was just totally absorbed in my work."

I was struck by the clarity of Anne's insight *and* by her lack of emotion or self-reproach. Never did I hear her say that she wished she had put less energy into her work so that she could have saved her marriage. Did work fill an emotional gap in her marriage, keep her safe from what felled her mom, or express the creativity of a core self? Or all of the above?

Although work may have conflicted with her intimate relationship, it did not preclude an active social life. Anne's social life centered on the house she owned with her husband, rather than on her partnership with him. It was a big Victorian house in which they had knocked down most of the interior walls, making it possible to have huge parties. Anne loved to entertain. She always gave big holiday parties for her large extended family and friends—holiday festivities that expressed the values of family, friendship, and community, which were important to her. Anne remembered: "I had this big dining room, and we'd break open the table and put in the leaves. The little kids would have their own table, and there would be a lot of noise. People were passing the potatoes and passing the pasta, and somebody was passing their baby. I had the weirdest kind of an image. I thought, 'I hope nobody mistakes the baby for an entrée as it's going around the table.'"

Besides her large family and wide circle of friends, Anne had a small group of close women friends who socialized together. They were mainly in the food trade, so they would be off from work in the daytime. Gathering at Anne's house with its big funky kitchen, five to ten women might start as early as 8:00 a.m. and hang out all day. The music would be on, and people would drift in and out. Mothers would bring their infants. Some would come with needlepoint or their ironing, and others would cook. There was always plenty of food. In the summertime, they would go out in the backyard to work on their tans while playing backgammon and drinking wine. They also had ladies' nights, when they would meet at somebody's house for a potluck dinner without children or men.

Anne's happiness during her twenties and early thirties was only slightly marred by a development to which she gives more importance in retrospect than she did at the time. Anne went into therapy in her early thirties because, despite her business success, she still had anxieties about who she was and her role in the world. She had fallen into marriage and a career at a young age without confronting the family trauma of her teenage years. Her aversion to caretaking now clashed with what turned out to be the traditional expectations of her husband. This conflict expressed itself in constant tension with John about housework. Anne worked much longer hours than John but without the numerous vacations he got as a teacher. After working a fourteen-hour day at a time when John was off from teaching for two weeks, Anne would come home to find the house a mess and the refrigerator empty. John didn't like a dirty house, but he thought that housework was Anne's job, that if she were a *real woman,* she would do it. Like Anne, John said that he didn't care about having children, but once he said to her: "You can never be a real woman if you don't have a child."

When issues about their marriage came up, Anne's therapist offered to see them together, but John refused to go. He said, "Men go to therapy only if they are crazy, or if they are war veterans, and have to talk about seeing their best friend shot." Anne did not insist. Nor could Anne and John talk about their differences and how they were exacerbated by his working-class and her upper-middle-class family background and by the seven-year disparity in their ages. Anne's values and views of the world were shaped by the women's movement and by the radical politics of the time; John, growing up as a working-class male in the 1950s, remained locked into a more traditional vision of married life.

Some married women in similar circumstances decide to accommodate—to do what will please their husbands—even if in the process they begin to lose their own sense of self.[27] Or they confront their husband and demand that they find a solution together. Anne did neither. Instead, she hired a housekeeper and went on with her fulfilling professional and social life.

The tensions in their marriage led to a decrease in their sexual satisfaction, but because she was so busy, and because she still shared many companionable activities with John—reading, traveling, hiking, and films—Anne did not mind. Anne's decline of interest in sexuality, her lack of emotional investment in her marriage, her satisfying career, and her active social life facilitated her decision to divorce, even though she was the first in her family to do so.

When Anne discovered John's affair, she was able to use the personal confidence she had acquired in business, combined with the introspective skills she had gained in therapy, to decide that she did not want to try to save the marriage. Given their distinct reactions to the gender revolution around them, Anne felt she would have to give up too much to stay with John.

After the divorce, the satisfaction Anne achieved at work, and the alternative forms of intimacy she developed through rich ties with friends and family, led her to the decision to further her autonomy rather than to focus on the daily intimacy of a coupled relationship. Anne, then an attractive, vivacious woman of thirty-five, had a number of lovers after her divorce and a four-year cohabitation. But she did not find a relationship with a man who, as she said, "incorporates passion and love, friendship and companionship." In using such general terms, Anne did not speak of missing the daily sharing of living together. She never indicated that she was lonely.

A few years before the divorce, Anne had sold her share in the restaurant and opened her own business—a restaurant, delicatessen, and catering operation—which was a five-minute walk up the street in what was becoming Berkeley's gourmet ghetto. After the divorce, she decided that the long hours necessary to own and run a small business didn't suit her. She sold the store at exactly the right time, just before the big supermarkets in the neighborhood added deli departments. With a nice financial cushion from the sale of her business, the self-confidence she had gained as a successful businesswoman, and nothing to tie her down, Anne decided to try a radically different type of work. Anne explained, "The food business is very hedonistic, which was great, but I had been raised in an intellectual environment, where reading, thought, and study were stressed. It was time for me to work those muscles again."

As she remembered it, Anne fell into filmmaking: "I was approached by a young documentary filmmaker who wanted to do a film on Berkeley in the sixties. I can't remember who sent him to me, but he was looking for people in the community to give him access. I had been dating people in the film world and hanging out with the Coppola crowd, so the whole project rather fascinated me. I thought, 'Why not?' So I became a researcher and associate producer of the film." When I expressed surprise at her interest in a political film, Anne revealed that after her marriage, while still an undergraduate and before getting involved in business, she had been an antiwar activist. Anne was never at the center of such radicalism, and John did not share her interest in social action, but politics was definitely in her blood.

She parlayed her filmmaking into a whole series of interesting positions: For four years, she beat the pavement as a field producer for a TV daily news show of a large network affiliate in San Francisco. She covered business, medicine, the environment, and high-tech news. At the same time, she produced longer-format news stories and TV documentaries. This media experience and her volunteer political work led to a one-year paid position in the top staff of a democratic candidate for governor of California. After they lost the campaign, Anne worked as a community liaison for the White House advance team for about twenty-five visits to the Bay Area by President Bill Clinton, Hillary Clinton, Vice President Albert Gore, and other White House personnel. Simultaneously, Anne worked on teams facilitating military base closings in the Bay Area and on Net Day 96 in California (a campaign to wire all the schools to the Internet).

The autonomy she developed by becoming a single woman, Anne believes, facilitated her entrepreneurial career.

I need to have this feeling of being a whole piece in the world. I have to understand the difference between me and the rest of the world. That was a huge battle for me. When I was married, I couldn't fully experience the distinction. Maybe part of it was that I was married so young. But there was always this tension about feeling whole. Only after I had been alone for a long time did I become aware where I started and somebody else stopped. I'm not sure I ever would have gotten the sense of being whole if I hadn't been single. I'm not sure I would have made that leap. Maybe I would have; there is no way of knowing. But I do know that it happened over the time I was single, and it was a fundamental change in me.

In turn, Anne's entrepreneurial life fostered the development of a personal identity and enhanced her autonomy. Sociologist John Hewitt explains this process: "The entrepreneur is beholden to no organization, but makes an autonomous way of life, creating a self as well as a successful business, rather than simply fitting the self to the enterprises of others."[28] Psychologists agree that individual autonomy is enhanced by "being able to control the environment and effectiveness in producing desired effects."[29]

When I interviewed her two years after the original interview, Anne had begun to question her frenetic work life. She recognized some of the negative implications of being an entrepreneur. "The downside," she said, "is that you never have colleagues who are with you for a length of time building a program. You don't have someone else to worry about your retirement, pay for your health care, or to upgrade your equipment. I have to keep marketing myself to get the next contract." She had decided that she needed to work less and in a more permanent position that would bring together her political, public affairs, and media work. She was turning down a lot of work, she said, because "it would have meant, once again, being totally married to work."

At forty-nine, Anne began to realize that she might never remarry or repartner, and she was just beginning to think through what that meant for her. "I'm not going to look for anybody, but just do my life," Anne declared. "I don't have the mental or emotional energy to be preoccupied with a question that is not answerable; it will either happen or not, depending on my destiny." This fatalism seems comparable to her sense that great job opportunities just fell into her lap. I believe, however, that her extroversion and competence ensured that she was in the right place for the jobs; she does not have the same confidence regarding an intimate relationship.

Interviewing Anne in her modest but attractive condominium in Oakland, I was struck by how different it seemed from the house she had lived in when she was married. The apartment was tastefully furnished, but the rooms were quite dark, with dim lighting, and the Pullman kitchen was tiny. This was a place of cool serenity, a place to escape into solitude from a bustling world, far different from a house open to the casual flow of friends and family that had made Anne so happy during her marriage. I sensed that Anne didn't really want such solitude. Indeed, during the four years that she cohabited after her divorce, Anne had re-created some of the same social atmosphere as in her marriage. She recounted how she would "have everything from baby showers to Christmas parties, or if there was some special on TV, we'd cook up some huge pot of beans and invite everybody over." But realizing she wanted her partner as a friend and not a husband, Anne broke up with him rather than marry him. She is pleased that they have remained friends, even as he has gone on to another committed relationship. But she admits that she misses the socializing.

As a single woman, Anne did not organize an active social life, and she found the holidays especially hard. One or another of her sisters now had the big dinner for Thanksgiving and Christmas, but it didn't mean as much to Anne as when she had the party at her own house. Even though some of her sisters are divorced and only five of her nine siblings have children, she did not feel completely comfortable at these family gatherings when she was not part of a couple.

Anne, recognizing the social deficit in her life, began to think about how to change it, how to create a personal life to supplement her larger work and political community. Anne said: "I don't think that any human being wants to be alone. So, the task is, How do you build a community around you that gives you the kind of emotional support you need?" She said she was spending more time with family and reaching out to friends. She didn't know whether she wanted to go on living by herself, but she did know that she had to have her own closet and bathroom. "That's fundamental, no compromise; I know that about myself," Anne declared.

When I contacted Anne in 2003, six years after the earlier comments and eight years after the first interview, she said on the phone, "You just caught me; I'm moving away for a matter of the heart." I immediately assumed that she had met someone. But when I talked to her in person, I found out that Anne, now fifty-five and divorced for more years than she was married, had decided to move to the Southwest. She was relocating not for a man or a job but because she had spent part of her childhood there and loved the climate, the skies, the culture, the art, and the aesthetics. She felt both physically and psychologically alive in Arizona. This is what "a matter of the heart" meant to Anne.

At first I was skeptical of Anne's decision, since I believe that friendship networks and community are crucial for long-term single women. As we talked, however, I came to see how this move not only would enhance Anne's self-fulfillment and autonomy but would probably improve her social and community life as well. Characteristically, Anne planned it carefully.

During the preceding five years, Anne had earned a six-figure salary in her first corporate job as communications director for a large company—a job that drew on her entrepreneurial and media skills. She initiated a lot of projects and then moved on to something new. Although she liked the job, met wonderful people, and learned a great deal, Anne saw the negative aspects of corporate culture. "A lot of behavior there is fear driven," she observed, "a lot of it driven by scarcity, competition, and the ups and downs of the economy." Moreover, "The inner circle is still white men, and it is almost impossible for women or people of color to enter that. You have the same old boys' network."

Anne asked herself if she was doing what she wanted to do.

Would she want to work there for the next five to ten years? Her answer was that the only reason she would want to stay was for the large
salary. But Anne had saved money and invested in retirement accounts. So during the economic recession of 2002, Anne let herself
be laid off. With her unemployment payments, she had enough to
support herself for two years without depleting her savings. She took
three months to decide what to do.

For the preceding two or three years, Anne had traveled all over
Arizona, thinking about moving. She decided she loved Tucson
and would relocate there. Whether Tucson would be a good place
to meet a man was a question that never entered her head. Rather,
Anne asked what kind of a life she would have there as a single
woman. Moving to Tucson, she concluded, made sense not only for
reasons of the heart but for more practical ones too.

Despite the economic downturn, Anne is confident of getting
another corporate job, one where she can work full-time for another
five years and save enough money to retire at sixty. Then she will
figure out how to link volunteer work with her new interests in art,
anthropology, and culture. She wants to find new retirement work—
whether paid or volunteer—that resonates emotionally and spiritu-
ally with her.

Anne persuaded her sister, who is divorced and retired and has
grown children, to move to Tucson too. In Tucson, each could afford
her own larger house with three bedrooms. Thus, together they
would have enough room for many family members to visit for holidays and vacations. Perhaps there Anne and her sister could replicate
some of the holiday sociability that Anne enjoyed both when she was
married and when she was cohabiting.

Not only would Tucson provide a hub for family, but Anne
has friends there already and the base to build a community. One of
her friends from the Bay Area is now a real estate agent in Tucson
and will help Anne first rent and then buy a house. Another friend,
a lawyer, is helping her locate a job. Anne has several other friends in
Tucson who belong to the national political organization in which
Anne has long been active. She feels that they would provide an in-

troduction to new friends and community. Anne envisions that in a smaller city it would be easier to get connected than in the larger Bay Area.

Anne discovered that the autonomy she cherishes cannot be sustained by work alone. With her new "adventure of the heart," she seeks a place to expand her self and connect with family, friends, and community. I think she will succeed.

Joy in Life and Death in Solitude

On a bright fall morning, I dialed the high school where seven years earlier Mary Bishop was assistant principal. Mary's home phone number had been disconnected, and I did not know if she was still in the area or at the same job. The young woman who answered, probably a student, paused when I asked for Mary. "Let me give you to my supervisor," she said. The older woman asked who I was and why I was calling. When I responded, she said quietly, "Mary passed away six months ago after a long illness." I was shocked. How could this hearty woman, so full of life when I had met her at the age of fifty-four, be dead? Then I remembered that at the end of the interview, Mary had alluded to some major health problems and said that she "did not want to become dependent on anybody."

I don't recall how Mary heard about my study. She didn't know any of the four other women in the room that evening in 1994. But her personality and story interested me. Of the forty-six women who participated in those initial group interviews, Mary was the only one who had been a nun and the only one voluntarily to bring up sexuality. Perhaps she did it to counter stereotypes of nuns, but she also felt comfortable with the topic.

Mary was a tall—about five foot eleven—handsome woman with short salt-and-pepper hair. She was outgoing and open. When remembering the fun she had had as a teenager in her convent boarding school, she broke into a hearty laugh. Born in Casper, Wyoming, Mary was the oldest of seven children. The rhythm method of birth control seemed to work for her Catholic parents, she commented, as there was a gap of exactly three years between each child, and girls and boys alternated. Mary was eighteen years older than her youngest sibling. Mary's accountant father and homemaker mother were in what Mary called an "extremely traditional relationship," one that was "neurotic but loving." Mary felt that the marriage clipped her mother's wings, and from a young age she resisted the idea of replicating her mother's life. Because Mary was often a surrogate mother for her younger siblings, she never felt the need to have her own children. She had "already done that," she said.

Entering a convent boarding school at fourteen was an escape for Mary—a retreat from the loneliness of living in the country with only a few friends and from the responsibilities of being the oldest girl. Mary loved the school; it was like a continuous slumber party. Life was fun with all these friends, and she appreciated being taught by independent and intellectual nuns. When she graduated from high school at the age of eighteen, Mary took her vows. Her decision had very little to do with God. She was attracted by the sensual mystery of the convent, by the long black robes and the chants. Looking back on it, she sees that not only did she want to continue the slumber party but she was "scared silly of sex." She never had a relationship with a boy in high school, and it seemed much easier to continue living with these fun women. Mary was appalled when she got to her new convent and found that one couldn't talk in the dormitories. She said with a laugh, "I thought that's what dormitories were for!"

Becoming a nun enabled Mary to get a good education. She graduated with a BA in English from a Catholic women's college in Chicago that later became part of Loyola University. Mary valued having been educated in an all-women environment where she was encouraged to be vocal and a leader. After college, she spent a few years teaching in girls' high schools in the Midwest, and then started working on a master's degree at Catholic University in Washington, D.C.

There, in the mid-1960s, when Mary was in her midtwenties,

her order, like many others, shed their habits. At the university, Mary met a lot of men and started feeling sexual urges that she had repressed as an adolescent. One summer she went to Central Valley in California to work with a parish youth group. There she fell madly in love with a priest and had a stormy affair. She was no longer afraid of sex, but she knew he would not leave the priesthood for her. Mary, however, felt she couldn't stay in her order; she felt like a fraud. So, at the age of thirty, Mary left the convent and "started being an eighteen-year-old in the world."

Many of Mary's friends left the order at around the same time, and most of them began to couple. Mary too expected to meet someone and marry. She didn't want to be "weird." Since she didn't care about having children, she envisioned combining a career in education with marriage. But Mary found that it was hard to find men who accepted her for who she was—"an outspoken woman with definite ideas." Moreover, she found that she didn't like who she became when she was in a relationship. "I felt like I was losing myself," Mary explained, "doing what he liked and doing what he wanted to do. Then I'd get up to here with that, and I'd say, 'Forget it.' So I'd try with someone else. I can remember that frenzy. But at some point I just settled down and said, 'It's okay to be me and me alone.'"

Mary's experience of losing herself in a romantic relationship that she hoped would lead to marriage is quite common among women. Considerable evidence points to how traditional marriage can lead to a loss of self, or a false self, as wives accommodate to their husbands without asserting their own needs.[30] Many divorced women in my study pointed to this loss of self in marriage. Jean McDonald, for example, separated from her husband when she was forty-three, after sixteen years of marriage. "One of the first things I did in my shock, grief, and anger," she explained, "was to make a huge list of every decision he had made that I hadn't been a part of. Then I made another list of the decisions that we had made together. The first list had forty items, and the second, two or three." Jean talked about how her accommodation started with little things: deferring to his sense of taste in furniture, to where he wanted the pictures hung. She "didn't want any conflict," so it was so much easier to do what he preferred. The second thing Jean did after the separation was to take back her maiden name. She felt she was taking back her self.

Single women, even autonomous feminists, may also experience a loss of self in romantic, sexual relationships. In Doris Lessing's 1962 novel, *The Golden Notebook,* the heroine, Anna Wulf, a divorced single mother and a budding feminist, had many intense relationships with men. In each, she "fought with a feeling [that] . . . the substance of my self was thinning and dissolving."[31] In a similar vein, the actress and feminist Jane Fonda declared in a speech to the National Women's Leadership Summit on June 12, 2003:

> Although I've always been financially independent, and professionally and socially successful, behind the closed doors of my personal life I was still turning myself into a pretzel so I'd be loved by an alpha male. I thought if I didn't become whatever he wanted me to be, I'd be alone, and then, I wouldn't exist. . . .[This] is such a common theme for so many otherwise strong, independent women.

Journalist Peggy Orenstein too found that high-achieving, single women in their twenties often felt they were "losing themselves" in relationships, unable to hold on to their sense of being a woman "who knows what she wants and is willing to pursue it."[32] Many of my students mention having this experience even in a dating relationship. All at once they don't know what they want to eat, where they want to go; they completely defer to the man but then feel bad about having done so.

Feminist psychologists trace women's easy loss of self to a childhood in which girls, from an early age, are expected to meet the needs of others—younger siblings, needy fathers, and unhappy mothers—while denying their own needs for nurturance and care.[33] Mary's childhood fits this analysis. Precisely such women have the most to gain with the autonomy that results from the process of building a viable single life.

Sometime in her forties, Mary let go of the expectation of finding a partner and getting married. She focused on her career. While teaching full-time, she worked for a master's degree in management. After she became a high school administrator, she began work on a doctorate in education, with the goal of teaching at the university level. In 1994, Mary, who was in her early fifties, was working on her dissertation, teaching a few classes to undergraduates training to be teachers, and holding down a full-time job as a high school assistant principal.

Although Mary loved her work, family, and friends, she valued the solitude of living by herself, especially after being with people all day at school. She admitted that is was not only the slumber parties but also the solitude and quiet that had attracted her to the convent. She remembered that she loved to walk in the walnut grove near their home to get away from a house full of kids. Mary's ability to enjoy solitude was *not* because she was temperamentally a loner. Far from it. In fact, it rested on the strong sense of self she had forged in adulthood as she built satisfying relationships with colleagues, friends, and family. Stephanie Dowrick, in *Intimacy & Solitude,* postulates that a person enjoys solitude when she is comfortable with her own self and secure in her social connections. She holds on to these connections in her head, even when no one is there. She experiences solitude as a calm, restful, and relaxed state, where she can fulfill her own needs and have a respite from meeting the needs of others.[34]

Mary remained close to many of her siblings and to her nieces and nephews. She was especially close to her brother Fred, who was three years younger. They fought throughout their childhood but became confidants and supported each other as adults. Mary's parents never fought; her mother just gave in. But Mary learned from her relationship with Fred that they could fight and still love each other—that fighting didn't mean rejection or the end of a relationship. With Fred and two of her sisters, Mary could share intimate concerns. They were friends as well as family. With other siblings, she was reluctant to share some parts of her life, but she still felt she could count on them no matter what.

In addition to her siblings who were friends, Mary had two other groups of friends. She remained close to a group of ten women who had been nuns together. Most of them had left the order, but a few remained there. They got together for a reunion about once a year, including the partners of those who were married or coupled. One of the husbands said that these reunions reminded him of his army buddies. Indeed, these women had bonded owing to their intense experience together—a "basic training" that had thrown them together twenty-four hours a day for a number of years. Mary felt closest to these old friends, but none of them lived nearby. She met most of her newer friends at her workplace. Although she saw them more often than the nuns and ex-nuns, she didn't know if she could count on them in times of need in the same way she could depend on family and her old friends. History, however, proved her wrong.

After learning of Mary's death, I interviewed her colleague Laurie, who had worked with Mary for three years and been a friend for two. Laurie talked about Mary's long struggle with colon cancer. Mary had had several operations, was in and out of the hospital, and worked only part-time for more than a year. Throughout the ordeal, Mary kept her sense of humor and personal strength. She was in charge of her own medical care and never complained. Mary didn't want to ask friends and family for help, but they rallied. None of her family lived nearby, but one sister came for six months and another for four. Mary's local best friend had died suddenly, a year earlier. But other friends, colleagues, and neighbors helped out—visiting, bringing food, and doing errands. Three weeks before her death, Mary had Laurie, another friend, and her sister over for dinner. Looking frail after having lost a lot of weight, Mary, who was in a wheelchair, insisted on doing the cooking and having an upbeat, fun evening.

Three days later, Mary went back to the hospital and never left it alive. During those last weeks, Mary asked her siblings and friends from out of town to come, one at a time, for a short visit to say good-bye. She did not want a lot of people hanging around. She told everyone she was ready to die and wanted to do so in peace and solitude. She died alone as she preferred. In death Mary was indeed a whole person, which May Sarton defined in *Journal of a Solitude* as one undivided "by conscience, by doubt or by fear."[35]

Mary requested that a memorial service be held in a nondenominational chapel, rather than in a church. All of Mary's siblings, nieces, and nephews attended, along with friends from far and near. The speakers—her brother, sister, a nephew, and a few friends—stressed her sense of humor, her dedication to education, her gifts as a teacher, and her love for her family. No one mentioned spirituality. Even in death Mary confounded the stereotype of a nun or ex-nun. As Mary desired, her ashes were scattered in Bodega Bay.

■ ■ ■

The autonomy that Elena Morales, Anne Rosetti, and Mary Bishop gained validates psychologist Anthony Storr's analysis that personal interests, and not just love, friendships, or human relationships, help make life worthwhile and lead to human happiness: "Interests, whether in writing history, breeding carrier pigeons, speculating in stocks and shares, designing aircraft, playing the piano, or gardening, play a greater part in the economy of human happiness than modern psychoanalysts and their followers allow."[36]

For some, work is where they express their interests and gain autonomy. Philosopher Sara Ruddick identifies the importance of loving one's work. Work that fulfills requires "love for oneself, love for the ideas and creations of others, love for the people one works with, love for the knowledge, change and beauty that work alone can achieve."[37] For other people, the positive aspects of daily life—cooking, gardening, caring for pets and the home—give meaning to life and provide enjoyment whether they do these things in solitude or with others.

Pursuing one's interests promotes autonomy, and, in turn, autonomy encourages one to engage in such projects. These three women, in pursuing their interests and maximizing their autonomy through work, created happy lives, but ones that were not as rich in intimacy or sexual/sensual pleasure as those of some of the other single women I studied. My research thus suggests an opposition between autonomy and intimacy, and between autonomy and sensual pleasure.[38] It may be impossible for most single women to simultaneously maximize autonomy, intimacy, and sensuality.

Autonomy, however, does not necessarily mean isolation or loneliness. Elena, Anne, and Mary pursued their interests in rich interaction with their extended family, friends, lovers, colleagues, and communities. Anne's political community, Elena's ethnic ties, and Mary's network of ex-nuns facilitated their enjoyment of their solitude. Their capacity to enjoy such solitude was a measure of their autonomy—of their inner security and emotional maturity.[39]

The strong sense of self these women came to possess resulted from challenges they faced at various points in their lives—for Anne her divorce, for Elena the isolation she endured in New Mexico, and for Mary the loss of self she experienced with lovers. When their sense of self felt most challenged, these women did not retreat into the dependence of relationships but sought to strengthen their autonomy. Their self-knowledge and self-acceptance did not come through romantic love. Rather than searching for a soul mate, these women claimed and enhanced their own souls.[40]

CHAPTER 6

"Will I End Up as a Bag Lady?"

Childless Single Women

Young women talk about the fear of not finding a soul mate; they do not express similar anxieties about having children.[1] In 2001 only 16 percent of young women and men in their twenties told pollsters that the main purpose of marriage was to have children.[2] Most single women find it easier to accept the possibility that they will not be mothers than that they might never be in a satisfying primary relationship. Similarly, women in my study who were over forty did *not* struggle with their status as nonmothers as much as they did with not having a partner.

A number of studies find that the rise of voluntary childlessness in the 1970s and 1980s was correlated with an increase in the commitment to the idea of the romantic couple.[3] In addition, the cultural supremacy of the couple shapes how social scientists and journalists view childless women: They focus their studies and discussion on married or coupled women who do not have children.[4]

Only in their thirties do single women struggle with whether they want to mother, and if so, whether they can do it without a partner. Thirty-something single women in my study answered these questions variously. Some, like Lanette Jones, the African American businesswoman, are clear that they would like children but don't want to become single mothers. Like her, many are unwilling to compromise their romantic ideals to marry a man just because he would be a good father. Others, like Elena Morales, are conflicted about whether to become a single mother if they do not find a partner who meets their romantic and family goals. Even women who have never had much of an interest in becoming mothers have to cope with the cultural ideal that happiness depends on family life with a soul mate and a child. In this chapter and in the next one (on single mothers), I follow three women in their thirties and examine how they resolved these issues.

I found, in contrast, that women over forty who say they would have liked to have children did not reflect on their past actions or think of new ways of becoming mothers.[5] Rather, they moved on with their lives, many finding other ways to relate to children and young people.[6] Other authors have found this also. Because a major study of ever-single women in the 1970s reported that motherhood was a major issue for unmarried women, journalist Lee Reilly expected a similar finding in the 1990s. She was surprised to find very few "biological tickings and quiet regrets."[7] Rather, Reilly ascertained that the vast majority of the ever-single women she interviewed "don't miss having children, and none has considered marrying for the sole purpose of having children."[8] As the title of this chapter suggests, and as I will explore in more detail, childless women's anxieties focus on whether they can sustain their autonomy into old age.

Why are single women able to resolve their feelings about childlessness by their mid- to late forties? I argue that neither social structural nor biological factors can explain this. Certainly, childless single women are more comfortable because they are surrounded by many others like themselves. According to the U.S. Census Bureau, in 2002, 18 percent of women aged forty to forty-four had never had a child. Among never-married women of this age (who represent 12 percent of this group), 63 percent were childless.[9] But this is not the highest rate in recent U.S. history. In 1950, 20 percent of women aged forty to forty-four were childless, yet they found themselves in a society that was especially hostile to single, childless women. They were marginalized by the marriage and baby boom of the 1950s, which had the highest U.S. rates of marriage and reproduction in the twentieth century.[10] Hence, we cannot be sure that the increasing rates of childlessness in the last ten years will prevail or that childlessness will become more socially acceptable on a permanent basis.

What about biology? One might conclude that the end (or rapid decline) of their reproductive biology explains why childless single women over forty put aspirations for mothering aside even though they do not abandon the search for a partner. But the years of my study (1994–2003) coincide with numerous breakthroughs in bio-technologies enabling older women to give birth. Yet in my study, no one in her forties considered in-vitro fertilization, using donor eggs, or even adoption. Only one divorced woman regretted not having had children during her sixteen-year marriage.[11] These single women's acceptance of their childlessness can be attributed both to the cultural primacy of the idea that being coupled is the major source of adult happiness and to other cultural changes.

At the height of second-wave feminism in the 1970s, many feminists questioned the widespread belief that motherhood was in-stinctual, *natural,* and necessary for women's identity and fulfillment. But by the 1980s feminist writers were more interested in reforming motherhood than in exploring childlessness.[12] Still, feminism had an impact. Femininity and female identity are no longer closely tied to maternity and nurturance. In an early 1990s study of childless women, psychologist Mardy Ireland found that motherhood is no longer "necessarily central to the development of women's sense of her adult self."[13] A forty-year-old woman in Ireland's study said: " 'There's nothing in me that has to have a child to feel like a woman.' "[14] Indeed, the sociologist Rosemary Gillespie found that voluntarily childless women often associate motherhood with a loss of female identity.[15]

The widespread availability of birth control and abortion is a precondition for separating reproduction from female identity, but to make this a reality, other possibilities have to open for women. The blossoming of career and work opportunities, especially since the ad-vent of twentieth-century feminism, has elevated creative labor as a source of female fulfillment.[16] In addition, femininity, for better or for worse, is defined now primarily by beauty, sex appeal, and empathy with a soul mate. To be feminine is to be sexy and to be empathic to another adult, not to be in a mother-child relationship. Today, we only rarely hear that women have an instinctive need to mother. Thus, most childless women no longer feel stigmatized as women.[17]

But culture is never monolithic, and older ideals linger. Despite cultural chatter about all the problems women have in combining work and child rearing, women still believe they should be able to have it all. Young women know that their mothers want them to have successful careers, but they also want grandchildren. As a society we still idealize family life, and *family* means a nuclear family, consisting of a parent and child. Psychologist Carolyn Morell points out that we accept the term "single-parent family," but we never hear of a "no child family." Such a narrow definition of family prevents us from seeing how increases in singleness and childlessness open opportunities to rekindle extended family ties, to remember the importance of being an aunt and a godmother.

These traditional cultural assumptions are especially hard on young women who already know that whether they couple or not in the future, they do not want to give birth or be a mother. When this topic came up in my class on single women, a few women in their twenties admitted that they already knew they did not want to have children. They were moved by an article we read in *Ms.* magazine, in which author Carolyn Megan responds to her boyfriend's belief that having children makes us human. Megan writes, "What makes us human is the ability to choose, to create in many different ways."[18]

When my students informed their mothers and others of their preference, they were told that they were too young to make that decision, that they were likely to change their minds. A Chicana in her twenties said that her mother told her she would have a sad and depressing life if she remained childless. Another young woman said that it was easier to lie by telling people that she thought she would be unable to have children. After that, she got a lot of sympathy. Feminist writer Bernice Fisher accurately pinpoints the impact of such attitudes: "The belief that women cannot truly choose to remain childless, that we do not know what we are doing, reveals a deep-seated misogyny. The voice that says childless women will regret their decision is the same voice that questions women's capacity to choose in any area.... It is the voice that undermines us as full participants in society, as makers of meaning in our lives."[19] Conversely, making a clear choice *not* to become a mother is to define oneself as a grownup, just as surely as the decision to have a child.[20]

Why Single Women Remain Childless

I found two types of childless, single women—those who had little desire to mother and those who did not want to be single mothers.

Having Little Desire to Mother

The new cultural emphasis on the couple as the route to happiness and a deemphasis on the joys of parenthood permit more women to admit that they never want to mother. Some women in my study acknowledged this to themselves at an early age, whereas others, with little interest in becoming a mother but reluctant to admit it, drifted into childlessness. Connie Crawford was a drifter. She was in a committed cohabitation for ten years, from the time she was twenty-six until she turned thirty-six. She reported that she and her partner never felt settled enough to consider the question of children. Only in retrospect does she admit that *not* making a decision was deciding. Thus, the process of ending up childless is for Connie and others a lot like becoming single: most women don't make a conscious choice, but other decisions and life circumstances lead them there.[21] Since she had "never had a passion for having children," Connie was happy with the result. She never felt attracted to pregnancy and considered raising children a lot of work. In her late thirties, as a single woman again, Connie had no regrets about not having had children. At age fifty, she still has no regrets. When Connie was in her midforties, her brother and his wife adopted a baby girl from China. Connie delighted in her new niece, considered this option for herself, but rejected it.

Dorothy Sawyer, the sexually assertive woman portrayed in chapter 2, also drifted into childlessness. She was married to her second husband from the age of thirty-five to forty-five. Her husband had a teenage son who got into drugs and alcohol. Dorothy didn't think her husband handled the situation well, and this discouraged her from having children. "Children didn't happen," she said. In retrospect, however, Dorothy, like Connie, recognized that she never had a strong desire to parent. She knows it would have interfered with her work and her sexual independence. Now in her fifties, Dorothy would like to have a twenty-something child with whom she would get along, but she would not like to have gone through the earlier years. "I don't know how mothers come home from work, cook, and interact with their kids," Dorothy remarked. "It's nice to come home and not have to deal with anything." Dorothy epitomized the new ideal of feminine identity based on sexual appeal rather than on an interest in, or ability to, nurture.

Those of my subjects who admitted that they were not interested in mothering included both only children, like Gillian Herald, and those who came from large families, like Anne Rosetti and Mary Bishop. They included those who were close to their mothers (Gillian Herald) and those who were estranged (Dorothy Sawyer) from them.

For all of these women, singleness served as a shield for prying questions and disapproval about their childless state, since women who are over forty and without partners are not expected to be mothers. After she divorced at the age of forty-five, Anne Rosetti, the autonomous entrepreneur, no longer had to face the family pressures she experienced while she was married. Ten years later, she can acknowledge that her choice to not have children—a choice with which she is content—has had both positive and negative consequences. She recognizes that "both opportunities and losses arise from choosing a direction in life." Anne cherishes her autonomy to pursue many interesting paths, but she misses some of the richness of family life that her sisters enjoy with their children. Such a recognition is *not* equivalent to regret; Anne knows she made the right choice for herself.

Coming to terms when single with one's lack of desire to mother can help a woman hold on to this conviction if she later becomes part of a couple. I interviewed Nicole Roberts, a petite and lively never-married woman, when she was thirty. She seemed to be a particularly grounded and self-reflective young woman, despite what she described as the unhappy, loveless family in which she and her three siblings grew up and her parents' divorce when she was in her early twenties. The oldest child, Nicole was seen as the responsible, maternal daughter who was going to get married and be a good mother. Instead, she became the first in her family to go to college and the first to live by herself and be self-supporting. At thirty, Nicole felt positive about her future, whether she remained single or became part of a couple. "I think I would be happy if I never married," Nicole said, "and I think I could also be happily married if there was a lot of mutual respect, a lot of communication, and if we were both clear about what's important to each of us and did not assume that it'll all work out after we get married." Until she met her boyfriend of six months, a man who was four years younger, Nicole had not dated much and never had a serious relationship. She felt conflicted about his desire to cohabit, because she was used to being independent and living in her own space.

Nicole was clear that she did not want to be a single mother and that she would probably be happy not being a mother at all. "The thought of being pregnant, having a baby, and being a mother just terrifies me no end," Nicole confessed. She believed that the fear came from "the responsibility of needing to protect a child from what I went through." She continued, "I do not want a child to grow up the way that I did, and I fear that I would not be able to change that." When I contacted Nicole nine years later, she was happily married to the same man, but they had decided not to have children.

Rejecting Single Motherhood

Single, childless women in their forties and fifties who would have liked to have had children but did not want to be single mothers came from both happy families and from those they considered unhappy or unhealthy or both. They expressed a variety of reasons for not becoming a single parent.

Lanette Jones, who came from a middle-class black family with divorced parents, said that her rejection of single parenting is the direct result of the negative social stereotypes of the black single mother. Nancy Dean, the flamenco dancer, declared that she was not physically strong enough to be a single mother and pursue her career too. Several other women agreed and/or said that they were not financially secure enough to consider this as an option. Rachel Brown, the single woman from an unhappy family whom we met in chapter 4, felt that she would have raised "a really crazy kid" if she tried to do it alone. Others from unhappy families felt similarly. Elena Morales and several other women from happy families, by contrast, expressed the importance of having had a loving father in their lives as they grew up. They found it hard to imagine raising a child without such a father. Another woman from a happy family felt it would be selfish to raise a child in less than ideal circumstances. She saw her disinclination to become a single parent as a selfless act.

Although not as conscious as Lanette Jones about how cultural ideas influenced their choices, indirectly all these women echo cultural themes of the late twentieth and early twenty-first century about the difficulties and dangers of single parenting. The overwhelming cultural message is that single mothers are financially and personally burdened and that their children are disadvantaged. This message is especially strong for black women and for other racial and ethnic minorities. The growing number of mature single mothers and the small but growing movement to support women's choice to become single parents are drowned out by the negative messages about single parenting. We'll consider, and critique, some of this cultural legacy in the next chapter.

When they more rationally consider the cultural bias against single mothers, along with the evidence presented about the joys, the intimacy, and the difficulties of single parenting, single women in the future may or may not be more open to this option. They may decide to explore other creative ways to integrate children into their lives. They may reject the notion that one can relate in a close, nurturing manner only with one's *own* children.

Integrating Children into the Lives of Childless, Single Women

I met and interviewed Emily Jacobs and Paula Little first in 1994 and then nine years later, in 2004. These women are eighteen years apart in age. I followed Emily, a bisexual, from the age of thirty-two to forty-one, and Paula, a heterosexual, from the age of fifty to fifty-nine. Emily was primarily single but cohabited with a woman partner for several years. Paula married at twenty-four and divorced at thirty-four; in her forties she had a serious relationship, which included a short cohabitation. Each woman's relationship failed between the two times I interviewed her, and neither wanted to talk much about it. Both were open, however, about their conventional families of origin, their expectations from an early age that they would marry and have children, why they didn't want to be single mothers, and the creative ways in which they had incorporated children into their lives.

Like many childless single women, Emily and Paula work in human services, which brings them into close contact with young people—Emily as a therapist and Paula as a music professor and choir director.[22] But they desired a more personal, one-on-one involvement with children. They have cultivated good relationships with nieces and nephews who live thousands of miles away, but they wanted additional ties to children. So both women found a way to form innovative ties with young people.

Emily Jacobs and the Magnolia Tree Club

Emily bounced into the room. A forty-one-year-old woman, her short stature and petite form hid her history as a nationally ranked soccer player when she was in her early twenties. Only her energy, and her direct, no-nonsense manner, pointed to this achievement, as did the difficulties she described in creating a mundane professional life after her athletic success.

Emily was the middle of seven children from an upper-middle-class Catholic family in Connecticut. Her father was a lawyer, and her mother a homemaker. From a young age, Emily loved sports and was the most athletic child in the family. When she was ten, she beat one of her older brothers at tennis. He threw his racket, and her mother reprimanded *her*. After that, Emily played mostly with and against girls. "It was okay if I played sports," Emily remembered, "as long as I was really feminine. I had long hair, and I wore it in a pony-tail with a ribbon. I smiled and didn't spit."

All the Jacobses were expected to go to Ivy League schools, and the father had enough wealth to pay for all of the children's tuition. Emily rebelled, wanting to get out of New England, to escape the control her father asserted with his money, and to play soccer. To her parents' distress, she turned down Harvard and Yale to accept a full athletic scholarship—still a rarity for women in 1980—at a less prestigious college in the South. Emily had a very rewarding academic and athletic experience there, but the school was more socially conservative than she had expected.

For eight years—in college and after—Emily played on the U.S. women's soccer team. These were wonderful years. Emily loved the close camaraderie with her teammates and their foreign travel as they competed internationally. Her parents came to some of the games and supported her as long as she remained feminine. "One year, when I was still in college but on the U.S. team and training intensely," Emily remembered, "my father had a fit that I was lifting weights, even though it was a required part of the training. He got my brothers a whole great weight set for Christmas, and I wasn't allowed to use it!"

After college, and while still on the team, Emily got a job at an elite New England boarding school (which had just become coed), which reflected her continuing attachment to her class and regional background. She was hired because the school needed a coach, but she also taught history and was a dorm counselor. Emily stayed at the school for two years, gaining experience and confidence as a teacher. When she fractured her leg and had to quit the U.S. team, Emily decided to enter a master's degree program in psychology at the University of California, Berkeley, switching after one year to the clinical PhD program. Although she liked teaching, she preferred what she perceived as the less stressful, and more independent, life of a therapist. She also hoped to gain personal insights through her education in clinical psychology. Moving to California, far away from her conservative family, permitted her to deal with her sexual orientation.

In high school and throughout her college years, Emily dated men and had several serious relationships. She held on to the idea that she would marry and have children. But toward the end of her senior year in college, she had a brief relationship with a woman. By the mid-1980s, gay and lesbian clubs had been established at some universities, but not at this southern college. Emily recalls too that there was still a lot of homophobia in women's athletics. "If you wanted to make the U.S. team, you stayed in the closet," she recalled. "The selectors of the team talked a lot about the image that we should present, especially when we're in other countries; there was just a lot of homophobia." After her move to California, Emily dated only women. But at age thirty-two she was still not out to her parents. She told two of her sisters with whom she has a close relationship, but they were not very supportive. One said, "Don't worry, it's a stage." The other sister, a practicing Catholic, tried to be nonjudgmental but suggested that Emily start going to church again, where she would find a good community.

In 1994 Emily did not feel ready for a committed relationship. She felt too unsettled, preoccupied with finishing her PhD and establishing a career, and with gaining more self-understanding. As a realist—someone *not* advocating a soul-mate ideal—Emily didn't

feel ready to make the compromises that she saw as part of any relationship. She didn't yet know what she was willing to compromise.
But Emily went on to say: "I can't imagine not having children. I can
more easily imagine myself as a parent than I can imagine the kind
of relationship I'm going to be in. I don't know why that's true, but
maybe it's because I love kids, and I've always wanted to have children. That's sort of a given."

Like a number of women in this book, Emily left the Bay Area
for several years, but had returned by the time I went looking for her
nine years later. On the phone, I learned she was now forty-one, still
single, and childless. What would I learn about her journey? Entering her small, but extremely pleasant apartment (an in-law unit of
a house owned by friends), I was met by Emily's two friendly Labs.
Emily herself looked and acted much the same—friendly, open,
skeptical, and still searching.

Unlike the autonomous childless women portrayed in chapter 5,
Emily is not personally ambitious. After taking a long time to finish
her PhD and complete the supervised hours necessary to become a
licensed therapist, she now works only part-time as a private family
therapist and teaches one course at a local college. Money is a problem, and she regrets that she can't afford to buy a house.[23] But Emily
has other priorities. "My career is not my primary concern," she said.
"I'd rather lead a balanced life and pursue all these other interests."
Emily breeds dogs, and recently she has taken up quilting. She is
learning about antiques and folk art. She likes gardening and hiking
with her dogs. Then there is her refereeing. During the soccer season, Emily is a referee for women's high school and college soccer
games all over the Bay Area, sometimes volunteering to referee eight
or ten games a week. "That is a big commitment," she said, "but I
love it."

Emily mentioned having been involved in two relationships
since I last talked to her—a serious one with a woman, with whom
Emily lived for two years, and a shorter relationship with a man,
whom she dated for about a year and a half, living together part of
the time. She had not dated for the previous three years but wanted
to start again. Emily said, "I miss the emotional connection." Her

emotional connection with someone, whether female or male, was more important to Emily than gender.

Although she would have liked to find a life partner, a companion to live with whom she could trust, Emily was not sure it would happen. Recently, one of her sisters died of cancer at the age of forty-five. Her brother-in-law, trying to figure out his future, asked her if she was happy being single. "I said to him, 'I have to say that I am. It is not that I wouldn't welcome the possibility of a relationship if it were a good one, but I'm not lost without it. Nor is my life empty in any way. I feel like I have a full and really fortunate life in all kinds of ways.'"

Hearing this, I reminded Emily of what she had said about her strong desire to have children. Emily said it was still a big issue. Given her precarious financial situation, she can't envision being a single mom. Although she has some vague idea that she might adopt in the future, she has faced the possibility that she won't have her own children. "I've become a little more accepting of things I feel I don't have control over; children are one of those things," Emily said. Then she pointed to framed photos around her apartment—large, artistic black-and-white photographs of children and teenagers engaged in outdoor activities. (Emily is obviously a good photographer too.) She told me of her ongoing relationship with the girls and boys in the Magnolia Tree Club.

Seven years earlier, Emily had been living with her woman partner in a town in northern California, where her partner had a job. Emily was working on her dissertation and "looking for excuses to procrastinate." She recounted the scene. "Lots of little kids were running around our disadvantaged neighborhood, with parents working two or three jobs and not around. Many were single parents. One mom had only a third-grade education; another had only finished sixth grade. I fell in love with the kids and practically ran a day-care center." The children were mainly Latino girls and boys, with one white girl and one African American boy. They met every day under a large magnolia tree and, after Emily became involved with them, came to call themselves a club.

After she moved back to the Bay Area, Emily kept in touch and now takes the kids on several trips every year. She takes six kids at a time, usually camping in the Sierras or on other outdoor adventures, but sometimes indulging their interest in amusement parks or other popular culture events. She has put in a lot of her own money, but also receives contributions from family and friends. Sometimes she goes by herself, but often friends (from her large network) or family come with her. Emily talked about a trip where her father accompanied her on a camping trip in the mountains one summer. "He was great with the kids, just sweet and adorable. Often I see only his patriarchal side, but I came to realize the things I have in common with him, and what I like and appreciate about him. This trip was a turning point in our relationship."

The Magnolia Tree Club's participants are now teenagers—one girl just had a baby and another is pregnant. Most have moved to other parts of town. "They have remained friends with each other, perhaps because of our shared experiences," Emily said. But despite the one hundred miles that separate them and the class differences, Emily envisioned a continuing relationship. Emily did not, however, see herself as a social worker or a mentor. Rather, she said, "I love kids; I love these particular kids."

A Network of Friends Integrates
Children into Paula Little's Life

Throughout this book, and more explicitly in chapter 9, I stress the importance of friendship networks in the lives of single women. Yet I had not anticipated finding that such networks can be important avenues for childless women to form significant ties to the next generation, especially when nieces and nephews live far away. Tracing Paula Little's life over time, I saw how she developed significant ties to friends' children. When I met her, Paula was fifty and her desire to relate to youth was satisfied primarily through her role as a teacher and a tenuous stepparent relationship to the eleven-year-old daughter of her partner of four years. Nine years later, no longer with a partner, Paula talked about the rich friendship network she had built, and how that led to more fulfilling relationships with a few children of friends.

Paula—tall, thin, pretty, quiet, and serious—grew up in a stable nuclear family (an older brother, teacher father, and musician mother) in the Southwest. She never imagined a single life without children. "You grow up, get married, have kids, and create a family," said Paula. "That's the way life is." Paula's love of music came directly from her mother, who played the organ for the choir in a Methodist church. For years, Paula and her brother sang in the choir. Later, they both turned against organized religion, but Paula is not surprised that she ended up with an MA in music and a teaching position in the music department of a small private college. She directs the choir and teaches voice and music appreciation.

As a young woman, however, Paula wanted some distance from her family. In 1964, she entered the University of California at Berkeley and was stunned in her first semester by the student revolt —the Free Speech Movement. Coming from a traditional family and a nonpolitical environment, Paula was overwhelmed by what she saw as the chaos at Berkeley. Her relationships with men were also turbulent and disorienting. Then, at twenty-three, she met her husband-to-be, who was practical and "kind of a guy-wire to the earth." Reflecting back, Paula concluded: "I don't think I would have married him had I not felt needy, because he wasn't the kind of person I enjoyed spending a lot of time with." Although she always felt constricted and restrained by him, Paula stayed married for almost ten years, taking the initiative to leave only at the age of thirty-four, after she had a career and a stable job. Because she was never satisfied with the marriage, Paula, in these prime childbearing years, never considered having children. Being part of the first generation to have reliable and legal birth control made this choice possible.

In her late thirties and early forties, without a stable relationship, Paula made a conscious decision not to have a child without a partner. "I had a strong relationship with my father," Paula said. "I really loved him, and I couldn't imagine a kid growing up without a father. I made what I considered an unselfish choice, because I felt it would not be good for the child."

Throughout her early forties, most of Paula's friends were musicians and artists and most did not have children. But in her late forties, Paula began a relationship with a divorced father who had a young daughter. During their four-year relationship, Paula grew close to the daughter, Mary, as she matured from ages seven to eleven. They had many good times together. About a year before our first interview, her partner, David, moved into Paula's house. Mary lived with David and Paula most of the time. Paula loved having a family, but David and Mary found it less satisfactory. Mary wanted to stay at her old school, more than twenty miles away, so David drove her to and from school every day, a burden he couldn't sustain. And Mary was separated from her friends. Nor did David and Mary ever feel at home in Paula's house. Only a month before our interview, they had moved back to the house he still owned in their old neighborhood. Paula was hurt but hoped the attachment would continue. When asked what her life might be like in ten years, however, she said she didn't know if they would still be together.

Through David, Paula became friends with several couples with children. She got to see close up what life was like with children and to appreciate both what she was missing and what she had that mothers did not—a stimulating career, freedom to travel, a wider diversity of friends. "I didn't put a judgment on it, whether my life or theirs was better," Paula recalled. "I just said it's kind of like chocolate or vanilla ice cream. Some people like one better and some the other." Getting close to families with children helped Paula come to terms with her own childlessness, but she didn't foresee that these friendships would create a new and more stable way to relate to young people.

When I reconnected with Paula, nine years later, she told me how she and David had drifted apart. They maintained a relationship for three more years, spending holidays and birthdays together and traveling twice to Europe. But Paula didn't like the lack of daily contact. "I felt split. I didn't feel like I had one center, but two," she said. Gradually, they moved apart, with "less contact, less intimacy, less family," and less of what Paula wanted. She grew more dissatisfied, and eventually they parted for good. David soon found a new relationship close to his home, and Paula was very hurt. She now feels, however, that their breakup forced her to come to terms with, and accept, her single life. "I didn't go into therapy," Paula told me. "I started reading spiritual books and ancient teachings, which opened my thinking and my heart. This exploration led me to be more open and more generous with people. I feel more connected to my students, more connected to my friends and my family."

Although Paula is satisfied with her life and happier than she has ever been, she would like "at least one more man" with whom to have "both physical and spiritual intimacy." I quoted Paula in the chapter entitled "Sex and the Single Woman" (chapter 2) because of her open and flexible view on what form this relationship might take. "It could be a traveling friend, someone to date, or he could live with me," Paula explained about her decision to try an Internet dating service.

Paula's introspection led her to focus on the importance of friendship. "I realized that in my relationship with David I had put all my eggs in one basket," she explained. "I didn't connect enough with women friends. Since that relationship has come apart, I have made a conscious and concerted effort to cultivate my women friends and friends who have families. I now have more than one or two close friends; I have a real network."

Paula was surprised that some of David's friends continued to seek her out. She began to see a lot more of a couple and their children with whom they used to go camping. "They invite me over for Thanksgiving and Christmas, and we still go camping together. They don't invite him. So I now have a real family connection with them." Although she didn't see much of David's daughter for a few years, Mary, now a sophomore in college, recently contacted Paula. "She wrote me a Christmas note saying how great it was that I was in her life, how much she loved me," Paula said. "Maybe as she gets older, we might have more contact."

Paula also increased her connection to her goddaughter, the daughter of a married woman friend. The goddaughter is graduating from college soon, and Paula is going to the graduation ceremony with the family, who have rented a house for them. In addition,

Paula has formed more personal relations with a few of her students, keeping in contact after they graduated. One ex-student with a baby comes now to visit almost once a week. Paula concluded, "I feel that I have created a large extended family, and that I've fulfilled the need to give to the next generation. I'm never lonely, and much more satisfied than I was nine years ago."

Do all single, childless women want to relate on a personal level with children or young people? Probably not. In retrospect, I realized that I didn't try to draw out women who might not want to relate very intimately with the next generation. One of my friends, a never-married, childless woman in her fifties, in a draft of an as-yet-unpublished memoir about her mother's death, wrote about the mixed feelings that arose in her when she lost her elderly mother. She has some regrets about not having a child of her own—an imaginary daughter who could replicate the close relationship she had in later years with her mother—but she has no interest in trying to find a substitute. "I like some of my friends' children," she wrote, "and even occasionally enjoy their company, but spending time with them is the *last* thing I want to do now; they're not what I need." Many more women undoubtedly feel the same.

When I showed the above paragraph to my friend, she said: "That is not the whole truth; let me show you another part of the memoir that you've never seen, a section where I talk about what teaching means to me." There she writes about the rewards of teaching at a small college where "you get to work closely with students, watch them grow up." Teaching young people, she said, "is what I've done instead of children, and that's okay—I'm a better teacher than I'd have been a mother." She concluded with a statement that epitomizes the life of a new single woman: "The art is in making the choice you can live with."[24]

The Specter of the Bag Lady

Author Irena Klepfisz projects the classic fear of single, childless women. "At the center of my bleakest fantasy is the shopping-bag lady," she writes. "I see her sitting on the subway, trudging along the highway, or crouched in a doorway at dusk. Invariably, she clutches her paper shopping bags close to her. From a distance her face looks blank, her skin gray. She is oblivious to the things around her, unresponsive to sounds and movements. She is particularly indifferent to people."[25] To Klepfisz, the bag lady represents the fear that as she ages she will lose connections and relations and become isolated. She writes: "I am afraid I too will end up alone, disconnected, relating to no one, having no one to care for, being in turn forgotten, unwanted and insignificant, my life a waste."[26] She notes: "For a long time I believed (and on some nonrational level still believe) that I could acquire immunity to the shopping-bag lady's disease by having a child. . . . In reality, of course, I know that many shopping-bag ladies are mothers, have families, have children. What is obvious to any mature, rational woman is that children are not a medicine or a vaccine which stamps out loneliness or isolation, but rather that they are people, subject to the same weaknesses as friends and lovers."[27]

I did not ask women in my study about their fears of aging, but three of the childless single women brought up the topic and explicitly mentioned a fear of becoming a shopping-bag lady. None of the single women with children referred to it. The three women—Lanette Jones, the businesswoman in her forties who is African American; Dorothy Sawyer, the sexually assertive woman in her fifties; and Anne Rosetti, the entrepreneur—are all economically secure and have planned for their retirement. They recognized the irrational component of their fears. Dorothy remarked: "My good friend, who is single and a senior VP making well over six figures, talks about being a bag lady too. So it is not about income; it is irrational. There is nothing in my past that tells me I will be a bag lady. But my generation (the early baby boom) expected to be married and not to have to work." Anne too acknowledges the irrational, and perhaps generational, roots of her fears about taking care of herself.

> Every year for thirty years, I've paid property taxes. I've never been delinquent. But every year, I have an anxiety attack around that, even though I have never overdrawn my account. I think

women still don't accept that we really can take care of ourselves. We never seem to be convinced that it won't all go away, that suddenly we'll be destitute. But now I'm getting to the point where I can say, "So it all goes away; you make up something else." I've gained that type of confidence. My irrational fears have become a friend, because they signal to me that there is something I'm worried about, that I need to pay attention to and try to figure out. So the bag lady becomes an ally.

Perhaps younger generations of women, raised with the expectation that they need to be economically self-sufficient, will be less fearful. Journalist Terri Casey interviewed Maria Rodriguez, a twenty-five-year-old Hispanic woman born and raised in Southern California who knows she doesn't want to have children. Maria envisions her old age as being surrounded by "friends and family and with the means to hire somebody to take care of me."[28]

As Maria recognizes, and Klepfisz articulates, economic issues are only one aspect of the fears that fuel the bag-lady image. Just as important is the fear of social isolation, of being alone with no one to care for us. Such fears have a rational element in a mobile society, where family obligations are the most lasting social bonds. Michelle Patenaude, a thirty-eight-year-old single childless woman, writes: "Secretly, I sometimes worry that I will spend my old age alone. Who will visit me in the nursing home? Who will look after my possessions when I die? Put flowers on my grave? Who will feed my cats, water my plants?"[29]

These questions and fears can be addressed. Chapter 9 provides examples of single women who became ill in their fifties and sixties and were cared for by circles of friends in a manner that far exceeded the care provided by most families. Gerontology research is reassuring, too, about extrafamilial support for single women over the age of seventy. Researchers find that "childlessness appears to be insignificant in determining happiness, satisfaction, or loneliness in the elderly; contact with friends is much more important than contact with children."[30] Research finds too that older childless women who were in long-term marriages are more vulnerable to isolation than are childless women who were single most of their lives.[31] Single women are more likely to have built social networks and relied on friends; probably they will go on doing so in old age and incorporate younger people into their friendship networks. Like Paula Little and Gillian Herald (see chapter 3), some single women in their fifties already are forging friendships with younger adults—friends who they hope will still be in their lives when they are in their eighties and nineties, when their peers may have passed away.

Alice, a middle-aged teacher who is single and childless, in an interview with Bernice Fisher, projects an optimism that lays bag-lady fears to rest. "She had given so much to others. She said, 'Someone will look out for me.'"[32]

CHAPTER 7

Without a Dad

Single Women as Mothers

> What I have is enough, at least for now. . . . There is the creak
> of the rocker, the luscious fact of my sleeping daughter. . . .
> I have friends and family whom I love in a town I love living
> in; I have wild roses climbing up the side of a house that
> belongs to me. The blossoms are a deep pink color, beautiful
> beside each other. Or by themselves.
>
> ELIZABETH BERG, *Until the Real Thing Comes Along*

The satisfaction of a single woman who has just become a mother—
a joy expressed by the protagonist in Elizabeth Berg's 1999 novel
Until the Real Thing Comes Along—is sustained by an increasingly intimate bond between mother and child as the child matures. This
pleasure, however, is accompanied by many hard tasks. Especially ar-
duous is the need for a single mother to be both the primary nurturer
and the disciplinarian. Even when she is surrounded by supportive
family and friends, and sometimes is aided by the child's nonresident
father or a father substitute, the single mother has the main responsibility for child rearing. As with other topics discussed in this book,
I don't want to exaggerate the differences between single mothers
and those who parent with a male partner. A lot of single parenting is
done within a marriage, for the majority of mothers in heterosexual
couples still have primary, sometimes sole, responsibility for raising
children.[1] Conversely, when both husband and wife are employed
full-time, they, like single mothers, often create networks of kin and
friends to help them parent.[2]

Of the thirteen single mothers I followed over time, only three
benefited from the biological father's active role in parenting, all of
them after a divorce. In addition to the inherent difficulties of parenting, all of us, divorced and unmarried single mothers alike, were

subject to the increasingly strident cultural messages that our children, growing up without an in-house father, would be disadvantaged and damaged. Even the term *single mother* is pejorative, since we seldom speak of a *married* mother.[3]

The impact of these negative cultural missives on us (an issue I'll explore in more detail later in this chapter) is only partly offset by the growing number of mature single mothers. Between 1980 and 2002, births to unmarried women rose from 18 percent to 34 percent of all births, and during this time births to unmarried women aged thirty to thirty-four jumped from 7 to 15 percent of all births. By 2002, two-thirds of all births to unmarried mothers were to women over the age of twenty.[4] The majority of single mothers, however, were divorced or separated. In 2000, 55 percent of single mothers were divorced or separated, and another 4 percent were widowed.[5] Looked at another way, 23 percent of all children in 2003 lived with only their mother (and another 5 percent with only their father).[6] Moreover, about 70 percent of children in the United States will spend some time in a single-parent family before they reach the age of eighteen.[7] Contrary to the stereotype, most single-mother families are *not* poor, with only 30 percent receiving welfare in 2000.[8] As a result of these demographic changes, all the single mothers in my study knew other single mothers, and all of our children had friends who were also growing up in single-parent households.

In the mid-1990s, when I began my study, most of the single mothers I interviewed were in their forties and early fifties, with children who were teenagers, and most of them were coping with their children's difficult adolescence. This was not a representative sample from which one can generalize about single mothers. I know single mothers, for example, whose sons and daughters were exemplary teenagers. But how single mothers cope with difficult teens is an important topic. Because the majority of these mothers were raising their children without the involvement of fathers, they were especially vulnerable to negative cultural texts. When our children were young, we, as well-educated and economically solvent women, could reject the ideological put-downs of single mothers. We could say to ourselves and others that because of their educational and economic advantages, our children would be fine.[9] But now that we were faced with troubled teenagers, our confidence faded. "I feel like my teenage son is a walking statistic," said one professional woman who had good economic resources and support from her friendship network and extended family.[10]

Dealing with our teenagers in a culture that told us that our children's difficulties stemmed from the lack of an involved father increased our anxiety as single mothers.[11] Such anxiety sometimes led us to questionable decisions to involve other men in our children's lives, men who subsequently damaged them. Even when we made good decisions, the insecurity with which we parented was counterproductive for our own and our children's lives.[12] If we could have anticipated my findings—that eight or nine years later most of our sons and daughters in their midtwenties would be leading good lives, sometimes with successes exceeding our expectations—we might have relaxed.[13]

If we had been aware of research demonstrating that a father's main contribution to family life is as a support for the mother,[14] that when he is involved with the children, he contributes most as an *additional,* rather than as a *male,* parent,[15] we could have been more confident about the positive role that friends and extended family played in helping to nurture our sons and daughters.[16] We would have seen how they could, to an important degree, substitute for "daddy."[17] Then we might have spared ourselves some of the negative impact that stepfathers and father substitutes had on our own, and our children's, lives.

This chapter explores the joys and hardships of single motherhood by narrating the stories of two middle-class, unmarried single mothers, my own story, and that of a divorced mother. After exploring the diverse paths we took in the process of becoming single mothers and the intimate bonds we forged with our children, I examine how we dealt with the daddy issue and how our children made the transition to adulthood.

The Process of Becoming a Single Mother

Deciding to become a mother without a partner who is committed to being a cohabiting parent necessitates accepting one's singleness, at least to a degree. Coming to terms with one's permanent status as a single parent, however, is a gradual process. Most mature women who accept single motherhood acknowledge that the biological father will play at best a marginal role in the child's life. But we fantasize, or hope, that a partner will show up for us, one who will also help parent. We let go of this idea as a result of both positive and negative experiences—the emotional intensity and satisfaction of being a mother and/or the disappointment, or worse, with attempts to bring new men into our own and our children's lives.

I will compare my process of adopting an infant as a forty-year-old single woman with that of Linda Woolsey, who, at the age of forty, twenty years after my adoption, is trying to get pregnant through artificial insemination. Both of us knew that biological fathers would not only be uninvolved in parenting but remain unknown, at least until our children became adults. For both of us the mechanics of becoming a mother were long and difficult. Our process was quite different from that of Janice Belmont, who got pregnant when she was not married or cohabiting. For Janice, pregnancy at the age of twenty-nine was accidental, but the decision to have the child was deliberate. She decided to keep the baby despite facing the strong probability that she would parent with an unknown—but probably minimal—amount of input from the father. Another distinct, but more common, route to single motherhood was that of Gwen Palmer after her divorce.

Becoming a Single Mother with an Unknown Birth Father

When I was thirty-seven, my purchase of a duplex with a couple, with the commitment that we would try to live with some degree of communal cooperation, was explicitly connected to my decision to become a single mother. I made it clear to my partners that I would have a child and that I wanted to create a household in which I could parent in some sort of family setting. There was even a day-care center in the meadow behind the house. My family was on the East Coast, and I knew that if I was going to be a single parent, I would need a support structure. I was right about that, but I failed to foresee that the communal household would not provide the support I needed. Nor did I anticipate the three-year struggle to bring a child into my life.

From the beginning, my preference was to adopt. I idealistically argued that I preferred to give a home to one of the many needy children who were already born. But I also knew that my Catholic, relatively conservative family would be more accepting of adoption than of my being single and pregnant.[18] Moreover, I wasn't dying to be pregnant, and I was scared of giving birth. I know that a lot of women want the experience of pregnancy and childbirth and feel bad if they don't have it, but I never felt that way. Yet I yearned to be a mother.

I started exploring adoption in 1978. A 1965 change in the California law permitted a single person to adopt through state agencies. I applied and was interviewed by a social worker. As part of the interview, the social worker showed me pictures of kids available for adoption and asked me to indicate those who appealed to me. I was attracted to a picture of two young Chinese girls who were sisters. The social worker said: "You would never get them because they are too desirable; as a single woman, you will only get a child who is hard to adopt, probably one with developmental difficulties." I told her clearly that I couldn't handle that. I had a demanding job and worked fifty miles from where I lived. So I said I would not accept a "special needs" child. As a result, I was never offered a child.[19]

I started investigating foreign adoptions, which seemed very difficult, especially for a single woman. Most of the agencies for overseas adoption did not accept single women or men. I considered organizing a foreign adoption on my own but discovered that I would probably have to stay in a foreign country for at least six months, hire a lawyer to deal with the bureaucracy, and probably bribe officials— a distasteful prospect. So I progressed to private adoption. I found that a new process had been established. You hired a lawyer or consultant to help compose and send out letters to gynecologists in small towns in Catholic areas of the United States. You wrote a story about yourself and hoped that a young pregnant woman would choose you. In 1978, however, the lawyer I went to, and other people I talked to, said it would be a waste of time for me to do this because a single woman would never be chosen. Discouraged, I stopped the process for several years. Was I on a fantasy quest? Although I talked about my desire to become a single mother with lots of friends, I knew no single woman who was deliberately trying to become a mother through either adoption or artificial insemination.[20]

Then in 1980, when I was forty years old, I decided to try again. Two factors encouraged me. First, I was awarded a fellowship by the National Endowment for the Humanities to do my own research. I didn't have to commute or teach for fifteen months, and I had complete flexibility with my time. Simultaneously, I heard about a single woman who was able to adopt by using the process of private adoption I described. I didn't make the right connections until late in the fall of 1980, almost six months after my fortieth birthday and six months into the fellowship, and I couldn't get an appointment with a lawyer until January.

Before the appointment, on January 2, 1981, I got a phone call from a married woman in Berkeley—a woman whom I had talked to on the phone about her two private adoptions. She said that her lawyer had heard about a baby in Louisiana. By January 5, I had agreed to take this baby, who was not yet born. The baby boy was born on January 10, and by January 15, I had him. So within two weeks I had a baby, but only after three years of frustration.

Here is how it happened. In a small town in southwest Louisiana, a seventeen-year-old white Catholic woman became pregnant. She was the youngest of five children from a working-class family, but all of her siblings had a college education, and one of her brothers, a priest, had a PhD. The birth mother, I was told, had had gynecological care since the third month of pregnancy and had then decided to put the baby up for adoption. Was it her choice not to get an abortion? Thinking the baby was white, the gynecologist planned to give it to his friends. But in the eighth month, the birth mother told her parents and the doctor that the father was black. The doctor remembered he had a letter in his file from a Berkeley couple who desired to adopt. He decided that it would be a good idea to get this mixed-race baby out of Louisiana. He called the couple, but the woman was now pregnant, and they were no longer interested. They, however, told their lawyer, who called the woman who remembered me. When I contacted this lawyer, he asked me to write a short biography of myself and to send a photograph. I played up the fact that I came from a Catholic family. The lawyer sent me a picture of the birth mother, and I agreed to pay for her medical expenses ($4,000), a small lawyer's fee, and the airfare for the doctor to bring the baby to San Francisco. He and his wife wanted a holiday in the Bay Area.

So my son, Marco, was delivered to me at the San Francisco airport by a southern doctor who complained about the uppity black waitress at the airport coffee shop. I immediately fell in love with the cute, cuddly infant. I was thrilled to have a baby with still nine months left of my leave. He was a healthy, easy baby, and I had plenty of energy. Friends quickly flooded me with used baby equipment and clothes and with presents.[21] No one in my leftist, academic, feminist community had done this, and everyone thought it was great. Even my extended family, who might have been embarrassed if I had given birth as a single woman, viewed me as having done a humanitarian deed. That wasn't my perspective, but if they needed to think that to be supportive, then so be it. I even got a tax break because a black child was seen as hard to adopt.

Twenty years later, when Linda Woolsey decided to have a child, the path she took was both similar to and different from mine. I met Linda when she was thirty-one and about to leave California for law school on the East Coast. Tall and blond, Linda combined a feminine style with an unusual self-assurance. When another woman in the group interview said that the deepest part of her desperately needed to be partnered, Linda responded that although she'd like a partner, she did not have a deep desire, certainly not a desperate one. She would never consider computer dating or answering a personal ad. Linda seemed to be one of the most independent young women I'd met.

Linda was raised by a single mother. Her father left when she was little more than a year old and her older sister was three. They saw him only a few times again as children and then lost all contact. Her mother remarried and had another child, a baby boy born when Linda was ten. Linda never liked her stepfather; she was pleased when her mother divorced him soon after. Linda said that she admired her mother and saw her as a positive role model for how to parent.

Linda was sure she wanted children sometime in the future, preferred to do it with a husband, but did not rule out becoming a single mother. Although she was still pursuing her education, Linda was beginning to feel some pressure. Her family and friends, and especially her grandparents, were always asking, "Haven't you met anybody?" She didn't like the feeling that she should "work" on a relationship with a man she was casually dating just because she felt her biological clock ticking.

Eight years later, I had some trouble locating Linda, finally contacting her through her law school. I found her living and working in the Bay Area again. I was not surprised that she was still single at thirty-nine and had earned both a law degree and a master's in public policy. Nor was I surprised that Linda, in the previous nine months, had been trying to get pregnant through artificial insemination after deciding to become a single mother. She told me that she'd had a number of relationships over the years and cohabited with a man for nine months, but nothing had worked out. She now had a long-distance relationship with a man in Texas, but she did not want to marry him, and he didn't want to be a father. Once she decided to explore the idea of having a child without a partner, she found a lot of support.

Linda bought a house in a smaller town outside the city. She had to commute to work, but the community there gave her a sense of place. She became involved in civic projects and made new friends. Linda's mother, who was living nearby, was planning to move in with Linda after her retirement the following year. Her mother, in her sixties and healthy, loved the idea of being the primary caretaker for Linda's baby, at least in the child's early years. Linda also joined Single Mothers by Choice, a national organization founded in 1986, which now has support groups in all parts of the Bay Area. Because she was not yet a mother, Linda went to a group of "thinkers and try-ers"; once she becomes a parent, she can join a mothers' group. She also enrolled in a Listserv, where she exchanged daily e-mail mes-sages with other single women trying to get pregnant. In addition, Linda started talking about her quest with a few female colleagues at work. She found support there too, including both single and cou-pled women in their late thirties and early forties who were using artificial insemination and other, more technologically sophisticated fertility treatments.[22]

Linda informed me that artificial insemination (AI) is now fully available to single women, at least in California, and is a much more open process than when I inquired about it in the late 1970s. She worked with a reproductive endocrinologist who was very support-ive. Through this doctor, Linda gained access to sperm at the Cali-fornia Cryobank, where she got a lot of information about the sperm donor. "There are baby pictures of the donor and a personal state-ment that they write," she said, "including their medical history up through the grandparents, great-aunts, and great-uncles." Linda has access to an audiotape of the donor responding to different questions, and she can look at psychological tests he took. No current, adult picture is provided, but there is a profile of facial features. In addition, the sperm bank does an attractiveness rating, with eight people eval-uating the donor's looks. "There is really a lot of information," Linda concluded, "permitting me to be more choosy than if I were having a child with a husband or partner."

But even with all this support, Linda, after nine months of try-ing, still had not become pregnant. On her e-mail list at Single

Mothers by Choice, everyone else had, including a forty-six-year-old. On the one hand, their success gives Linda hope, but on the other hand it made her ask, "What is my problem?" She wished she had started when she was younger, thinking that maybe she would have if she hadn't bought into the couples ideology. But she acknowledged that she might have had the same difficulties conceiving when she was thirty, and at the time she had not yet finished her education.

When I contacted Linda again in late 2004, almost eighteen months later, she was at a decision point. She was now forty-one and for two and a half years had tried to get pregnant with artificial insemination—she had been pregnant only once, for eight weeks, before suffering a miscarriage. She was more determined than ever to be a mother. Her forty-two-year-old married sister had just given birth to twins through in-vitro fertilization after ten years of trying different types of infertility treatment. "It's fabulous," Linda said. "I went down last week for ten days to help her. I loved it. It reinforced [my feeling] that I really want to do this."

Linda has given up on artificial insemination and decided that in-vitro fertilization is not a good bet for her. At her age, and with only one ovary, there is only a 5 to 10 percent chance that she will get pregnant, at a cost of $10,000 a try, plus $2,000 for drugs. "If I had unlimited financial resources and time, I would do it, absolutely, but I have neither," Linda said. Rather, she has decided to use eggs donated from a woman in her twenties, which will be fertilized with donated sperm, and then have an embryo implanted. Linda explained that it will cost about $23,000, but a number of embryos can be frozen so Linda can have multiple tries. Her reproductive embryologist has about a 60 to 70 percent success rate with this technique, so Linda is feeling very optimistic. She is apprehensive, though, since there is also about a 20 percent chance of having twins.[23]

Feeling that she can't undertake more than one daunting process at a time, Linda will move on to consider adoption only if this method doesn't work. She has no time limit for trying to become a mother, although she may reach a financial cutoff point.

I think about the childless single women I have interviewed. They would probably be amazed that a single woman could go to these lengths to become a mother. Even I, who went to a lot of trouble to adopt, can't quite imagine myself doing what Linda is doing. Linda admits that the process has been very difficult and emotionally draining. "I think it is particularly hard for women who have had some success in their life," Linda said. "You map out a plan. You say that if I want to achieve this objective, these are the things I need to do, and you think that with diligence and staying the course that you'll get there. But this is one area where it doesn't necessarily work that way."

Yet Linda believes that the process would be even harder if she were coupled and having trouble conceiving. The reproductive endocrinologist's waiting room is a very emotional place. "You see these desperate couples clinging to each other," Linda said. "I thought, 'Boy, I don't want that; I'm glad it is just me, and that I don't have to deal with the dynamic between two people.'"

Becoming a Single Mother with a Known Birth Father

We met Janice Belmont on the first page of this book; she was talking about how, in her fifties, she had given up her quest for a soul mate. Originally from a Midwestern middle-class family of four children, Janice moved to California with her family when she was ten. In her late twenties, she dated an African American man for two years. They had an emotional commitment, but they did not live together and never discussed marriage or parenting. When she was twenty-nine, Janice, a college graduate and a struggling artist, found herself accidentally pregnant. Her boyfriend would not make a commitment but did not press her to get an abortion. When she was three months pregnant, they broke up, and Janice made the decision to have the child, knowing, in all probability, that she would be a single mother. "I love children and I wanted to have a family," Janice explained, "but I always had mixed feelings about marriage." She didn't ask for child support but hoped that the father would play some role in her child's life.

After the birth of her son, Isaiah, Janice went on welfare so she could stay home with him. A year and a half later, however, she went to work part-time, receiving only partial welfare. When Isaiah was three, Janice took a full-time job as a secretary. Only after Isaiah was seven did Janice go back to school to get an MA in fine arts. She hoped to obtain a job teaching art in college while pursuing her goal to be an illustrator of children's books. Although Janice never obtained a permanent teaching position, she pieced together a barely adequate income from several part-time college teaching positions and occasional income from her illustrations.

Janice's siblings were supportive of her decision to become a single mother, but her mother was upset, especially because her son was biracial. Her father, who was more liberal, had died when she was seventeen. Janice's mother was disappointed that Janice would never be a conventional wife and mother and worried about what others might think. Later, her mother became very attached to Isaiah, but she never lost her concern about the social stigma she had to endure because of her biracial grandchild.

Becoming a Single Parent after Divorce

Gwen Palmer's route to single motherhood, at a younger age and after a divorce, was quite different from the other three of us but representative of many single mothers. Gwen grew up in a small Midwestern town as the youngest of three in a working-class family. Her father was a telephone repairman and her mother a housewife. Embedded in a tight community that was based on an evangelical church, Gwen was very religious as a child. But her small and secure universe was shattered when she was sixteen, for her mother died. Gwen's close bond to her mother could not be replaced by that to her grumpy, emotionally remote father or by her much older siblings, who had already married and moved away. Nor did family members help Gwen deal with death. "We didn't talk about it, and we didn't cry about it: we just went to our separate corners and tried to survive," she remembered. Gwen's only salvation was the mother of a boyfriend who tried to become a surrogate mom for her. Although Gwen soon left the Midwest, never to return except for short visits, she kept in contact with this woman.

Gwen graduated from high school but had an emotional breakdown during the first week of community college where she had started a secretarial course. She was in a "crazy" relationship with a man who was four years older. A married friend was leaving for California, driving with a male friend of her husband, and urged Gwen to come with them. Gwen thought that her surrogate mom had convinced her father that it would be good for her to get away. Six months after graduating from high school, Gwen, aged eighteen, married the friend. She wasn't in love with him but didn't know what else to do with her life. The marriage lasted six years. Telling me about it at the age of forty, Gwen remembered only an emotional blur. She recalled working at jobs she hated, at a gas station and as a retail clerk, and searching self-help books for hints on how to spark their emotional and sexual life. Despite her misery, Gwen, retaining some of her religious values, believed marriage was forever. So once they were financially a little better off and able to rent a small house, Gwen stopped taking the pill. She got pregnant easily and gave birth to a daughter a few months before her twenty-second birthday. Gwen had not consulted her husband or consciously thought out her path but had assumed that starting a family is what one did as a married woman. She didn't think becoming a parent would "save the marriage"; she just thought she might become more reconciled to it. Gwen considered her decision to have a child the best she ever made. Indirectly, it gave her the confidence to leave the marriage.

Gwen loved being pregnant and being a mother. She was happy to be able to take four months off work to be with her daughter, Kate. During this time, she came to terms with something she had been repressing—her husband was either drinking all the time or sleeping off his drink. That was why none of her efforts to rekindle their relationship had worked. Before confronting him, Gwen decided to go to meetings of Al-Anon, a support group for the families and friends of alcoholics. There she met Jeanne, who was divorcing her alcoholic husband.

With support from the group and from Jeanne, Gwen left her husband when Kate was a year and a half. For a while, she shared custody with her ex-husband, but once when he brought Kate back, he was quite drunk. Gwen panicked, acknowledging that she was putting her daughter in jeopardy. Since she had sole custody (which her husband had not challenged when they divorced), Gwen restricted the time and conditions under which he could see Kate. Soon her ex-husband remarried and drifted out of their lives, even though he continued to live only a few miles away.

After the divorce, Gwen decided to pursue her education and attended a community college. She enrolled Kate in the day-care center there and then obtained a part-time job at the center. With this job, welfare, $75 per month in child support, some school loans, and strict economy, Gwen, now in her midtwenties, felt her life was finally on track. Jeanne, the friend she met at Al-Anon, had remarried, and her large family (her two kids, her husband's child from a previous marriage, and the child they had together) took in Gwen and Kate. Kate called her Aunt Jeanne, and Jeanne's children called her Auntie Gwen. Ten years older than Gwen, Jeanne became another surrogate mother, and Gwen felt that she had found the best family she ever had. Kate never related much to Gwen's family in the Midwest, but, now in her twenties, she still has a strong relationship to Jeanne. Kate can talk to her about things she doesn't want to share with her mother.

With her two-year degree completed, Gwen got a secretarial job at a nearby high school. She loved the camaraderie with the staff and teachers, and the convenient hours gave her lots of time with Kate. When I first met and interviewed Gwen, she was still working there, having finished her BA and risen to the position of administrative assistant to the principal.

The Intimate Bond between a
Single Mother and Her Child

We have seen how commitment and success at work lead to autonomy among single women. Sexual expression too can foster autonomy, as can the decision to not have children. For all the single mothers portrayed here, deciding to become a single parent or choosing parenthood knowing they would probably be single mothers, fostered relational autonomy. Taking on a lifelong commitment to a child as a single individual elicited personal strengths we didn't know we possessed as we faced our many trials.[24] But single motherhood also fostered an intimacy that was very satisfying. It gave us an outlet for love, sharing, and care that we had not found at work, with friends, or in adult relationships.[25] Caring for a child without the obligation most women feel to give emotional support to a husband or partner fostered an intense bond between mother and child.[26] But we were told that too much intimacy, especially between mothers and sons, is unhealthy. How did we experience intimacy with our children and yet deal with our fears of too much intensity?

Because of her youth and inexperience, Gwen thinks she wasn't a great mother when Kate was young and that Kate had "to coraise" Gwen. Still, they were always close, and Gwen called Kate "an old soul in a little body." After Kate was sexually abused at the age of twelve (see the next section), Gwen truly became the parent and consolidated a deeper bond with Kate.

When I reconnected with Gwen, she was forty-nine and Kate was twenty-six. Gwen told me that Kate moved out for several years between the ages of eighteen and twenty, but then moved back home, where she had lived for the last six years. Kate worked full-time at a good job, paid half the rent and some of the household expenses, and had lots of friends, a busy life, and a boyfriend who stayed over several nights a week. Neither Gwen nor Kate is a "snuggle bug," and they are not "touchy-feely kinds of people"; nevertheless, they talked intimately and enjoyed spending time with each other. They usually had breakfast together and sometimes dinner, and usually they connected before bedtime. Gwen said of Kate: "She is my best friend, the main thing in my life; I love it that we're so close."

Recently, however, Gwen concluded that they needed to develop more independence. She decided to buy a one-bedroom condo in a new cohousing development twenty miles away. The twenty-nine units in the building are organized around common spaces, and the residents will have three meals a week together and serve on committees for common governance.[27] Although she won't move in for nine months, Gwen is already a member of the community life committee and enjoying the experience. Gwen is attracted to the cohousing philosophy and hopes to find new friends and more of a community so that she can consolidate her life as a single woman. Kate found her own two-bedroom rental house and for the first time is living alone.

■ ■ ■

Like Gwen, Janice feels that she and her son "grew up together." Janice always lived only with her son. During our first interview, when she was forty-five and Isaiah was sixteen, Janice said: "I've gotten so much from my relationship with Isaiah; the two of us have a real sense of family. Even though I've been without a partner all these years, I've never been alone." Because Janice's closest friends live far away—in Seattle, Arizona, and Paris—her relationship with Isaiah has been intense. We'll see later how this deep bond played out as he became an adult.

I can say about my twenty-three-year-old son, Marco, what feminist Robin Morgan said about her son: "He is the only man I truly love."[28] Our emotional bond is very deep; no one can make me feel so happy or so depressed and anxious. The bond was there from the beginning, but it deepened during Marco's middle childhood. I loved it that he was so warm and cuddly, much less physically reserved than I am. How great that he was so emotionally astute about other people's moods and desires. Even though I found it hard sometimes to hear about situations that made him feel unhappy, embarrassed, or disappointed, as well as those he felt good about, how wonderful that he could share with me in a way that I have never been able to do with my parents.

Both Marco and I look back on the years when he was between five and twelve as an idyllic time when we were both very happy. We both loved the small, alternative private school he attended from kindergarten through sixth grade. Fourteen out of the twenty children in his class attended the school for the entire seven years, and five of them were, like him, a mix of African American and white. The school became a community for both of us, as did other activities in which he participated—junior rangers (a group of both girls and boys in a hiking and backpacking program run by the regional park service), sports, summer camps, and theater and music programs.

Another feature of his childhood that deepened our connection was the trips we took together, sometimes with other families, but often just the two of us. We both love the outdoors, hiking, and backpacking. Marco enjoys fishing too, which I don't, but I could always take a book with me. We hiked often to the high sierra camps out of Tuolomne Meadows in Yosemite. We had at least three wonderful vacations in the Southwest, hiking the Grand Canyon and in Zion and Arches National Parks, among other places.

With Marco, my friends, and my work, I had a full life, with no time or emotional space for a romantic relationship. Sometimes, Marco told me he wished I would get married, but he liked my men friends only if they were interested in him. He also said he wished he had siblings. Yet, when the single mother of his good friend had another child, Marco (then aged ten) wasn't so pleased. "Babies," he told me, "cried too much and were a lot of trouble."

Still, in the 1980s and early 1990s, as the single mother of a son, I was affected by the strong cultural ideals warning that close mother-son relationships were bad for a boy. As a feminist, I wanted a sensitive and responsive son, and I certainly didn't believe that a mother who was involved with her son would lead him to homosexuality. I was pleased that he combined athletic ability and physical adeptness with more "feminine" qualities. He liked to play with dolls when he was four, chose to take modern dance lessons at age eight, loved fashion even as a preteen, and was always emotionally very open. I loved these qualities, but sometimes I also felt anxious. Would these traits make it harder for him to be a male in the world? Once, when he was eight or nine and playing Little League baseball, he came over to the spectator area and sat on my lap for fifteen minutes—not two or five but fifteen! I was both pleased and uncomfortable.

A few years later, I was relieved when I read therapist Olga Silverstein's *The Courage to Raise Good Men* (coauthored with Beth Rashbaum) and found that she rejected the concept of "overcloseness" in mother-son relationships.[29] The psychologist William Pollack, in his book *Real Boys,* presented a similar point of view. Pollack asserted that a close relationship with a loving mother makes it more likely that "a boy will become a free, confident and independent man, a man who likes himself and can take risks, and who can form close and loving attachments with people in his adult life."[30]

I believe, however, that a close bond is only one factor that makes separation in the teenage years difficult for both single mothers and their children.

Seeking a Daddy or a Male Role Model

Single mothers are the most vulnerable on the topic of raising a child without a father (or a father substitute) and the most susceptible to ideological pressure—cultural exhortations that are often deeply internalized. Let us examine the cultural milieu in which we found ourselves before looking at our individual responses.

Starting with the famous Moynihan Report of 1965, a pathology of matriarchy thesis gradually became pervasive in the United States both in social science and in popular discourse. This theory, first applied only to poor and black single mothers but later extended to everyone, argues that "the absence of a father is destructive to children, particularly boys, because it means that children lack the economic resources, role model, discipline, structure and guidance that a father provides."[31] Feminists in the 1960s and 1970s denounced the racism and sexism of this statement, fought for increased government support for poor mothers, and defended the importance of good, affordable child care for all working mothers. But the main thrust of feminism in this period was to get men to participate more fully in family life as equal parents and partners. Thus, indirectly, feminists contributed to the cultural denigration of single mothering. Influential feminist texts from the heyday of second-wave feminism in the late 1970s and early 1980s demonstrate this tendency.

Letty Pogrebin, in her influential 1980 book *Growing Up Free: Raising Your Child in the 80s,* insisted that "kids need fathers" and that "the best mothers are less mothers."[32] With no foresight of the continuing decline of the nuclear family during the 1980s, and with a condescending tone toward those in alternative family forms, Pogrebin declared: "Because eight out of ten children do live with *two* parents, most of the ensuing discussion will be pegged to that family constellation; however, I encourage single and blended families to adopt as many suggestions as possible to their own special situations."[33]

Pogrebin's views were echoed in best-selling accounts by other feminists. Adrienne Rich, in her rich and complex account of mothering in *Of Woman Born* (1976), ends her chapter called "Mother and Son, Woman and Man" with an extended discussion of how men have to be more involved with children. Jane Lazarre concludes *On Loving Men* (1978) with a strong disclaimer about the impact she could have on her sons: "Because I am a woman in that world, I am incapable of giving them certain things that only their father can give them."[34]

Academic feminist theorists reinforced these views. Nancy Chodorow and Dorothy Dinnerstein independently developed psychoanalytic arguments about how women who mothered infants structurally and unconsciously reproduced gender differences, creating dependent, nurturing females and independent, assertive males. Again, their solution to such sex-role dichotomies was to get fathers involved in infant care.[35] Coming from this perspective, feminists were unprepared to defend middle-class single mothers when they came in for public criticism in the 1990s.[36]

In 1992, then–vice president Dan Quayle attacked TV character Murphy Brown's decision to bear a child out of wedlock and to raise her son as a single mother. This led to a huge public discussion and debate. At the time, as an ever-single mother of a ten-year-old son, I welcomed the publicity, since I felt it gave recognition to mothers like me. "Better to be in the spotlight, even when it was seen by many as negative, than to be invisible," I thought. But I did not anticipate the deluge that would follow.

In the 1993 *Atlantic Monthly* article "Dan Quayle Was Right"—an essay that gained wide publicity—Barbara Defoe Whitehead set the agenda.[37] She gathered all the academic studies she could find to support the idea that growing up with a single mother damaged children. A few months later, a *Time* magazine cover story on fathers informed us that some unnamed psychologists "suggest that boys without fathers risk growing up with low self-esteem, becoming overly dependent on women and emotionally rigid."[38] By 1996, a Gallup Poll had found that 79 percent of a national sample of adults in the United States agreed with the statement "The most significant family or social problem facing America is the physical absence of the father from the home."[39]

Feminists continued to support the rights of single mothers and fought against government pressures to push marriage as a solution to their poverty, but they did not develop a coherent response to the ideology about the need for a father. Indeed, popular feminist studies in the 1990s about married women's difficulties in combining work and family life, studies that made popular such terms as "the second shift" and "the price of motherhood," made single motherhood seem even more problematic.[40]

Lost to public scrutiny was any evidence that challenged these ideas about fatherlessness. Such evidence did exist. Books by psychologists (Olga Silverstein's *The Courage to Raise Good Men* and William Pollack's *Real Boys*) argued that a single mother could raise good sons, and that a son or a daughter could successfully reach adulthood without a father or a dominant male figure. Articles by sociologist Timothy Biblarz, who with several collaborators published quantitative studies in major sociology journals, found that if one controls for the educational and occupational level of single mothers, their sons do as well (in terms of educational and occupational achievement) as those growing up with two biological parents, and *better than* sons who grow up only with their father or in a stepfamily with either their own father or a stepfather present.[41] But evidence that single mothers were doing good jobs dropped into cultural oblivion, even as the numbers of single mothers increased.

In this milieu, single mothers in my study were worried about the impact on their children of being raised without dads—men who were emotionally involved with their children and would help raise them.[42] Mothers of sons in my study were more concerned about the lack of a dad than those who had daughters. Unmarried— as opposed to divorced—single mothers were more overt in articulating their belief that they needed to involve the father or find a substitute.[43] Divorced women who had left alcoholic, violent, or abusive husbands were usually relieved if these fathers were not involved with their children. But often they looked for male role models, and if they remarried, hoped that their new husbands would become dads.

Few single mothers are aware of research showing that children in families with a stepfather do worse that those living with only their mother.[44] The stepfather may bring his own children with him, and even if he doesn't, he now takes some of the mother's emotional and physical energy. Researchers document that a man's contribution to running the household is about equal to the extra work he creates.[45] Moreover, as Gwen was to learn, stepfathers are one of the primary perpetrators of child sexual abuse within the family.[46]

I document four cases of failed attempts to find dads or intimate male role models for our children. We were all strong women, but still vulnerable to the societal opinion that a child needs *one* primary male in his or her life. While we invested much energy in these doomed endeavors at finding dads or male substitutes, our children benefited from the parenting efforts of women friends and family members and from the men they came in contact with in the course of their daily lives. All of us, however, would have benefited from cultural messages that encouraged us to put our efforts into cultivating relationships between our children and a number of supportive adults in our friendship networks and communities rather than those that told us to be both self-sufficient single mothers (not a burden on the state) and to find a dad for our kids.[47]

Our fathers, brothers, and male friends and our children's teachers, coaches, and counselors, although not as close or as involved as a father, provided powerful and positive images of what it means to be a man.[48] We, their mothers, were good role models too, demonstrating to our sons as well as to our daughters human beings who were "strong but gentle, firm but caring."[49] As a result, the children of single mothers in my study, like those in others, had no trouble becoming men and women with appropriate gender identities, but with behaviors that often were more flexible than those prescribed by traditional notions of masculinity and femininity.[50]

Janice Belmont hoped that the African American father of her mixed-race son would be a dad and that his parents and siblings would provide family ties. She put a lot of energy into fostering these paternal bonds but was disappointed. Significantly, she did not put as much effort into building a network of adult friends for herself and her son as did mothers who were divorced or had decided to become a parent without knowing the birth father. Janice's friends gave her moral support, but her closest friend with a child lived one hundred miles away. Thus, she did not have friends nearby to help her with day-to-day parenting, as Gwen and I did. Janice had no equivalent of the strong network of support created by Julia Cohen, the divorced mother discussed in chapter 3.

For years, Janice tried to get Isaiah's father to become more involved. The father visited occasionally and took Isaiah to see his mother, but he never asked his son to stay over at his house. Isaiah sometimes went for more than a year without seeing his father. When the father did turn up, Janice often felt that he was more interested in her than in his son. She never asked the father for child support, but she wanted him to love Isaiah.

Janice felt bad about this situation. "I'll always regret that he didn't have a dad, a man in his life who was committed to him and loved him. I think that's really important for a young man," she said. But Janice admitted that if she had stayed with Isaiah's father, he probably wouldn't have given those things to Isaiah either, and then her son would have seen fights and a bad relationship.

The father often invited Janice and Isaiah to a big holiday party at his mother's or sister's house, attended by his many siblings and their children. Janice, as the only white person there, sometimes felt uncomfortable, for some of the relatives seemed distrustful of her. She understood how this experience came as the result of a long history of racial segregation in the United States, but this knowledge did not make it easier for her. Isaiah wanted to belong to this family, but he too felt that he never really fitted in. As Isaiah grew older, he and Janice stopped going to the father's holiday gatherings, since Janice's mother, sisters, and brothers had moved to northern California and lived nearby. Holidays with them held tensions, too, but these were more relaxed times for Janice and Isaiah.

When Isaiah was fourteen, however, he started reaching out to his father, to his half brother, who was eleven years older, and to his grandmother. Janice encouraged this—especially his visits with his father—putting Isaiah on the bus for the hour's ride to his house. But by the time he was sixteen, Isaiah had become disenchanted. He came to the same conclusion that Janice had earlier: He couldn't turn his father into a dad. "My father can't do the job that you are doing as a parent," Isaiah told Janice. Although Janice always found it hard to both nurture and discipline, she now recognized that being a single mom "brought out qualities" that she didn't know she had. When her son subsequently went through a crisis, she reached out for help from others, but she had the strength to bear most of the burden herself. Isaiah's father died of cancer when Isaiah was eighteen and a freshman in college.

■ ■ ■

When adopting a male baby as a single woman, I too worried about finding a father substitute. When Marco was four, I obtained the name of his African American birth father.[51] But all I had was the name of a man residing in Louisiana or Texas; we still know nothing about him.

My father, then in his early seventies, first met Marco when he was five months old. From then on, they always had a special bond. But he lived three thousand miles away, and we saw him only once or twice a year. In retrospect, seeing the grief Marco felt this year when my father died at ninety-four, I believe that bonding with a grandfather, even an elderly and distant one, can be a powerful force. If I'd known that, I might have relaxed my efforts to find male role models for Marco.

One of my explicit reasons for buying a duplex with a couple and trying to live communally was to have a man in the household. As it turned out, this was my most ill-fated attempt to find a father substitute. My housemate was never interested in Marco and favored his own son. When he was three, Marco asked me why the other boy had a father and he didn't. I gave a lame answer, pointing out other children he knew who did not have a father either. I feel fortunate that the household broke up when Marco was only four.

All through elementary school, Marco had contact with wonderful men. Among them was Victor, the Ghanaian after-school teacher; Dave, one of the leaders of the junior ranger program for hiking and backpacking; Michael, his piano teacher; Russell, the African American man who coordinated the summer musical theater program; and my friend Robert, who helped Marco learn to fish. (As I was writing this, I couldn't remember several of these men's names; when I called Marco, he named them right off.) As a child, Marco was very open with me about all his disappointments, but after we moved out of the communal household, he never mentioned being concerned about the lack of a father. (Of course, he may have had feelings he didn't disclose to me or with which he was not in touch.) Still, I worried that he needed a more intimate bond to a man. So when he was nine, I applied for him to join the Big Brother program.

The man assigned to us was an African American man in his early thirties who was openly gay. He had moved to the Bay Area from the Midwest several years earlier and worked for UPS. Marco

liked him and enjoyed going places with him, but I never felt comfortable with this man. I didn't think I was homophobic, so I attributed my discomfort to age, class, and racial differences. I was
troubled that he had no family in the area and did not introduce us to
his friends. He was not interested in coming to dinner or meeting
my friends. After a few months, he asked me if Marco could stay
overnight. I refused. A few weeks later, he asked on the phone if he
could take Marco to Disneyland, a trip that involved an overnight
stay. I was upset that he had already talked to Marco about the possibility, and when I said no, he became verbally abusive. He called a
few days later to pressure me and was even more abusive. This time,
I recorded the conversation. I decided that I did not want this man
in our lives, but before terminating the relationship, I confided in a
lesbian friend. "Was I being homophobic?" I inquired. "Absolutely
not," she said. "Would you have allowed your son to go with a single
heterosexual man you didn't know very well? Would you let a heterosexual man talk to you like that?" When I called Big Brothers to
terminate the relationship, they were not very sympathetic, and they
refused to assign someone else. Marco was upset when I told him he
would not see the big brother again; all I told him was that the man
and I didn't get along. For a few weeks, Marco brought up the subject to see if I would change my mind, but then he seemed to get over
it quickly, involved as he was with all the other people and activities
in his life.

Even though the name of the organization (Big Brother) does
not suggest a dad, many single mothers, at least middle-class ones,
join for that reason, as I did. In her study of mature women who
chose to become single mothers, Melissa Ludtke reports that one single mother was so frantic to find a father figure that she contacted Big
Brother when her son was three even though the organization accepts only boys who are over the age of eight.[52] Another problem is
that a man commits to being a big brother for only one year. My
friend's son found a good relationship with a married man through
this organization. But when the year was up, the big brother ended
it. In joining the program, he had imagined helping an underprivi-

leged young boy, not one with the education and advantages of this one. He also participated to see whether he wanted to become a parent. He found out that he did. His wife then became pregnant, and he wanted to save all of his energy for his child. But my friend's son felt abandoned. This was not a positive experience for him.

Because of my limited personal encounters, I don't want to condemn the Big Brother organization. I'm sure others have positive stories with which to counter these negative ones. What I do question is the single mother's anxious search for a "dad" for her son or daughter. Jane Mattes, the founder of Single Mothers by Choice and the author of a popular self-help book by that name, believes that single mothers can raise sons and daughters without a father but urges them to find a man who can become intimately involved with their children at an early age. Her criticism of Big Brother is that the organization should accept younger children. I believe that Mattes's advice can be counterproductive, especially when it increases mothers' anxiety and insecurity.[53]

Marco found familial relationships with my single friend Judy and her son, Carl. Carl was born three weeks before Marco. I had been trying to become a mother for more than two years when Judy got pregnant. She was prepared to parent without marrying, cohabiting, or getting much financial support from the father. After we both ended up with sons, and after my communal household broke up, Judy and Carl, her brother, sister-in-law, and nephews became an alternative family for Marco. He stayed with Judy and Carl when I needed to travel for work and when I wanted to get away for a short vacation without him every couple of years. When Judy traveled, however, Carl stayed with her brother's family. So ours was not a completely reciprocal relationship, but both Marco and I benefited from Judy's connection to Marco.

Later, tensions arose between Judy and me. We had different parenting styles and divergent expectations of the relationship. As a result, our vacations together with the boys didn't work out as well as our trips had as single women. By attending a few therapy sessions together, we worked out a less intense relationship between us, but one where the boys would see each other just as often. Now as young men in their twenties, Carl and Marco are still close friends, despite their different personalities and divergent interests. Several years ago, Marco rode the bus from California to Ohio to attend his "brother" Carl's graduation from Oberlin College.

In looking back, I see that all these relationships that happened naturally—built on family and friends, both male and female, and on Marco's interests—were essential supplements to my efforts as a single parent.[54] Conversely, the ties that I tried to create just because I thought Marco needed a father substitute failed at best and might have been harmful. As for myself, I received emotional support from a large network of friends (mainly female). I could always talk to them —whether they were mothers or not—about my concerns as a parent. I often got contradictory insights or advice, but talking to them permitted me to sift through my feelings and come to my own conclusions about what path to take at critical junctures in child rearing.[55]

■ ■ ■

Gwen's second husband harmed her daughter. As mentioned earlier, Gwen had divorced her alcoholic husband when she was in her midtwenties. Like many young divorced mothers, Gwen had a number of boyfriends, one of whom cohabited with her for a short while. Then when Kate was six, Gwen fell in love with Gabe, an artist who made a good living working with an alternative energy company. From the first date, however, he never wanted to spend time with Kate. He always pressured Gwen to send Kate to her friend Jeanne's house so they could be alone. Nor did Jeanne like Gabe. Gwen remembers crying sometimes about her divided loyalties to Gabe versus Kate and Jeanne. But she was in love. Gabe soon moved in and married Gwen when Kate was eight. As they settled into family life, Gwen was relieved that Gabe and Kate seemed to get along better.

Within a couple of years, Gwen found out through friends that Gabe was having affairs. He admitted as much when Gwen confronted him but said that he would stop. Gwen desperately wanted to prevent another divorce. Only later did she discover that the affairs continued. "Oh, my God," Gwen told me, "my husband and I didn't use condoms; he was risking my life."

When Kate was about twelve, Gabe casually told Gwen that he had fondled Kate's breast when she had fallen asleep on his lap as they were watching TV together. Gabe said that he wouldn't do it again and was working on it with his therapist. Gwen was angry, wondered what more might have transpired, and talked to her therapist about the incident. The therapist downplayed it and advised Gwen not to pursue the topic, for it might ruin her relationship with Gabe. In retrospect, Gwen is angry with the therapist and herself. She knows that by law the therapist was required to report this incident (which she did not) and that she, Gwen, should have talked to Kate.

A few months later, Gwen's suspicions were aroused again one morning when Kate was really angry at Gabe. Gabe had offered to take Kate to school, and Kate angrily replied, "I'm not going anywhere with you." Gwen suddenly faced reality. She asked Kate what was going on. Kate told Gwen that the night before she had woken up to find Gabe putting his hand down her pants. Gwen immediately took action.

"I believed her positively," Gwen said. "There was not a doubt in my mind." Gwen confronted Gabe and said: "You are out of here." Gwen soon filed for divorce. With Kate's consent, Gwen decided to involve the legal system and formally charged Gabe with sexual abuse of a minor. Because he admitted the charges, there was no court trial. He spent a short time in jail and a longer period in community service. Kate never saw him again, and a few years later she asked Gwen to cut off contact with Gabe's mother and his other family members.

Gwen and Kate went into therapy together, to a competent therapist this time, and talked about what had happened. Kate's biggest fear was that she had been sexually assaulted other times when she was asleep and had not woken up. They concluded that it probably didn't happen, but the sexual molestation had a huge impact on both Gwen and Kate. Gwen, now forty-nine, has never again lived with a man and has dated only off and on. For many years she put all her energy into helping Kate, with support for herself from friends and colleagues. Kate had a troubled adolescence, running away from home once for four days, using alcohol and drugs, and being sexually promiscuous. During this time, Gwen, still feeling that a man's presence would help, asked Jeanne's husband to take a more active role in Kate's life. He refused, telling Gwen it was not his responsibility. Gwen now knows he was right. By then in her late thirties, Gwen needed to rely less on these parental substitutes. Through her discipline and her positive support of Kate, Gwen forged the basis for a close and continuing bond.

An isolated single mother with an only child is not an optimal environment for raising a child. But the solution is not just to find a father or an intimate male role model. In the novel *About a Boy,* twelve-year-old Marcus, living with his depressed mother, says that his problem is not that he didn't see his father much but that two "wasn't enough."[56] Marcus wanted a larger family; "he didn't care whether the family he wanted were all men, or all women, or all children. He simply wanted people."[57] Later, he realized that the friendship network that he had forged with both adults and other teenagers provided more security than a nuclear family. "You can find people," Marcus said. "It's like those acrobatic displays, . . . those ones when you stand on top of loads of people in a pyramid. It doesn't really matter who they are, does it, as long as they're there and you don't let them go away without finding someone else."[58] The film based on the book doesn't include these quotes and focuses exclusively on the importance to Marcus of one adult male friend.

I question whether a father equivalent is essential, especially if a number of good people are involved in a son's or daughter's life. We need more research on this topic—research that focuses exclusively on single mothers in different situations. Because lesbian mothers usually parent without the daily involvement of a father, often relying on a network of friends and extended family, they are important subjects for study.[59] What difference does it make if the father is known or unknown, involved a little or not at all? What is the impact on the child when she or he is raised without a father but in a network of friends and family (including men), in a situation where the mother does not actively seek out male role models or feel anxious or guilty about this situation? What do grown children of single mothers say about their experience?

Transition to Adulthood

Does the absence of a father, and the intimate bonds between a single mother and her child, make the son's or daughter's transition to adulthood more difficult? Maybe so, but my study indicates that the transition, in most cases, is made successfully. By their midtwenties, most children raised by the single mothers in my study had productive adult lives *and* continuing close ties with their mothers.

What is striking about the data in my small sample is that almost all the adult children of single mothers live within an hour's drive of their mother, and usually less. The one exception is the daughter of Julia Cohen, the lesbian mother portrayed in chapter 3. Her daughter went to an elite college in the East and then settled there. But think of all the others: Maria Cardoza, whom we met in chapter 1, has a son in his early twenties who lives twenty miles away; the twenty-one-year-old son of Myra Detweiler (chapter 2) lives with her; of Wynona La Blanc's four children (ranging in age from the late thirties to the early forties) (chapter 3), three are married with children and live nearby and one daughter lives with Wynona and her child; Beth Gilman (chapter 4) has a single daughter in her early thirties who lives fifty miles away and a twenty-five-year-old married son with two children who lives in the next town; Gwen Palmer, who decided to move away from her daughter, will now live only twenty miles away; my twenty-three-year-old son lives two miles from me; Janice Belmont's twenty-six-year-old son lives with her; Karen Mills, whom we will meet in the next chapter, has two adult daughters in their early thirties, one of whom is living with her and the other a few minutes away with a partner and two children; and Diane Epstein (chapter 9), before her death at sixty-one, lived in the same city as her twenty-four-year-old daughter. Does the desirability of living in northern California have any bearing on this proximity? Only research on single mothers in other locations will let us know.

Many of these single mothers were not particularly close to their own mothers, and about three-fourths of us moved thousands of miles from our families of origin. Just as the strong, dependent bonds of our parents' traditional marriages enabled some of us to easily pursue a satisfying single life, our autonomy facilitated our children's choice for closer family bonds. In this, we benefit too. As single mothers, most often of only children, our families are small, but they are lasting.[60]

I don't want to tell my son's story as a teenager or young adult, since he and I, unlike everyone else in this book, do not have anonymity. Let me just say that I've learned a lot about the travail of young black men in this society. I now know personally about racial profiling and the perils of driving if you're black. But I also know about the opportunities offered to a smart, talented, attractive middle-class black man like him. I'm proud that he has sustained a relationship for more than six years with a lovely young woman. I know I'm lucky to have a son who is usually kind and loving toward me, who has never hurled the insults that adoptive parents fear, and who has tolerated the anxiety and disappointment that I often expressed about the paths he took.

■ ■ ■

During our first interview in 1995, Janice's story about her sixteen-year-old son was more distressing than any others I had heard. Isaiah had always done well in school and sports and had many friends. But at fifteen, when his efforts to connect to his black father were failing, he started acting out. He was irritable, angry, and sometimes depressed. Never aggressive, he was now getting into fights and was arrested for shoplifting. After a period in which he was having delusions, Isaiah was diagnosed with a mood disorder and put on lithium. Six months later, at the time of the first interview, Isaiah seemed better, but Janice was still anxious. She found a history of mental illness in his father's family, and there was a similar history in her own family. In addition, Janice felt that some of Isaiah's difficulties stemmed from his attempt to separate from her when there was no one else on whom he could count.

Fortunately for Janice, this crisis brought her closer to her two brothers, who provided emotional support for her and some guidance and help for Isaiah. In addition, Isaiah's father agreed to pay child support for the first time—$200 a month to help Janice with Isaiah's legal fees and other expenses. He provided financial aid for more than a year until he was diagnosed with terminal cancer and had to quit his job.

Eight years later, I found Janice Belmont, at fifty-four, again living with her son, who was twenty-four (he had lived away from home during college). He was with her out of financial necessity rather than choice. When he was seventeen, Isaiah had stopped taking lithium without telling Janice, with no ill results. Doctors later concluded that the diagnosis of mental illness was a mistake. Isaiah had dropped out of high school, but he took the GED and SATs and attended a state university. It took him six years to finish college (for reasons I explore in the next paragraph), but he had just graduated with distinction and was about to enter a PhD program at Stanford. Janice was proud of these achievements but recounted a more difficult transition in his personal life.

During high school, Isaiah had a white girlfriend from a born-again Christian family. He wanted to break up with her before going to college but found out that she was pregnant and would not have an abortion. Isaiah refused to marry her, but when his son was born during his freshman year at college, he agreed to pay child support and help raise the child. This meant that he had to work, go to school, and care for his son two days a week. When his son was three, Isaiah tried to get back together with the mother to see if they could be an intact family. Unfortunately, the relationship didn't work out, but in the process his girlfriend got pregnant again. When I talked to Janice, Isaiah's daughter was six months old and his son, five. Isaiah now has joint legal custody of both children and physical custody for two days and two nights a week. He pays almost a $1,000 a month in child support, which is why he is living with Janice again.

Janice is proud of the responsibility Isaiah takes for his children. She supports his decision not to marry after he told her that his ex-girlfriend "was not the person with whom I want to spend my life." Janice likes living with her son, especially since the rental house they share is large and the bedrooms are far apart. She loves the children and wants to help provide a home for them. "I like to have fun with the kids, but this is a bit more responsibility than I want," Janice explained. Janice's dream is to own her own small house with her son living nearby and the grandchildren visiting often. "With two grandchildren, you don't have to worry about being lonely," Janice concluded, "but now I have to try to protect myself and be sure I have some solitude."

■ ■ ■

The portraits of middle-class single mothers presented here do not glamorize their lives, but neither do they pathologize single motherhood. We were all adversely affected by the cultural denigration of single mothers, sometimes leading us to try to distance ourselves from those who were younger and poorer. I, for example, was a subject in sociologist Jane Bock's study of mature, middle-class single mothers by choice. When I read her article reporting on the study, I was startled by her analysis, which opened my eyes to something I had never considered. "By appropriating the term *single mothers by choice*," Bock writes, "mid-life, middle-class single women implicitly...imply that other single mothers do not enter parenthood by choice or, at least, not by a choice as responsible as their own. Thus, the label itself serves to separate this population from other single mothers, those who allegedly are the 'real' problem."[61] I never again used the term *single mothers by choice.*

A culture that accepts and supports all single mothers would help married mothers as well. Journalist Ann Crittenden, in her influential book *The Price of Motherhood,* cites a study of seven developed countries that found that nations providing generous benefits for single mothers and their children had a higher percentage of married women who stayed home with their children. Crittenden concluded that "married women feel that the risk of staying home is worth taking when the consequences of marital failure are not economically devastating."[62]

Although my sample is not large enough to present reliable findings, the openness and honesty of the single mothers in my study, and the insights gleaned by following the fate of their children as they became adults, raise provocative questions for further study. Let us have more longitudinal studies focusing on different types of long-term single mothers, rather than always comparing two-parent and single-parent families with the assumption that any differences we may find will mean that single-parent families are deficient.[63] Let us compare mothers (both single and coupled) who have the aid of a network of friends and/or extended family with those who are mothering in an isolated household.[64] Does a network of support make a difference to the children?

Such research, I believe, will help us discern the parameters that make single motherhood a more viable life option, one with its own specific strengths and weaknesses—not a path all women will want to take, but one where knowledge about those who have gone before can help those taking this route. Single motherhood, rather than being seen as deviant and problematic, will come to be seen as an important link in the reinvigoration of extended families, friendship networks, and community.

CHAPTER 8

The Cultural Divide and Social Continuum between Single and Married Women

My married friends consider me single
and my single friends see me as coupled.
MARIAN

When I first envisioned a book about single women, I drafted a critique of the institution of marriage. I soon abandoned this approach, however, first because I saw that it detracted from studying singleness in its own right, and second, by including longtime married women in my initial group interviews in 1994–95, I discovered a polarization between single and married women that I wanted to avoid. I found that many married women were just as dissatisfied with their lives as were single women. Their husbands were not soul mates. Those who had quit work and cut back or limited their career aspirations to care for children felt that their choices were not socially valued. They all knew single women they admired, and some felt that single women had more exciting and fulfilling lives. Their attitudes, like those of single women, seemed to be at least partly shaped by cultural norms that sharply divide single and married women and place them in competition with each other.

In reality, however, single and married women today are *not* two distinct, lifelong groups. By age forty-four, the number of single women who have married and divorced is larger than those who have never married,[1] and even many of the never-married women have cohabited, some for long periods. Most women today spend part of their lives coupled, cohabiting inside or outside of marriage, but they also spend increasing blocks of time as singles, especially before marriage and after divorce. I found, however, that the word *single* incorporates a variety of living arrangements, and sometimes who is single and who is coupled are not easily discernible.

What I discovered challenged the strict demarcation between single and coupled women. Instead, I found a continuum, with many ways to exist between being a married, cohabiting couple and an individual residing by herself. But I simultaneously observed that the cultural rhetoric developing after the mid-1990s more strictly categorizes women as married or as single/divorced and sees these two types of women as rivals and threats to each other. On the one hand, defenders of marriage denigrate the lives of single and divorced women. On the other hand, those who extol the virtues of single life disparage marriage. Both sides try to claim cohabiters as belonging in their camp—either as the equivalent of married people or as having rejected marriage and identified themselves as single. Contrasting the rhetoric about the stark differences between single and married women with the continuum I found in real women's lives opens the possibility for a new cultural dialogue, one that values both coupled lives and single lives and everything in between.

The Cultural War between Married and Single Women

A culturally conservative movement for family values arose in the 1980s, sparked by the work of a handful of academics, public policy professionals, and religious spokespeople.[2] In the mid-1990s, these same forces turned their focus to marriage,[3] a strategic move, since research consistently shows that Americans never wavered in their commitment to family, although cultural disagreement about the institution of marriage has increased. Moreover, in refocusing on marriage, cultural conservatives have attracted some liberal allies.[4]

Like the movement for family values, the marriage movement is not a grass-roots social movement but an ideological attempt by intellectuals to influence cultural norms. Their goal is to decrease the divorce rate and to increase the number of children growing up in two-parent families.[5] Although these goals are unobjectionable, the supporters of the marriage movement seek to achieve them by touting the *benefits* of marriage versus the *detriments* of single life— especially for single women and single mothers.[6] Then, in a spate of counterattacks in the 1990s and early 2000s, feminist intellectuals began to defend single life by denigrating marriage. Some commentators on each side of the fence built a polemic for or against marriage, and others, in more scholarly books and essays, offhandedly incorporated negative assumptions about single life or about marriage.

In articulating the main themes in the rhetoric of both those who belittle single life to defend marriage and those who critique marriage in order to champion single life, I do *not* attempt to establish the truth or validity of these claims in any detail. Rather, I seek to highlight the oratory and the use of unproven and overgeneralized assumptions. I want to expose the manner in which this cultural debate is detrimental to both single and coupled women, driving them apart and leading to feelings of competitiveness and envy while obscuring the similarities and continuities in their lives.

Denigrating Singleness and Critiquing Marriage

To make my point, I have picked a few books by scholars and journalists on both sides of the debate, all of which gained popular exposure in the media. Before focusing on their rhetoric, let me characterize the books and their authors.

Sociologist and demographer Linda Waite (who views herself as a liberal Democrat) chose journalist Maggie Gallagher (a well-known conservative)[7] to coauthor a 2000 book entitled *The Case for Marriage: Why Married People Are Happier, Healthier, and Better Off Financially.*[8] The title itself sets up married people and singles as two competitive groups. Waite and Gallagher identify with the marriage movement and argue in support of new government policies to benefit marriage and to punish the divorced and the single. But they have inherited a long tradition, from both popular journalism and social science, of pitting married and single women against each other.[9]

Nor are Waite and Gallagher alone in the quest to condemn single life in order to bolster their case for marriage. Hostility to singleness intrudes more subtly in the work of two prominent social psychologists who study divorce. Judith Wallerstein, Julia Lewis, and Sandra Blakeslee, in *The Unexpected Legacy of Divorce* (2000), and E. Mavis Hetherington and John Kelly, in *For Better or for Worse: Divorce Reconsidered* (2002), conducted longitudinal studies of divorced women and their children over a twenty-five-year period.[10] Unnoticed in the media attention and debate about Wallerstein's more pessimistic and Hetherington's more optimistic assessments of divorce is their negative view of long-term single women—divorced mothers who don't remarry and unmarried adult women from divorced families. Whereas Wallerstein and Hetherington only indirectly denigrate singles, recycling negative stereotypes without much thought, journalist Danielle Crittenden, in *What Our Mothers Didn't Tell Us* (1999), argues directly against single women.[11]

Directly opposed to these books are those which condemn marriage. I must admit that I first reacted with a rush of positive feeling to the books by journalists and academics that critiqued marriage in defense of single life. I found it so refreshing to read well-written, often witty, accounts condemning married life as an antidote to all those authors who portrayed single women in negative terms. Only when some of my married women friends and students told me that these works made them angry did I begin to consider the larger cultural and political implications. I saw how these authors too contributed to a cultural divide between single and coupled women—a separation that harms us all.

Journalist Dalma Heyn's *The Erotic Silence of the American Wife* (1992) and *Marriage Shock: The Transformation of Women into Wives* (1997) argued that women lose their voices, their selves, and their sexual pleasure when they enter marriage with traditional expectations.[12] In the latter book, Heyn cites statistical studies to stereotype

married and single women, exactly the opposite of the statistics that
Waite and Gallagher use.[13] Heyn writes, "I'm for marriage; I'm married myself, happily,"[14] but then she provides only negative statistics
and examples of married women and positive ones for singles.

Taking an even more radical stance toward the disadvantages of
marriage, Jaclyn Geller, a single woman in her thirties and a PhD
candidate in English at New York University, published in 2001 *Here
Comes the Bride: Women, Weddings and the Marriage Mystique.* Geller
develops an interesting critique of the wedding and relationship
industries and has smart insights into her own and other single
women's lives. She could have written this book without rejecting
the institution of marriage, but she chose otherwise. "We must stop
repeating the absurd mantra, 'it's okay to be single,' Geller proclaims,
"and adopt the more aggressive stance that 'it's not okay to be married."[15] Geller admits up-front that she indicts "the woman whose
personal taste or private inclination leads her to marry."[16] Even more
critical of marriage is the 2003 book *Against Love: A Polemic,* by Laura
Kipnis, a Northwestern University professor of media studies.

Single Women Are Unhappy, Isolated, Immature, and Selfish

Before turning to the more explicit polemic in *What Our Mothers
Didn't Tell Us,* let us look at some examples of how the more academic books slip in negative stereotypes of single women.

Waite and Gallagher go beyond their statistical comparisons to
conclude (without statistical support) that singles lead a life "without
meaning or purpose," with no one to help out in a crisis.[17] "Man was
not meant to live alone, and neither was woman," write Waite and
Gallagher. But they seem to view single people as all-powerful adver-
saries who now can lay claim to "many of the rights and benefits previously reserved to the married."[18]

In *The Unexpected Legacy of Divorce,* Wallerstein argues that
women and men whose parents divorced when they were children

(and who were between twenty-eight and forty-three years old in the late 1990s) have great difficulties forging personal lives, even though most of them are successful at work. Wallerstein's measure of "success in personal life" is achieving a stable marriage and becoming a committed parent. Only 60 percent of the ninety-three "children of divorce" she follows have married (compared with 80 percent of all adults at their ages), and only 38 percent have children. Reporting in depth on only five composite individuals (only one of whom is single), Wallerstein presents Lisa, a thirty-one-year-old never-married woman.

Wallerstein considered Lisa, as she was growing up, to be her best case—a little girl whose divorced parents devoted themselves to her. Lisa always seemed well-adjusted and happy. Now Lisa has a successful career, which she loves, and is cohabiting with a man who treats her well but whom she admits she does not love. Lisa tells Wallerstein that she probably will not have children and that she has "pretty much decided to remain single for the rest of my life."[19] Lisa lists some of the positive attributes of being single: she is independent and strong, she thinks for and relies on herself, and she can work with all kinds of people. To me, such a straightforward statement, one that goes against the cultural pressures for women to marry and have children, indicates a strong sense of self-worth, a trait that psychologists usually value. But Wallerstein reacts very negatively: "I couldn't help thinking how distressed I would feel if Lisa were my daughter and had decided to forgo ever finding a man she could love. Having been in a happy marriage for fifty-three years, I knew how much she would be missing."[20]

At least Wallerstein is honest about her personal judgment and is not trying to pass it off as scientific. But I'm still astounded that she assumes her readers will unquestioningly accept her opinion. Wallerstein does not ask Lisa why she stays with her partner. Does he meet her sexual needs or desire for security? Does she have friends, family, coworkers, and community that meet her other needs? What needs does she have that are not met? Instead, Wallerstein goes on to press Lisa as to whether she is really sure, at age thirty-one, that she will never fall in love or find a man who will love her. Under this psychological pressure, reinforcing the societal ideals she has heard all her life, Lisa says yes, that finding love is what she wants more than anything in the world. She does not say that she wants to be married or have children.

Wallerstein contrasts Lisa with another child of divorce, Karen, who did not have such an easy time growing up: "She and Gavin [her husband] enjoy a stable, loving relationship, a sweet child and a promising future. By any measure, they are a success story for our times."[21] Wallerstein maintains that Karen and other children of divorce who establish long-term commitments exhibit a "major achievement that reflects their greater maturity and increased self-esteem."[22] The contrast between Wallerstein's judgments of Karen and Lisa could not be starker.

Mavis Hetherington, rather than focusing only on the children of divorce, studies the divorced women and men themselves and how they have changed and developed over time. Hetherington divides the divorced into six categories in terms of their long-term adjustment to divorce. These categories are not presented neutrally but include Hetherington's evaluative conclusions. Hetherington labels those she considers to have made the most positive adjustment to divorce (20 percent of her sample) *enhancers.* These divorced people (mainly women) were "competent, well adjusted and self-fullfilled," and they had made happy and successful second marriages.[23]

She designates a second group (10 percent of her sample) who also made a positive adjustment *competent loners.* These divorced people (both women and men), too, were "well-adjusted, self-sufficient, and socially skilled," with "a gratifying career, an active social life, and a wide range of hobbies and interests."[24] But they had not remarried and were not particularly interested in doing so. Why does Hetherington label them *loners,* when she admits they are socially skilled and have an active social life? She offers no evidence that they spend a lot of time alone or consider themselves loners. Rather, their disinclination to remarry seems to be the key. Hetherington writes that they "have little interest in sharing their lives with anyone," but then she goes on to give an example of a divorced man who has a committed relationship with a widow.[25] Neither wants to cohabit, but they share a lot. Hetherington, while arguing for the possibility of positive outcomes for divorce, indirectly valorizes marriage—even if it is a remarriage—and stereotypes long-term single life.[26]

Danielle Crittenden views the increasing numbers of single women as the direct result of second-wave feminism, which, she writes, promoted a unilateral program of autonomy and career success for all educated women. In contrast, she advocates a return to marriage and motherhood as central to *all* women's aspirations. As a result, she paints a negative portrait of single women's quest for independence.

> Once you have ceased being single, you suddenly discover that all that energy you spent propelling yourself toward an independent existence was only going to be useful if you were planning to spend the rest of your life as a nun or a philosopher on a mountaintop or maybe a Hollywood-style adventuress, who winds up staring into her empty bourbon glass forty years later wondering if it was all damn worth it.[27]

For Crittenden, the single woman seeking autonomy is really prolonging immaturity. "Too often," she declares, "autonomy is merely the excuse of someone who is so fearful, so weak, that he or she can't bear to take on any of the responsibilities that used to be shouldered by much younger but more robust and mature souls."[28] Single women, Crittenden writes, have no responsibilities and are selfish and immature: "By spending years and years living entirely for yourself, thinking only about yourself," she proclaims, "and having responsibility to no one but yourself, you end up inadvertently extending the introverted existence of a teenager deep into middle age."[29]

In such a portrait, single people have no friends, family, neighbors, or colleagues to whom they have any responsibilities or from whom they gain support. Indeed, Crittenden writes, only by taking up the roles of "wife, husband, mother, father," do we "build our identities, expand our lives, and achieve the fullness of character we desire."[30] Crittenden concludes that "lifelong independence can be its own kind of prison."[31]

In contrast to these negative views of single life are the uniformly positive accolades for single life by those who criticize marriage. For example, Heyn, in *Marriage Shock,* writes that a single woman has a "lusty, powerful, loving, sexual self."[32] She goes on to paint an even more idealized view of "the comfortable and happy relationships" of single women,[33] who never lose their voice: "In single life, the interior voice of women's knowing, like a soprano solo, is strong enough to resist domination; single life is unprecedented, ungoverned, free space; there may be a behavioral debate about etiquette, but essentially the culture is disinterested in her life when no men or children are in it, so she may express herself as she wishes."[34]

Married Women Are Imprisoned in a "Domestic Factory"

In contrast to these satisfied single women, Heyn writes, married women are depressed because they lose themselves as they try to be good wives. "What I know is that wives conventionally prescribed 'goodness,'" Heyn writes, "what we now call the 'morality' that supposedly keeps entire families together—kills self, and then pleasure, and then inexorably, relationship."[35] From this observation, Heyn jumps to a pessimistic generalization about marriage as an institution. "Marriage will continue to exist—institutions rarely die," Heyn concludes, "but will sink to the status of a sort of sanctified one-night stand, as modern women race into it for all the reasons women always have and then, shocked, race out."[36]

Jaclyn Geller's negative view of marriage stems from her observations of the full-time housewives of the 1960s and early 1970s in the upper-middle-class suburb of Scarsdale, New York, where she grew up. Characterizing such a married housewife as "a glamorous, anesthetized doll," Geller sees her as held in "domestic captivity" in an isolated nuclear family.[37] Geller, in direct opposition to Danielle Crittenden's view that long-term single life is a prison, labels these married women as living in a household prison.[38] In an even more polemical view, Geller concludes that there is a "fundamental rottenness at the heart of the marital contract" and that "marriage is destructive."[39]

Like Geller, Laura Kipnis sees the coupled household as a prison, with spouses as "each other's jailers, and house arrest the basic condition of modern love."[40] This "domestic gulag," based on a "security state model,"[41] is legitimated by the denigration of single life: "The well-publicized desperation of single life—early death for men; statistical improbability of ever finding mates for women—is forever wielded against reform-mined discontented couple members," writes Kipnis, "much as the grimness of the USSR once was against anyone misguided enough to argue for systematic social reforms. . . . '*Hey, if you don't like it here, just see how you like it over there.*' "[42]

Kipnis goes on to compare the coupled household to a highly regulated industrial workplace. Marriage, writes Kipnis, is "a domestic factory policed by means of rigid shop-floor discipline designed to keep the wives and husbands and domestic partners of the world choke-chained to the status quo machinery."[43] In the domestic couple with its "demands of labor-intensive intimacy and 'working on your relationship,' now it's double-shifting for everyone."[44] Married sex is also subject to the work ethic, with husband and wife "plugging away at the task year after year like diligent assembly line workers (once a week, same time, same position) aided by the occasional fantasy or two to get the old motor to turn over, or keep running, or complete the trip."[45]

Continuing the analogy, Kipnis see therapy as the enforcement wing of the love-takes-work ethic and "adultery as the sit-down strike" against it.[46] Not needing a factory manager, the domestic couple polices each other, regulating each other's daily lives:

> From bathroom to bedroom, car to kitchen, no aspect of coupled life is not subject to scrutiny, negotiation and codes of conduct. . . . You can't leave the house without saying where you're go-

ing. You can't not say what time you'll return. You can't go out when the other person feels like staying at home. You can't be a slob. You can't do less than 50 percent of the work around the house, even if the other person wants to do 100 percent more cleaning than you find necessary or even reasonable.[47]

Kipnis provides pages of additional examples.[48]

After such a litany, the single person can't help but feel superior, and those in a couple either devastated or angry.

Bridging the Cultural Divide

Are coupled and single women destined to be portrayed as perpetually at war with each other? Will "the grass always tend to look greener on the other side of the marital fence," as sociologist Norval Glenn predicts?[49] I think not. If negative rhetoric about single life and marriage ceases, or at least decreases, and is replaced by cultural expressions validating both, women will be able to discern the similarities and continuities between married and single life. Examples of such an alternative perspective can be found both in more polemical and in personal writings.

The earliest, and most comprehensive, expression I have found of an attempt to bridge the cultural divide is in the 1974 book *The Challenge of Being Single,* written by Marie Edwards and Eleanor Hoover. In "The Singles Manifesto" at the end of the book, the authors proclaim:

> I will, by choosing to live a free single life, be helping to raise the status of singlehood. In doing this, I will be strengthening rather than weakening marriage, for when we truly have the option not to marry, marriage will be seen as a free choice rather than one demanded by a pairing society. Finally, I will do my part in every way to promote good will between marrieds and singles, because misunderstanding will be diminished only when each of us, as a unique human being, realizes that being self-aware, autonomous,

free, self-fulfilled, and whole has nothing whatsoever to do with being either married or single, but, in the final analysis, comes from being ourselves.[50]

The increasing number of women who now experience long periods of singleness before they marry or settle into a long-term cohabitation, or who become single after years of marriage, helps breaks down the cultural divide. Individual women are beginning to write about their dual experience. In her essay "Married at 46: The Agony and Ecstasy," writer Nancy Wartik notes that "love and marriage are as much a struggle as single life, just in a different way."[51] But Wartik knows from experience that single women are still more stigmatized and that being a single woman is hard. "I never want to vanish so far into coupledom," she writes, "that I . . . forget just how valid —but how difficult—a choice staying on your own can be. I've always come down on the side of those who prefer to fight through loneliness and other ghosts of solitude rather than compromise too much in love. Had I not met Dennis, I think there's an excellent chance that's the fight I'd still be waging."[52]

In a similar vein, a younger woman, Lisa Miya-Jervis, the editor and publisher of the magazine *Bitch: Feminist Response to Pop Culture,* wrote "A Celibate Sexpot Ties the Knot." From her teenage years, Miya-Jervis expected to remain single, and all her family and friends accepted this. Thus, everyone was surprised when she married. But Miya-Jervis believes that this early conditioning explains her continuing identification with single life.

> Now that our first anniversary has come and gone, "my husband" trips off my tongue as easily as "my Good Vibrations video rental account," but I still find myself identifying with single women more than married ones when the conversation turns to commitment, independence and the pleasures of being alone. "I'm not one of them, those smugly coupled women who think that true happiness comes only to those who pair up like Noah's animals," I want to protest. "I know your single life is just as fulfilling as my married one because I lived it."[53]

Katherine Graham, a very different type of woman, first experienced marriage and later spent years as a single woman. Widowed young after her husband's suicide, Graham took over as publisher of the *Washington Post*, becoming the most influential and powerful woman in Washington, D.C. She never remarried; the reason was, in her own words, that "I was married to my job and I loved it." But Graham continued to have many close married friends: "I enjoy being around married people who really love each other, are constantly polite and caring about each other, and between whom you feel a real and supportive relationship," she explains.[54]

The movement for gay marriage is another arena in which to contest the current cultural polarization between single and coupled people. Many commentators on the fight to legalize marriage for gays and lesbians recognize that such a social change, whether seen as radical or conservative, risks reinforcing inequality between single people and those who are coupled.[55] A personal proclamation by a lesbian couple, Martha Ackelsberg and Judith Plaskow, makes the political point very effectively.

> We love each other, and we've been in a committed relationship for nearly twenty years. We are residents of Massachusetts. But we're not getting married. We fully believe that gays and lesbians should have the right to marry, and we celebrate the fact that a significant barrier to our full citizenship has fallen. In not taking advantage of this new right, however, we can more comfortably advocate for the kind of society in which we would like to live.

Ackelsberg and Plaskow go on to say,

> Were we to marry, we would be contributing to the perpetuation of a norm of coupledness in our society. The norm marginalizes those who are single, single-parents, widowed, divorced or otherwise living in non-traditional constellations.... At this moment, where there is so much focus on celebrating the right to marry,

we want to hold up a vision of a society in which basic rights are not tied to marriage, and in which there are many ways to organize one's intimate life, marriage being only one of them.[56]

All of these statements seek to end the competition between single and coupled life, but none of them has anything concrete to say about nontraditional constellations. Geller, however, points toward a more complex reality. She imagines:

> In an optimal future, no single model of relationship would enjoy privileged status. Some people would naturally gravitate toward lifelong, monogamous sexual partnerships, others toward a series of such partnerships, others toward celibacy, others toward multiple sexual relationships. Some might choose to live with their lovers, others to live with biological relatives, others to live alone; still others to live communally with friends. Law and social custom would respect and reward all models equally.[57]

The reality that I discovered—a continuum between single and married life with many in-between ways to live—is more complex than any of the current cultural representations. Reality points toward a need for the cultural change that Geller envisions.

The Social Continuum between Singles and Cohabiting Couples

What does it mean to be an in-between—someone who is not exactly single or part of a cohabiting couple? And to be so for a long time? Although this question was not the focus of my research, unexpected, interesting data emerged. I divide my findings into three topics: the lack of cultural categories for those not conventionally single or coupled, maintaining a long-term, committed sexual/love relationship without cohabiting, and cohabiting without sexual involvement.

No Cultural Labels for the In-Betweens

All the women in my study considered themselves single, or they would not have volunteered to be interviewed. Only when I began talking about my work to friends and acquaintances did I discover that it is hard to predict whether a woman considers herself single or not when her situation does not fit neatly into our current categories.

I've known Deborah (who is in her late fifties) for many years. Although she has never married, she has been in a monogamous coupled relationship with Jim for more than ten years. They live together only during part of the summer and every other weekend because of the travel involved in her work. Both admit, however, that they prefer having two houses. Jim likes the country and Deborah the city, and they both like a lot of private space. But they are registered as domestic partners, and Jim receives health benefits from Deborah's insurance.

Deborah, however, considers herself single and presents herself as such to colleagues and clients. When I ask her why, she replies proudly: "I have never been married and never been financially dependent on a partner." She owns the two houses in which they live, and she supports Jim, until he finishes and sells his novel, something that Deborah admits may never happen. If they had the same living arrangement and he supported her, Deborah would not consider herself single.

I was surprised when another acquaintance—someone I considered an admirable single mother and who sometimes cohabited—told me that she always considered herself coupled. "Why?" I asked. "Because I'm always with a partner or looking for one," she replied.

In contrast with women who label themselves decisively either single or coupled when to an observer their situations seem more ambiguous, there are women who admit they can't classify themselves. One acquaintance, Marian (also in her fifties), is quoted at the beginning of this chapter. Marian, who is in an eight-year committed relationship but does not cohabit, remarked to me, "My married friends consider me single and my single friends see me as coupled, but I feel in between." A more public discussion of lives that fail to fit neatly into the categories of single or coupled may lead to a richer language than "in between."

Maintaining a Long-Term Sexual/Love Relationship without Cohabiting

Some married couples (sailors, traveling salespeople, and migrant workers) always have spent a lot of time apart because of work demands.[58] We now have increasing numbers of commuter marriages as more married women seek careers.[59] But these phenomena have not challenged the cultural assumption that couples prefer to cohabit. When there are no work constraints, a person who states a personal preference for being coupled but lives apart from the partner is likely to be questioned, and not readily accepted, by family, friends, and colleagues. Moreover, with the increasing social acceptance of cohabitation, some people have become more suspicious of unmarried couples who do not live together, especially when they have been in a relationship for more than a couple of years. We can all point to examples (in chapter 4, Beth Gilman's four-year noncohabiting relationship with Jose) where one partner in fact is nonmonogamous and not committed. Faced with such suspicion about their motives, many long-term noncohabiting couples defend living apart by referring to career demands or, when one partner already has children, to their needs. Both Julia Cohen, the lesbian mother portrayed in chapter 3, and Deborah and Jim, made such justifications even though one or both of the partners preferred privacy and distance. I found a lesbian couple in their fifties who live apart, not because of career or childcare issues, but because of preference.

Jolene Gibbs, aged fifty-four, strode confidently into my class on single women in April 2003. Recruited by another participant for a panel called Living Outside a Couple, Jolene, tall and attractive, was articulate and engaging. She shared some of her background to underscore the fact that her conventional upbringing would not necessarily lead someone (including herself) to predict her present life—a lesbian in a ten-year committed, but noncohabiting relationship.

Jolene, the eldest of five children from a Catholic family in a strong Catholic community in Southern California, married right out of high school. She was sexually attracted to her husband, but she soon found him too domineering and demanding and married life too staid. So after a couple of years, Jolene left the marriage, fled to northern California, moved in with friends living in a rural area on a piece of land owned by one of them, and became a hippie.

Later, in her thirties, Jolene moved back to a small city, owned a retail store for ten years, and then, at the age of forty-five, desiring more financial security, obtained her real estate license and joined a large firm. She's been there for the last eight years and plans to stay until retirement. Jolene did not discuss when and how she came out as a lesbian, but she did say she was in and out of cohabiting relationships all her life. Fifteen years ago, however, she moved into her own apartment just to regroup but found she liked it. She has lived by herself ever since. Jolene rents a small apartment in a complex of ten units. As people moved out, her friends moved in (one of her best friends lives next door) and established relationships with other residents. Recently, she realized that all the tenants live by themselves, even though some of the women and men have significant others and children who visit. Inadvertently, Jolene helped create a community of singles.

Jolene loves coming home after a busy day to the quiet of her own space. "I light a few candles, turn on the music, do yoga, and think," Jolene said. "I don't like being with someone all the time." But she loves having close friends nearby to take in her mail when she travels, to call on in an emergency, and for informal socializing.

When Jolene met Lucy, her current partner, ten years ago, Lucy was living with her ten-year-old son. Neither Jolene nor Lucy thought they could live together. When the son moved out several years ago, Jolene did not want to give up her apartment, and Lucy liked having her own space. So they decided to continue their arrangement. Jolene and Lucy live only a mile apart and have no rules about how often they see each other. Typically they spend Saturdays and Sundays together. Lucy has become friends with Jolene's best friend and next-door neighbor, Jill. The three call each other wives, partly as a joke but also because they take care of each other. Jill has a girlfriend who lives about four hours away and whom she sees only a couple of times a month. So Jill is often available for social activities. Sometimes all three go out together, but more often Jolene sends Lucy and Jill out so that she can have more time at home. Jill and Lucy share an interest in baseball and the theater, about which Jolene is less enthusiastic.

Jolene and Lucy find another advantage to their living arrangement: they don't have to get involved with each other's families. Jolene is close to her four sisters and her eight nieces and nephews. She loves to visit them, but Lucy, who has just finished years of intensive child rearing, isn't interested in going. Lucy is happy to spend time with her many friends when Jolene visits her family. Jolene also finds it easier to visit her mother without Lucy. Jolene is very close to her mother, even though her mother has not accepted her sexual orientation. "My mother is still wondering when I'm going to get married again," Jolene recounted. "I'm fifty-four, but it's never too late." Jolene commented that her family prefers to think of her as single than as a lesbian. Jolene summarized the advantages of her situation: "You need a variety of people in your life, all kinds of people, because relationships enrich you."[60]

Cohabiting without Sexual Involvement

Even more socially hidden are unmarried pairs who cohabit, are more than roommates, but are not sexually or romantically involved. I discovered the two cases I describe here accidentally, one in a follow-up interview with a divorced mother and the other in a conversation with my hairdresser.

Exes Sharing a House and Family Life

In 1994, at the age of forty-eight, Karen Mills, a spirited woman with short brown hair, arrived for her interview directly from work, dressed professionally. Although still completing her PhD, Karen worked part-time as an economic analyst in a San Francisco planning department, a position, I learned, she still holds, now as a full-time permanent employee. In 2003 I was at her home in the early evening, where Karen lounged in sweat clothes, tired after a long day at work, including almost an hour's commute each way.

I found that Karen still has a close relationship with her two daughters. In 1994 Karen, as a divorced mother for twelve years, loved living with her daughters, then aged nineteen and twenty-one. "I am much closer to them, and they are much closer with me, than I ever was with my parents," Karen declared. "We talk about what's going on in their personal lives, which I never did with my parents. They don't want to leave home, they are happy, and I am too." Although she had been in a few relationships since her divorce, mostly with men who did not live nearby, no boyfriend had ever met her daughters. Karen said clearly, "I don't see myself getting married again; I like being independent and I like the sense of freedom." But she didn't want to live by herself.

Thus, I was not surprised in 2003 to find that one daughter had moved back in with Karen (after living in the East for four years), and that her other daughter lived a few miles away with a partner of four years and their two young children. Karen loves being a grandmother and takes care of her grandchildren three or four times a week. I met both daughters, and I could see the obvious affection between them and their mother.

But I was startled to find that her ex-husband also lived with Karen, since her previous account of their relationship would not have led me to expect that they could live together again. Karen said that he moved in temporarily after cancer surgery so that her daughters could help take care of him. I assumed that this had happened recently, but it turned out that the surgery had taken place almost six years earlier. Karen was quick to add, "It's my house, and we are not back in a relationship at all."

Eight years into the marriage, when their daughters were in first and third grade, Karen recognized that her husband, Jason, was an alcoholic who became angry, abusive, and intimidating when he drank. But Karen wanted Jason, despite his drinking, to be a father, so she tried to maintain a friendship for their daughters' sake.

Despite tensions for a number of years, twelve years after the divorce (in 1994), Jason and she were "pretty good friends." She was pleased that her daughters got along with their father, who had never been abusive to them. Karen said, "He's a nice guy, but I don't want to live with him; I don't like to be around when he is drinking, but it's fine to have dinner with the kids." He repaired her car and helped out with house repairs, but when I asked if she considered Jason family, Karen replied, "That makes me cringe a little bit."

Yet a little more than three years after this remark, Jason moved into a house that Karen had bought, and he stayed. I probed to find out what this meant to Karen. For Karen, ownership of the house is important. She said: "He has his own room and does not dominate the household. We don't eat together much. If I feel like cooking, I cook. I never feel obliged. Whoever is here when I cook, there is plenty. He doesn't cook, but he will fix something for himself. Financially, we are completely separate. He does work on the house, but he has no equity or ownership of it." Karen continued, "We have no formal arrangement about work and finances. He'll do the yard work and heavy stuff. When the furnace went out, he called a guy in, and then he got the part and fixed it. I'll buy the parts for the renovation, and he does the work. He buys all the incidentals to get the job done. It seems to work."

The arrangement is viable because Karen is happy with celibacy. "I don't have any anxieties about not being in a relationship," Karen said, "or any desire to put energy into seeking one out." In answer to my question about whether Jason has any other relationships or sexual liaisons, Karen said she doesn't know or care. What Karen likes is family life. She has never lived alone and doesn't want to do so. Living with her daughter and her ex-husband, and having her other daughter and grandchildren nearby, makes Karen very happy.

In addition, Karen has replaced the small-town community she had when the children were small with a new community she has made through eight years of participation on a women's softball team. The team plays competitively and travels to state and national tournaments. Karen loves this activity and has made a few close friends. She socializes with them and goes to ball games and other events. Jason never goes with her. Some of these friends know that he lives with her, but no one has met him or thinks of her as coupled. Nor does Karen; she definitely identifies herself as single.

Karen admits that neighbors and extended family may have more trouble understanding their living arrangement. She mentions that Jason's sister from Germany visited the year before and asked whether they were a couple again. Neighbors don't ask, perhaps assuming that a woman and a man who live together, especially when they used to be married, are a couple. Since a number of married couples undoubtedly cohabit with a similar lack of intimacy or sexual involvement, Karen can be seen as more honest than most, recognizing how her situation deviates from social norms for both single and coupled life.

Women Cohabiting with Nonromantic Significant Others

My hairdresser, Delia, has a very different type of cohabiting relationship, one that is more intimate and committed than Karen and Jason's but, like theirs, one that does not involve a romantic or sexual bond. Delia, an extroverted, pretty woman in her midfifties, has been with her partner, Angie, for thirty-two years, living together for the last twenty-eight. But Delia is neither sexually/romantically involved with Angie nor a lesbian. They own two businesses and a house together, and both have long-term relationships with a man (for eleven years for Delia and twenty for Angie). "We are a nonromantic, significant other (an NRSO) for each other," Delia explained. "I've never heard this term from anyone else, but it describes us."

Delia comes from a traditional family on the East Coast; she grew up thinking she would get married, be supported by her husband, and raise kids. Right after college she was married briefly but soon left the relationship. Now, thirty-seven years later, her ex-husband lives in Los Angeles and is a friend. He ended up as a single father, and Delia helped bring up his son. "I consider myself a mom to Nathan," Delia said, "and I consider them my extended family." Angie is happy that Delia has a child in her life. They considered the idea of adopting or fostering a child together, but they couldn't figure out how to fit it into their full and independent lives.

Delia and Angie met in the women's movement in the 1970s and decided to go to beauty school together. They worked in the same shop before buying their own store. But their attraction went beyond the business partnership. "I was completely attracted to Angie, but not sexually," Delia explained.

> With her, I felt that I could be who I wanted to be. I respected who she was and I wanted something she had. I wanted to learn how to be in touch with my feelings, to be more honest. She wanted to learn to be more practical and not spend money like she did. . . . When I met her, I felt like I'd like to live with her. I said it once, and she said: 'Are you crazy?' Yet here we are twenty-eight years later. What makes attraction? It is not always about sex. I always had girlfriends, but I had to learn that friendship means something, that it stands for something, accounts for something. It is not about my friends being around until I find the real thing. They are the real thing. We are here for each other. I've just been going through something hard. My boyfriend has been wonderful; he'll hear me, but he doesn't process the same way. He is more a wonderful escape with great sex.

The relationship between Delia and Angie evolved slowly, without a road map. In the early years, Angie, who had been married twice, often had a boyfriend, and this caused problems. Delia recalled:

> We became really good friends when she was separated one time from her husband. When they got back together, we stopped talk-

ing on the phone. I called her and said, "It is not okay to be my friend when your husband is not around and not my friend when he is in your life. I'm in your life, and you talk to me and I matter, or I don't." Angie sat up and said okay, but I still had to deal with the jealousy that came up because of her being with someone. I felt, "What's wrong with me that I'm not in another relationship?" Over time, I came to realize that I was whole just as I was. I didn't have to be defined by a sexual or romantic relationship. As a result, I realized that I have a great life beyond my wildest dreams.

But how do their male partners deal with this atypical arrangement? Delia's lover, Mark, lives fifty miles away and has a situation similar to hers. He owns a business with his ex-wife. Although Mark and his ex don't live together, they see each other every day and are each other's nonromantic significant other. Their grown son works in the business too and lives in a separate house on their property. Delia has become friends with Mark's ex-wife and enjoys spending time with her. Delia and Mark see each other almost every weekend and Wednesday evenings, usually at his place. "I'm crazy about this guy, I love being with him, and we have a really good relationship," Delia explained, "but I don't want to be married or even to cohabit. One of the benefits of not living together is we really look forward to seeing each other, but two or three times a week is plenty. Seeing Mark, and then getting separate time at home, with Angie and with friends, makes me feel like I get my cake and can eat it too." Delia concluded: "I really don't believe anyone can get everything from one person."

Angie's romantic involvement is different. She has been in a relationship for twenty years with a married man. His wife of forty years knows and accepts their relationship. She calls Angie her wife-in-law. Angie sees him once a week, and once in a while they go on a vacation together. Angie occasionally talks on the phone to his wife; she likes her but would not want her life. She abides by the wife's rules that Angie and her husband do nothing to embarrass her. They don't hold hands in public. Fortunately, their social circles are quite distinct. Sometimes he comes to a party with Angie and is introduced as her boyfriend, but they have never met any of his or his wife's friends. Angie loves him and likes this limited relationship, but she knows that it would not have been enough for her if she did not have her life with Delia. She doesn't think her relationship with her lover would have lasted if both of them had been single and he had wanted to cohabit; she couldn't live with someone who is domineering and a neatnik. Although initially Angie's parents did not approve of her being involved with a married man, now they like him better than either of her two former husbands and enjoy spending time with him. They love Delia and treat her like a daughter.

Delia's family has found it harder to accept her relationship with Angie. "My father on his deathbed said that he would be so happy if I met someone who wore a suit and was Jewish," Delia remembers. "My mother still has trouble trying to understand and accept the significance of Angie in my life; she wants to think of her as a room-mate. She doesn't want to give me money to buy a new couch be-cause she would be buying it for Angie too. If she were my husband, that wouldn't matter. My mother doesn't understand how we do money. She comes to visit and asks: 'Who is paying for this? Whose milk is it in the refrigerator? Who pays the phone bill?'" But Delia and Angie have found a fair way to divide their expenses. "Tradi-tional husbands and wives have to figure out how to share expenses and everything else," Delia noted, and "we do too." Delia did not tell her mother that she and Angie plan to share with each other what little inheritance they get from their families. Despite these difficulties, Delia remains very close to her mother. She talks to her every day on the phone. Often Angie's and Delia's parents plan to visit at the same time, and once they all went on a cruise together. "We've said to them, 'This is the closest you are going to get to in-laws.'"

Delia and Angie share family in another way. They both are very close to Angie's niece, now a forty-year-old MD. The niece lived with them off and on when she was in her twenties, and both Angie and Delia contributed financially to her medical education. She calls them both aunt. As a single woman, she takes her aunts as role models for how to craft an unconventional but satisfying life.

Over the years, friends have come to accept that Delia and Angie are in a permanent relationship as significant others. "We have a large circle of friends whom we have known for a long time," Delia explained, "and we are always invited as a couple, even if it is a friend who is closer to Angie. Sometimes she goes with her boyfriend, but everyone sees us as an old married couple." Delia's lover lives farther away and doesn't seem interested in socializing with her friends, which suits her just fine.

Delia and Angie did not find it difficult to compromise on how to live together, but they have had more problems in their joint work life, in managing the two businesses they own together. Delia is more aggressive, has a higher energy level, and takes the lead, but then she becomes stressed and resentful that the more relaxed Angie isn't doing enough. Delia's ideal vacation involves work-related activities, whereas Angie prefers to get away from it all. They have learned to talk about their resentments, to experiment with different solutions (sometimes Delia is paid more), at times to make more formal agreements, and to better utilize their temperaments and skills.

Overall, being nonromantic significant others suits them. Delia is surprised at how her life has turned out; she never would have envisioned it this way. But she is pleased that she kept an open mind and was willing to challenge preconceived notions of how happiness is supposed to look. A mutual friend, who lived with Delia and Angie for a while, summarized her view of why it works: "They entertain each other. They are both characters and enhance each other's lives."

Delia recognizes that she has a richer family life than most people. "Someone once said to me that I collect families," she said. "I have Angie. I have my boyfriend. I have helped my ex-husband bring up his son, and I consider them my extended family. My friends are also like family. In addition, I have my family of origin on the East Coast. Since my father died several years ago, my family there consists of my mom and my siblings, nieces, and nephews." With so many families, Delia feels confident she'll have a support base as she ages.

Younger women, too, are experimenting with living with a nonromantic significant other, although they don't use the term. In a 2001 article in *Ms.* magazine, Pagan Kennedy struggled with the namelessness of her situation, one very similar to Delia and Angie's. Kennedy and her partner, Liz, both in their late twenties or early thirties, both heterosexual with boyfriends, have made a home together for two years, with a commitment beyond that of roommates. Kennedy recounts how her dissatisfaction with cohabitation with a boyfriend led her to look for something different. "He and I had completely different ideas about what we wanted from a living space," Kennedy writes. "He thought of an apartment as a desktop where we could scatter papers, coffee mugs, and computer parts. What I regarded as a mess, he saw as a filing system that should under no circumstances be disturbed. Meanwhile, I drove him crazy by hosting political meetings in our living room, inviting ten people over for dinner at the last minute. We loved one another, but that didn't mean we should share an apartment."[61]

Vowing never again to drift into such a domestic catastrophe, Kennedy developed a vision of the household she wanted and how to achieve it: "I would find someone to share my passion for turning a house into a community center—with expansive meals, weekend guests, clean counters, flowers, art projects, activist gatherings, a backyard garden, and a pile of old bikes on the porch, available to anyone needing to borrow some wheels. My friend Liz seemed like the right person. And so I proposed to her."[62] During the first year, they began to run several businesses and a nonprofit group out of the house, but they also spent holidays with each other's families and dealt with many people's assumptions that they were lesbians.

Kennedy and Liz have no long-term commitment to each other, no vision of the future, and no adequate word for their household.[63] Hearing Delia and Angie's story and how such a household arrangement can last may provide a model for them and others.

As we break down the hierarchy and division between those who are coupled and those who are single, we need to reconsider the inequality in our evaluation of romantic relationships and friendships. Perhaps a time will come when nonsexual, committed friendships will be seen just as important as romantic relationships. Someday we may say "just lovers" as casually as we now label ourselves and others "just friends."

CHAPTER 9

Friendship Networks as a Source of Community and Care

> We create communities on this
> long extension cord of friends.
> ELLEN GOODMAN AND PATRICIA O'BRIEN,
> *I Know Just What You Mean*

A large network of friends, and not just a best friend or a small circle of friends, ensures that a single woman will live, as well as die, well. Although a best friend may provide a lot of intimacy, she is not a good source of security. Expecting one best friend to meet most of one's needs is often unrealistic. Like a divorce, a breakup with a best friend can be devastating, and friendship, unlike marriage or even a cohabiting partnership, is not protected by law and social custom. In contrast, a single woman who has a number of good friends is not so devastated when one friendship no longer works. In a wider network of friends, she can find support for a range of personal interests and for different types of intimacy; she can be surer of daily help and aid in a time of crisis.[1]

A network of friends involves more than just numbers, and more than only good friends. Unlike a close circle or a clique, a network is open to friends leaving and new ones entering. In such a network, not everyone knows everyone else, certainly not well, but most people know of each other. A network of friends incorporates overlapping friendship circles from work, childhood, church or politics, and shared recreation. These circles intersect when a few friends from work know your childhood friend, or a friend from church knows your golf buddy. A network usually ranges from very intimate friends to those with whom you socialize, to others with whom you share a particular interest but don't share intimate details of your life, to even more casual and recent friends. Such a friendship network fosters individual autonomy but also provides bonds of support. Research finds that such a network of different types of friends is especially conducive to health and well-being.[2]

In addition, friendship networks are key to community building. Rather than seeing a contemporary community as based on a set of shared values among people who live near each other and experience face-to-face interaction on a regular basis, sociologists now emphasize a personal community as being defined by social networks that provide companionship, social support, a sense of belonging, and trust.[3] Although a personal community usually does not have a cohesive moral or ideological purpose, it is built on bonds of belonging and care—connections that, as we will observe, can be activated into common action.

Four types of ties—between friends, kin, coworkers, and neighbors—create the networks that sustain a personal community, and of these, friends provide the largest number of bonds.[4] A personal community based on networks is not limited to a concrete group, organization, or neighborhood. Friends often are made in such settings (at school, college, work, church, the gym), but networks of friends transcend a particular setting. A community based on friendship networks, in turn, becomes a source of new friends, as we meet friends of friends.

Social commentators often bemoan the increase in singleness, seeing it as a sign of social decay, but research finds that single people in the United States have more friends and see them more often.[5] The friendship networks of singles thus can be seen as promoting the renewal of community in advanced industrial societies.[6] Since currently women in the United States are better at friendship and at building friendship networks,[7] single women can be seen as critical creators of community.

A personal community does not have to be geographically based, but geographic proximity (within an hour's drive) is important to single women for both daily care and crisis help. You can get emotional support and practical advice over the phone or the Internet, but that is not the same as having people nearby whom you can see on a regular basis or who can come quickly and often when there is a special need. Because single people are more dependent on their friendship networks and personal communities, many find it harder to move geographically than do their coupled peers. Perhaps someday professional single women will negotiate a career move only if the prospective employer helps find jobs for several of their friends too.[8]

Friendship Networks at a Time of Life-Threatening Illness

In *Bridget Jones's Diary,* the best-selling British novel (and later film) about the travails of a single woman in her thirties, Bridget expresses her fear of "dying alone and being found three weeks later half-eaten by an Alsatian."[9] Whether spoken or not, such anxiety plagues many singles, accounting, I think, for why this line is quoted so often. I discovered, in contrast, that single women die alone only if, like Mary Bishop, they so desire. I found that the friendship networks that single women create over a number of years provide the basis for excellent care in a time of severe illness and impending death—care that in many ways exceeds that available in a family.

Over the course of my study, one participant, Diane Epstein, died, as did the best friend of another, Lynn Rostow. Both Diane and Lynn's friend, Wendy, died over a two-year period of metastasized breast cancer. Both were embedded in networks of friends who helped family members support these two single, divorced mothers. But the two networks functioned quite differently, adapting to the distinct personalities and personal styles of the dying women. Tracing the progression of illness and death of Diane, who was sixty-one and had a twenty-four-year-old daughter, and of Wendy, who was fifty and had two sons, aged eighteen and twenty-two, demonstrates how friendship networks provide excellent care and how such care, in turn, strengthens these networks and builds community.

Dying in a Cocoon of Friends, Community, and Family

On a cold, wet December Sunday afternoon, I rushed into a nonde-nominational community church in Oakland, California, hoping I wouldn't be late for Diane Epstein's memorial service. A large color photograph of a smiling Diane graced the front of the craftsman-style hall, reminding everyone of her upbeat, incredibly warm personality. I heard musicians warming up. In an adjoining room, I deposited the salad I had brought as a contribution for a potluck meal to follow. Expecting a small, cozy gathering, I was overwhelmed by the large crowd of more than three hundred people. Were all these people close to Diane, the insecure single mother whom I had first interviewed seven years earlier when she was in her midfifties? Was this the same woman who had trouble making ends meet with her jobs as a teacher in a Jewish preschool and as a part-time massage therapist?

The numbers began to give me insight into why I was unable to see Diane several months earlier, even when I offered to bring food or to do errands. I had heard through the grapevine that she was terminally ill, and I wanted to talk to her one more time. Once, I did have an appointment, arranged through a friend, but it was canceled because, I was told, too many close friends and family members were visiting. At the time, I thought Diane probably was too sick or depressed to visit with a mere acquaintance and a researcher. Now, I perceived that she was, in fact, too busy, with too many friends clamoring to see her. Both the memorial service—warm, personal, moving, and humorous—and a subsequent interview with one of Diane's good friends, Joan, helped me fill out a picture of Diane's life and how she died.

Diane grew up in Beverly Hills in a Jewish family, with a college-educated, businessman father and a high school–educated home-maker mother. Her parents were originally Roosevelt Democrats, but they lived in a neighborhood filled with leftists. Diane's mother loved the community and became very political. Exposed as a teenager to progressive politics and to the strong community among Jewish leftists, Diane quickly identified with the New Left movements of the 1960s, especially the antiwar and peace movements she encountered as a student at the University of California in Los Angeles and Berkeley and at Mills College. But Diane didn't join any left-wing organization; she found most of them much too doctrinaire. Although she regularly attended antiwar marches and rallies, and sometimes those for other causes, Diane characterized herself "as always on the edges" of politics. She joined a small women's consciousness-raising group, but not a feminist organization.

Given Diane's assessment of herself, I was surprised that many of the friends speaking at the memorial service stressed her political activism, as did an obituary in the *San Francisco Chronicle* entitled "Advocate for Peace" and the headline of a story in the *San Francisco Jewish Bulletin,* which read "Peace Activist and Teacher Dies at 61." Diane's friend, Joan, confirmed that Diane was not a joiner but hypothesized that friends, colleagues, and acquaintances saw her as very political because she was so vocal about her political values and because she did indeed participate in a huge number of marches and demonstrations. Diane marched for the last time in the anti–Iraq War march in San Francisco on October 26, 2002, just a little over a month before she died. Under her tutelage, Diane's preschool students wrote letters to the environmentalist Julia Butterfly Hill, sang workers' songs, and told their parents it wasn't such a good idea to shop at the Gap. Coming from someone else, this might have been seen as doctrinaire, but not from Diane, who at other times used puppets, costumes, and wigs to tell elaborate, fanciful stories to the children, then would kneel down, look them in the eye, and truly listen to what they had to say.

Diane presented herself as an ever-single woman, so I was surprised to learn in the first interview that she had been married briefly at twenty-three, a marriage that was annulled after nine months because her husband would not consummate it. "He was a nice man," Diane recounted, "but we were both very naive." Diane had a big wedding, and she "was shattered and disappointed" when the marriage did not work out. She went to Israel for two years and lived with a man there, but that relationship, like many other affairs and several more serious bonds, did not last. Diane said she was always looking for a permanent relationship, but she never put her life on hold. Surrounded by friends, Diane always had fun.

At a gathering of friends the week before she died, each person was asked to pick a word to describe Diane. They picked *a beam of light, radiant star, social conscience, community, queen of laughter, playfulness,* and *sparkler* among others. Diane chose for herself *party girl.* Every year she had five or six parties for her birthday, organized by different groups of friends, and she always gave a costume party at Halloween. The first time that Diane was hospitalized, more than twenty-five years earlier, for a hysterectomy, Joan found sixteen people in her hospital room after her operation. Diane had not yet heard that she did not have uterine cancer, but nonetheless she wanted to sing and have a party. Even as she was nearing the end of her life, Diane mobilized friends to help organize a sixtieth birthday party for her sister.

More than a partner, Diane desired a child. She wanted to build on the close family ties she enjoyed with her mother (after her father's death some years earlier), a sister, a niece, and a number of cousins. With much trepidation, Diane, in her late thirties, began to contemplate becoming a single mother, encouraged by Joan's conscious decision to get pregnant and parent without a partner. Diane tried artificial insemination for a year, feeling lucky to have found a doctor who would give sperm to a single woman at a time before it had become acceptable to do so. But Diane didn't get pregnant, and then she had the hysterectomy. Now she became determined to find a child to adopt.

Feeling too insecure to adopt an infant, Diane looked for an older child. Joan recalled: "Diane called me from an orphanage in Mexico, saying she had seen this darling little girl who was the right age (four), but she was scared that she couldn't handle being a mother. I reassured her and said this might be her only chance." In my first interview with Diane, when her daughter, Celia, was sixteen, she talked about her insecurities as a mother, even though Celia, until she became a teenager, was an easy and delightful child. Joan confirmed that Diane lacked confidence about many decisions. Although Diane was a warm and loving mother, she was in therapy continually and always needed friends around to advise and help her. "She was so lovely that people came and helped her, always getting back in fun and sociability whatever they gave in practical help and advice," Joan said. Despite the difficulty, Diane considered that having a child was the best thing she had done. Her last words, Joan reported, were "Celia, Celia."

After becoming a mother, Diane went to work at the Jewish preschool. Her experience working with a small group of women teachers, who became her friends, bolstered her confidence as a parent. It also initiated her integration into a Jewish community that was more religious and less overtly political than the one in which she grew up. Becoming a mother strengthened her family ties too. Diane became closer to several cousins. She spent holidays with a cousin and her family who lived about ninety miles away, bringing Celia and her mother, and sometimes her sister and her family too.

At the memorial service, these family ties were in strong evidence. Two cousins, a niece, and Diane's sister spoke, as did Celia, now a beautiful twenty-four-year-old woman with a thick braid of rich black hair down her back. Celia spoke in a strong, if tearful, voice. Claiming that she didn't know 95 percent of the people there, Celia acknowledged that her mother touched all those present. She recalled how her mom adopted her out of an orphanage when she was poor and had nothing, where the orphans were trained to be maids and servants. Celia regretted that she took her mother for granted, was ungrateful as a teenager, and gave her such a hard time. "I will always cherish the precious moments and years I had with my mom," Celia said. "If I have children, I will want them to know about their grandmother." Celia said that even though Diane was not her biological mother, she will always be her one and only mother.

The nonfamily members at the memorial service belonged primarily to a large network of friends whom Diane linked together into her own personal community. Joan, in looking over her photos of Diane from the previous thirty years, found that they were almost all pictures with Diane in groups of friends. The rabbi started the memorial service by saying, "Everyone here thinks she or he was Diane's best friend." Diane's friendship network was built from five different sources: (1) Long-term friends whom Diane had met in college or in activist circles in the 1960s. (2) Seven colleagues who worked with Diane for all or part of her seventeen years at the preschool and met as a group to celebrate birthdays and other celebrations, often with special rituals. (They called Diane the crone of the group; she was the first to turn fifty, then sixty, and the first to die.) (3) A woman's group informally named the Golden Girls, which started with five women in the 1980s and later added four more women. (The group, consisting of both coupled and single women, all but one of whom were mothers, met once a month for many years primarily to talk about themselves and their lives. This group was important too in helping Diane overcome her anxieties as a mother.) (4) Friends from the progressive, left-wing synagogue in which she was a member for about fourteen years. (5) Finally, new friends Diane picked up wherever she went and whatever she did. Joan commented that Diane made more new friends in her fifties than anybody else she knew. Another friend recounted that if you went for a walk or hike with Diane, you would have to stop seventeen times to talk with people whom Diane knew. From these overlapping groups of friends, Diane drew the resources to deal with her cancer.

Diane was diagnosed with breast cancer and had a mastectomy four years before her death. Two years later, the cancer had metastasized. At that point, Diane retired and gave full attention to her health. In her dealings with doctors and cancer specialists, Diane's insecurity was apparent, as she was at first easily intimidated by their authority. Friends, however, always accompanied her to doctors' appointments and chemotherapy treatments, and with their support, Diane learned to confront the doctors to get a medical team she respected. The first time she fired an oncologist, she was very anxious, but by the time she had fired the fourth oncologist, she had grown confident. A friend remarked at the memorial service that "out of the cancer experience, Diane gained a self-confidence, a toughness, she did not possess before."

I met with Diane for the second time, about a year before she died, after she had had eight chemotherapy treatments. She told me that she preferred to rely on friends rather than family members. Although her daughter had moved back in with her, Diane wanted her to have her own life. Diane's mother was eighty-six, and her sister and cousins lived several hours away. Diane shared her fears more intimately with her friends, for she felt that they could handle her illness more objectively and philosophically. Family members got too upset and made dealing with the cancer more difficult for her. The family seemed grateful to be able to hand the burdens to others.

Unlike another woman dying of cancer whom we will meet in the next portrait, Diane wanted to organize the help of friends herself. One friend commented that Diane did "breast cancer by community," but she wanted to orchestrate it. Diane did permit her group of colleagues from the preschool to organize meals, but otherwise she took the initiative. She called friends to accompany her to doctors and to help her with tasks. She wanted to invite the friends (sometimes up to five) who would stay in her apartment the night after her chemotherapy treatments. "She figured out what people were good at doing and asked them for their help," Joan said. For example, Diane chose as executor for her will a man she had met in the synagogue, along with a woman friend who was a lawyer. Diane chose to talk about dying with a male friend who was dying of colon cancer, rather than with her more intimate women friends.

Because Diane knew so many people who offered help, some of her oldest friends did not play a major role in her care. Joan understood, but another old friend resented it when she found it hard to see Diane. Still, Diane's upbeat personality, something she retained until the end, made her dying process a positive experience for most of her friends.[10] Eight days before her death, friends organized a ritual with her to say good-bye. A participant remembered, "She wore her pink bed jacket and pink wig and she was radiant, not depressed or despairing. Two days before her death she was still singing 'Just One of Those Things.' In helping her through her illness, we all felt uplifted being in her presence."

The spontaneous participation of Diane Epstein's network of friends in her dying process is different from the experience of another woman in my study. Lynn Rostow helped organize a more formal support network for her dying friend, a friend who was much more angry and difficult than Diane.

Sharing the Care of a Dying Friend

Despite her Harvard education, and after living in California for many years, Lynn Rostow retains her Brooklyn accent. With her curly dark hair and high energy, she is very direct and displays a wry sense of humor. Lynn married a classmate during her junior year at Harvard, and they both graduated in 1968. After another year in Boston, the couple moved to California when Lynn's husband was accepted for graduate school at the University of California at Santa Barbara. The turbulent times, however, led Lynn in a different direction. Attracted to women's liberation and the counterculture, Lynn joined a feminist consciousness-raising group and worked at an alternative newspaper.

A year after moving to California, when she was twenty-three, Lynn left her husband, packed everything she owned into her Volkswagen bus, and drove up the coast looking for a place to settle with a leftist and feminist counterculture. She ended up in Portland, Oregon, attracted to the city by the presence of her brother and his partner, who lived nearby, and by its alternative media, a women's clinic, feminist businesses, food coops, and natural food groceries. Living in a cooperative household, where expenses were low, Lynn worked at odd jobs—for the recycling center, an alternative newspaper, and then in a cannery for a short while.

In Portland, Lynn met Wendy, who was five years younger. Immediately drawn to Wendy's enthusiastic enjoyment of life, Lynn remembers the woman who became her friend: "She got great pleasure from noticing a new bird in the yard, or a brief warm conversation with a stranger at a restaurant, or a good program on NPR, and she shared her enthusiasms." Lynn recounted how she met Wendy:

> We were in overlapping circles. Wendy was living with a group of people I knew from the underground paper. One person in her household revealed to them that he was a fugitive and with the Weather Underground. Wendy and I joined a support group for him, and we both were sexually involved with him, she more seriously than I. At some point, she and I moved into the same collective household with two other men. With Wendy's death, all the others have died of cancer—one man of liver cancer, the other of brain cancer, Wendy of breast cancer, and I have had breast cancer too. It makes me wonder. We lived in that house maybe one or two years.

When Lynn became involved with a woman and started to identify herself as bisexual, she and Wendy drifted apart. Wendy met and married David and moved to the Bay Area. A few years later, Lynn and her partner followed, but Lynn did not seek out Wendy, even though her partner and Wendy both worked as nurses in the same hospital. However, Lynn and Wendy heard about each other. Lynn knew that Wendy had two sons; Wendy learned that Lynn's partner had given birth to a baby boy with a commitment to equal coparenting with Lynn.

> When we were looking for a preschool for Joseph, we were interested in one where I heard Wendy sent her kids. So I called her. She told me that our friend, the fugitive, had been caught and was on his way to prison but was staying at her house for a few days. She asked if I wanted to come over to see him. I went, and Wendy and I had such a good time with each other that both of us wanted to renew our friendship. She had broken up with David and I had just left my partner, so we were both now single mothers, she with two boys and me with one. One of her sons was a little older than Joseph and one a little younger. So it was perfect.

During their years apart, Lynn had returned to school, become a therapist, and returned to heterosexuality. Wendy supplemented her nursing income with work as a yoga and meditation teacher and had become heavily involved with a Tibetan Buddhist group—interests that secular Lynn did not share. But the two women loved to hike together, and they enjoyed music and films. They went camping with the boys, shared family meals, and organized holiday rituals.

The year they reconnected (1988), Wendy was diagnosed with breast cancer. After a year of trying alternative therapies, she ended up with a mastectomy, chemotherapy, and the prognosis that she had less than five years to live. During this time, six or seven of her closest friends met to talk about how they could support her. Lynn didn't know most of the others and doesn't remember much about what they did for Wendy in that period. "I did some cooking for her," Lynn recalled. "I remember making a dish for her that she really liked, and then when she got well she couldn't stand it because it reminded her of her illness."

Seven years later, in the mid-1990s, Wendy had a recurrence of the cancer. This time she had a terrible reaction to the chemotherapy and was miserable. Lynn gave Wendy a lot of emotional support and found a therapist for her teenage sons. With another of Wendy's friends, Lynn again organized a network of support, now consisting of twelve to fifteen people who for three months helped with the shopping and cooking, accompanied Wendy to doctors' appointments, and just visited. Then, in 2000, Wendy was diagnosed with a metastasis and given an unknown but limited time to live. For the first year, a similar loose organization helped Wendy, but in the last year of her life, from September 2001 to October 2002, Lynn was the central organizer for a much larger and more highly structured support network.

Wendy was worried that she was going to burn people out, that she was too needy, and that people would get tired of taking care of her. "There was an objective basis for her fear," Lynn agreed. One day, in an elated state, Wendy called Lynn to say she had found a book about how friends organized a support group for a single woman in her forties who was dying. Lynn bought the book, *Share the Care:*

How to Organize a Group to Care for Someone Who Is Seriously Ill, written by Cappy Capossela and Sheila Warnock,[11] and agreed that this offered a plan that would work. With a larger and more highly structured group, no one would be overburdened, good friends could do more, but acquaintances or those with other burdens in their lives could still do a little. People could choose tasks they liked or wanted to do at times that fitted into their lives and schedules. Participants in the group could take care of each other.

Share the Care emphasized the importance of the first group meeting and provided elaborate plans on how to run it. Lynn followed the instructions; as recommended, she selected another woman to be a coleader, one of the other women who, like herself, had been involved in the informal support network for years. About twenty-five people came to the meeting, which was held the Sunday before the September 11 terrorist attack. Wendy's ex-husband, David, the father of her children, who had become a friend over the years, took an active and important role in the care network, as did her sister, an engineering professor who lived an hour away, but most of the participants were friends and colleagues from various circles. They included friends she had made through her children, several other nurses with whom she worked, friends from the Buddhist group, several women, who like Lynn, knew her from Portland, and a number of her yoga and meditation students. Although most of these former students were not close friends, they were personally devoted to Wendy because of the intensity and excitement with which she taught yoga, meditation, and Buddhism. A few of these original participants dropped out over the course of the year, but others joined, so that about thirty people in all participated.

As *Share the Care* suggested, Lynn conducted several exercises with participants, where they could express their feelings about being close to someone who was dying and say what they would get out of being in the care network. The latter was especially important to ensure that Wendy would not feel like a charity case and to reaffirm the notion of friendship as reciprocal and egalitarian. Lynn remembered how the participants responded: "Some said that Wendy had given them so much that they wanted to be able to give something back. Others said that death was a big mystery to them that they wanted to demystify. A few said that family members had died and they hadn't really processed it; they thought participating in this group would help. Everyone wanted community in their lives."

After these exercises, Wendy talked about her needs, and Lynn proposed an elaborate structure. Wendy wanted a separate medical team, composed of one friend who was a doctor and several of her nurse friends. Sometimes they needed an additional person to accompany Wendy to an appointment, but usually they operated independently of the care network. For the care work—shopping, cooking dinner a few times a week, errands, and so on—participants were organized into four teams, each responsible for one week a month. At this first meeting people signed up for what they wanted to do. Some people signed up for more than one task, and others preferred to be on call to fill in. Each team was headed by cocaptains, who were responsible for reminding people it was their week, finding substitutes when people couldn't do it, and filling in when Wendy needed something that wasn't on the list.

To get a different perspective on the network, I interviewed Cathy, another friend of Lynn's, who too knew Wendy from Oregon but was not close to her. Cathy decided to become part of the support network because of her close friendship with Lynn and because, as a single woman, she wanted to learn how to support her own close friends if any of them needed help. Cathy recounted the flexibility of the system: "I decided I didn't want to do shopping, and I didn't feel like I knew Wendy well enough to go to the doctor with her, and I couldn't with a full-time job. But I could do the calling and organizing as a cocaptain. I did that for a few months, until I was diagnosed with breast cancer myself, and then someone else stepped in. I didn't do anything for months during my own chemotherapy and radiation, but then I came back at the end to do some cooking and calling." Cathy's main role, however, was to be an emotional sounding board for Lynn's more conflicted experience.

Lynn orchestrated an e-mail list, an innovative addition to recommendations found in *Share the Care*. Through e-mail, Lynn kept everyone up-to-date about Wendy's health and new developments (positive and negative). "That list became a form of communication," Lynn recalled, "not just for the share-the-care team, but for her siblings and parents, who did not live here, her college roommate, who lived in LA, and some of her colleagues who were not part of share the care. So when a particular drug stopped working, everyone knew about it. When she tried something else, everyone knew."

Both Lynn and Cathy, from their different perspectives, felt that the care network worked amazingly well. People were responsible and consistent in fulfilling their commitments, with only a few problems over the summer when many of them went on vacation. There were a few minor mishaps, but nothing significant. As Wendy's health deteriorated, however, she was in a great deal of physical pain and was very frightened. She needed more and more help, but she resented her dependence on others and sometimes expressed this frustration by criticizing her friends.

Lynn recalled: "Wendy was critical of some people who did the shopping—feeling that they did not follow her instructions; she didn't like the way some people cooked. So I had to use some tact in figuring out how to shift people around. I had to say to somebody, 'You know there is someone else who really wants to do this.'"

In May 2002, nine months after the care network had started and after Wendy had been hospitalized for five days, Lynn called another meeting of the whole group, for it was clear that the medical situation was changing and had become much more fluid. Wendy attended the first half of the meeting. "It was great for her to be there for that hour and hear all the loving things people said," Lynn reported. "I think it extended her life by about four weeks. After she left, we talked about things that were challenging for us." A new need arose: having someone stay in the hospital with Wendy. "She wanted people there twenty-four hours [a day], and we were able to do that," Lynn said. "We had a cot in her room that someone could sleep on." No one knew when she would be in the hospital, so rather than doing specific assignments, the four teams had to be more flexible. Captains would call their own team members first, but if they couldn't find someone, they could call anyone on the list.

Cathy recalled her experience as the cocaptain of one of the teams during the last weeks of Wendy's life:

> It was an incredible experience. For three weeks, we lined up peo-
> ple for twenty-four-hour care, seven days a week. I thought it was
> going to be hard, because these are busy people. But it was so easy
> to get the coverage. I had more people wanting to be there than I
> could schedule. No one talked about burnout even though people
> were exhausted. People's children and partners accepted this as im-
> portant. My son accepted that I'd spend the whole day shopping
> and cooking for Wendy. One woman did say to me, "I'm fine with
> not seeing her again, because I'm so disturbed after seeing how this
> has changed Wendy's appearance. If you don't need me, I'd prefer
> not to go. But if you need me, I can do it." Other people didn't
> even mention that; people were so generous.

Lynn's experience as part of a core group of five women was more complex. Part of what made Wendy's dying so hard was that she had been so very alive—intellectually, emotionally, physically—with a wide range of interests and passions. But as her health dete-riorated, Wendy could not accept that she was dying, rejected the advice of her medical team to get hospice care, and became more difficult to support. Lynn recalled the last month of Wendy's life when she was in the hospital about three-fourths of the time: "What she wanted was impossible. She wanted to know stuff that nobody knew. She wanted to receive treatment that didn't exist. She wanted to be nurtured in ways that you couldn't figure out." Sometimes Wendy yelled at people, criticizing what they had done, making them feel inadequate. Lynn used her skills as a therapist to try to run interference to keep the network functioning. "One time, when someone called wanting to quit because Wendy had been upset with her for buying five tomatoes rather than four, I reassured her that Wendy got upset with everyone." Several months before she died, Lynn, along with a nurse and a friend from the Buddhist community, met with Wendy to counsel her and help her deal with some of her anger. Lynn felt it was good for the three of them—a therapist, a medical adviser, and a spiritual adviser—to be all together in one room with Wendy, but she was not sure that it helped.

Share the Care had not prepared Lynn for anger and hostility on the part of a dying woman, nor for her own feelings when Wendy turned on her. "One time when Wendy was in the hospital," Lynn recounted,

> I had some free time because a client canceled, so I decided to just go over to the hospital and get a list from her of whom she did and did not want to stay with her there. I walked into the room, and Wendy looks up and says: "I can't have people dropping in on me like this." She said: "Susan was just here and I had to kick her out." I said to myself, "Susan has known you for a year, and I've known you for thirty." I was really hurt, but it helped that within a couple of minutes her sister and I went out in the hall, and she comforted me. Often when I left Wendy, I would call someone to decompress and talk about what was going on. People really supported each other in dealing with Wendy's temperamental and often hurtful ways.

Lynn was hurt again when Wendy did not include her among the four people—three friends from the Buddhist group and one of her nurse friends—she wanted to have in the room when she died. Wendy didn't want her sons and sister either. Considering Wendy her *best* friend increased Lynn's sense of rejection. Cathy commented: "I don't think Wendy would have distinguished best from other friends. I don't. I have a series of friends and recognize what I get from each of them, but I don't rank them. I suspect Wendy was more like this."

Hearing these stories from Lynn, Cathy was relieved that she had no contact with Wendy during those last weeks. Cathy admitted, "My relationship to Lynn and to the other people in the group kept me in it, not my relationship to Wendy."

I asked both Lynn and Cathy how Wendy's family dealt with the Share the Care network. Cathy said, "They were so appreciative." "They were profoundly grateful," Lynn said, "profoundly grateful." Wendy died at the age of fifty, when her mother and father were still in their seventies and healthy. Wendy's mother came several times from the Midwest for a week or two and wanted to help more, but Wendy did not feel close to her mother and did not want it. One of Wendy's sons was away at college, and the other was just out of high school when his mother died. They were part of the network, but they could not have done it all. At the evaluation meeting after Wendy died, one of them said, "Your network allowed us to have a relationship with our mother that was not just shopping, cooking, and worrying about the details of life. We could be normal teenagers."

At a final meeting of the network—a potluck dinner a month after Wendy died—people talked about Wendy's positive characteristics, her zest for life, her insight and compassion, and also about how difficult she had been as she got sicker. Everyone who attended had only good things to say about the share-the-care network. Those who were close to Wendy felt that they could not have dealt with her demands and anger without the group process. Lynn became much closer to one of the nurses, someone she had known before, but not as a friend; she also became friends with Wendy's sister. These new friendships helped fill the hole that Wendy had left in her life. Those like Cathy who were less close to Wendy felt that participating in the group had given them a new sense of community and more confidence that friends would be there for them. A relative of Wendy's was so impressed by the network that she got her church to develop a Share the Care ministry to formalize help for needy members of the congregation.

Thus, an informal personal community built on friendship networks provided a model of activating an ethic of care—a model from which an established organization, a church committed to care and community, could learn. Even with such a difficult object of care, the network held and friends supported each other. Such a friendship network can be activated in an emergency, however, only if the bonds have been established. "This care network was only possible because Wendy had a large network of friends that had come together over many years," Cathy remarked. "We could not have put it together if that didn't exist."

Singles Build Friendship Networks in Their Twenties and Thirties

Building a friendship network takes time and necessitates some stability in one's life, but even singles in their twenties and thirties recognize the importance of a network of friends. Journalist Ethan Watters, while in his thirties and single, wrote about his "urban tribe"—a loose network of single friends who socialize, help each other out, and provide intimacy and emotional support.

> We constantly kept track of each other in a never-ending e-mail thread. On an average week, among my group of twenty-five friends, there were hundreds of one-to-one e-mails, a dozen group e-mails, and perhaps fifty phone calls exchanged.... We shared food together, not only on every Tuesday night at the Rite Spot Café but in a constant series of impromptu dinners and barbecues.... There were book groups, poker nights, wine tastings and cocktail hours, weekly sporting events, and gatherings to watch television shows.[12]

These friends also helped each other move furniture, paint apartments, and gather money to help somebody in financial need. They encouraged each other to take personal risks to meet their individual goals.[13] Watters recognized that his friendship network had links to other networks in a way that formed a community.[14] "After more than a decade," Watters reflects, "my sense of living as a single person in a modern American city was that of belonging to an intensely loyal community of people."[15]

While important for day-to-day social support, friendship networks can also provide aid in a medical crisis for a younger single person. Linda Woolsey, the woman we met in chapter 7 who was trying to get pregnant by artificial insemination, told a story that illustrates the importance of such assistance. When I first interviewed her, Linda (at the age of thirty) was especially self-reliant, lived by herself, and hated to be a burden. But when she broke her leg on a rafting trip with eighteen friends and was on crutches for two months, she needed help. She got some assistance from family members who lived nearby but relied mainly on her large network of friends. Friends drove Linda to work, shopped, cleaned, and fixed meals, but they also took her to a movie or stopped by for a chat. In my interview with her, Linda remarked that some people might see such a health crisis as a catalyst for finding and living with a partner. But Linda felt the opposite. Even though she was looking for a partner, she felt that neediness can be very hard on a primary relationship. She doubts that her friends would have been as forthcoming if she had been living with someone.

Watters believes that these large friendship networks formed by single people in their twenties and thirties will not last, as most singles marry or couple by their late thirties. Sasha Cagen, a writer in her late twenties who stresses the positive aspects of single life, also sees friendship as a phenomenon that will be subordinated to "marriages, parenthood, career and myriad responsibilities" as people age.[16] "It becomes weird in middle life (and to a lesser extent in old age) to put friendship at the center of your life," Cagen concludes.[17] My research suggests that both Watters and Cagen are too shortsighted.

The friendship networks that young people build in their twenties and thirties may not last a lifetime, but even so, they provide a model and help hone the skills needed to re-create friendship networks in one's forties, fifties, and beyond. A young person who has enjoyed a rich communal life will be less afraid to remain single, and if she does couple, she will be less likely to retreat to an isolated nuclear family and cut off her single friends.

Friendship Networks Are Not Families

In Diane's and Wendy's caregiving networks, a clear distinction was made between friends and family. In both, friendships sustained the caretaking, while family members were included when appropriate. Likewise, Ethan Watters, in calling his network a tribe, avoided family terminology. Yet in written accounts of similar phenomena, I found many examples of family terminology used in the context of friendship networks.[18]

The word *family* has more cultural value than *friend*. Social psychologist Lillian Rubin notes that *friend* is "used to refer to a wide range of relationships with varying degrees of closeness and distance"; by contrast, we have a "rich set of descriptive terms for family relations—*mother, father, aunt, uncle and cousin.*"[19] In interviewing people about friendship, Rubin found that over and over again people said that their close friends were like family. "The idea of kin is so deeply and powerfully rooted within us," Rubin observed, "that it is the most common metaphor for describing closeness."[20] Because friendship has no explicit obligations of care or firm expectations of permanence in our culture, using family terminology seems to give friendship networks more legitimacy.

Using family terms for nonkin relationships, however, reinforces the invisibility of care provided by friendship networks and contributes to the insecurity that those with weak family ties feel. We obscure the manner in which a network of friends can provide care without taxing individual friends or family members. In addition, as political theorist Martha Ackelsberg argues, "using the language of kinship to describe powerful . . . non kin bonds . . . obscures the social inequalities that are often perpetuated through families."[21] We often forget the harm done in numerous cases—husbands' and fathers' domination, parents' abuse, and so on.

The strength of friendship networks—and their ability to promote community—rests on their separateness from family and cohabitation. In this regard, friendship networks are very different from the communal households formed in the 1960s and 1970s. If Ethan Watters had lived in San Francisco in that era, he would have joined a communal household and not formed a tribe. Although those who joined communes were motivated both by a desire for community and by the search for an alternative to the nuclear family, the latter reason prevailed.[22] But if Watters had joined such a commune, it would have been, in all probability, much less stable than his looser network of friends. The communal households of that period, whether urban or rural, large or small, were formed primarily by white middle-class youth who grew up in intact nuclear families, and most lasted no longer than two or three years.[23] Those who were the first to leave communes, according to sociologist Benjamin Zablocki, were looking for an alternative family, compared with the more limited and pragmatic views of those who stayed longer.[24] In rejecting the nuclear family in favor of a vague communal alternative, these participants in communal households did not consider balancing individual autonomy—a strong American value—with their need to be part of a larger community.

The reason that my own communal household lasted for eight years can be attributed to the fact that it was small (three people), that we were older when we formed it (in our late thirties), and that we maintained separate living spaces, permitting some autonomy. Like most of my contemporaries, however, I was looking primarily for an alternative family—a search that left me deeply disillusioned when the household disintegrated. Unlike larger communes, which often weakened their ties to friends outside them,[25] my very small communal household facilitated and strengthened friendships and became the center of our community. But the breakup of this household threatened the community and made its dissolution more painful.

I and many others have found a more stable basis of community in looser friendship networks and a source of security that supplements but is distinct from our family life.[26] My desire to clarify the distinction between friendship networks and family, however, may apply only to mainstream U.S. and European culture.[27]

The Wider Significance of Friendship Networks for Caregiving

Although friendship networks are not substitutes for family, they may be increasingly necessary to sustain not just single life but also family life. "A growing body of research demonstrates that the crucial difference between functional and dysfunctional families," argues historian Stephanie Coontz, "lies not in the form of the family but in the quality of support networks outside the family, including the presence of non-kin in those networks."[28]

Because many of us no longer live close to our siblings, parents, or adult children, let alone extended family, friendship networks are important to married couples (or those in long-term cohabitations) too.[29] Catastrophic illness in even the most stable marriage and nuclear family can quickly lead to an experience resembling that of a single person. When her husband was diagnosed with terminal brain cancer, a fifty-two-year-old friend in a long-term marriage said to me: "I almost instantaneously became single, but with the burden of total responsibility for the care of a dying adult—a process that lasted two years. If I had to rely only on my nuclear family—two children in their early twenties—or even on my small extended family, it would have been hell." She was fortunate to have a network of close friends and colleagues who helped care for her husband and provided the emotional support and practical help that she needed. Another married friend with a strong friendship network was surprised at how helpful (and necessary) friends were when she was injured in a serious automobile accident. These personal examples are reinforced by quantitative studies demonstrating that a significant portion of personal caregiving in the United States today occurs outside the nuclear family.[30]

These studies document the unprecedented mobilization of networks of people not related by traditional family ties to care for gay men with HIV/AIDS. Within the contemporary gay community, care is provided primarily by those not traditionally seen as caregivers; young men between the ages of twenty and fifty give care to peers who are not related by blood or legal marriage. Using large samples, these studies find that friends provide about as much care as live-in lovers and far more than family members. Networks of gay men who provide care for lovers and friends believe that a similar network will care for them if they become ill.[31] The authors of one study concluded: "Researchers and policy makers have begun to recognize the valuable contributions of this nonprofessional, nonpaid national health resource."[32]

Researchers who have reviewed the literature on older adults find that friendships are more important than family relations for morale and well-being in old age. A network containing a number of friends is especially important for well-being among the elderly.[33] Thus, the care provided by friendship networks bridges the private world of the family, the public world of the market (care we pay for), and the state (Medicare, Medicaid, welfare, and disability support). Care provided by a network of friends is more public than family care but more personal than paid or state-provided care. Informal friendship networks can provide the personal and empathic touch too often missing from state and market care and can furnish shared personal care beyond that of a small family group. But care through friendship networks does not obviate the need for market- and state-supported caregiving.

Not everyone has the ideal friendship networks depicted here. Making and keeping friends and building friendship networks require skill and attention.[34] Today, if we figure out how to create such networks, we do it in a hit-and-miss fashion. Although we have huge numbers of books, therapists, workshops, and so on, on how to find romantic partners and improve family relationships, few books and, to my knowledge, no therapists or workshops specialize in how to find and improve friendships.[35]

Even if we have strong friendship networks, they cannot provide effective care in every instance and cannot compensate for the social and economic inequalities in American society.[36] Nor are friendship networks reliable sources of long-term care for the disabled or very elderly, who cannot meet the ideals of equality and reciprocity that we hold.

Changes in Public Policy to Support Caregiving through Friendship Networks

At the same time that we fight for better state-funded caregiving and for market-based care that is both high quality and affordable to all, we must advocate a change in public policy that currently sees all private care as based only in the nuclear family. The significant amount of care now provided by friendship networks (which often include extended family members) is unsupported by public policy. Hospitals, for instance, often admit only immediate family members (which in progressive institutions now include domestic partners) to intensive care units and the rooms of those who are seriously ill or dying. Caretakers who do not live in the patient's household are excluded.

Workplace bereavement policies do not include paid time off to attend the funeral of a friend. Even the most progressive family leave policies provide time off only for the care of family members, whether defined broadly or narrowly.[37] Time off to care for friends is available only very rarely and then indirectly. Some living wage ordinances at the municipal level include provisions for paid and unpaid days off to be used for "sick leave, vacation or personal necessity."[38] However, caring for a friend would cut into one's own vacation time or sick leave. A few union contracts and a small number of large companies now include provisions for paid or unpaid time off that can be used for any reason.[39] Such plans are a step forward but grant no legitimacy to friendship networks as a source of care.

Rather than taking an individualistic perspective that encourages people to be more responsible for their own care, we can propose policies that recognize and promote new communities of care—care provided beyond the parent-child bond by networks of friends and extended family. Policies that allow employees to take time off to care for *any* child and *any* other adult, not just for themselves or close family members, foster such an alteration in values, as do policies that encourage employees to donate paid time off or sick leave to their fellow workers or colleagues in need.[40] Public policies that help build networks of care will improve the life of all adults, whether single or coupled, while also assisting in the reinvigoration of community life.

Challenging the Soul–Mate Ideal

> If we could discover a word that meant "adventure" and
> did not mean "romance," we ... would be able to free
> ourselves from the compulsion always to connect yearning
> and sex. If ... a woman finds herself longing for something
> new, something as yet not found, must that something
> always be sex or till–death–do–us–part romance?
> CAROLYN HEILBRUN, *The Last Gift of Time*

My contention that a life focused on the search for an idealized partner, a soul mate, is not the route to happiness could be labeled anti-
romantic. I reject that label. Rather, I argue that coupling with a soul
mate has many negative consequences and that romance can be
redefined.

The internal, interpersonal focus of the soul-mate couple incorporates and reinforces a higher degree of individualism than the
friendship networks of single women.[1] Moreover, the emphasis on
intense communication with a soul mate reinforces class and ethnic/
racial separation, for we are more likely to be able to share deep communication with someone with whom we have a lot in common,
such as our level of education and the way we spend leisure time.[2]
I agree with Wendy Langford's argument that this romantic ideal
obscures the continuing inequality in the power dynamics between
men and women.[3] In addition, I concur with sociologist Eva Illouz's
thesis that romance has been incorporated into the capitalist market
and that love has been infused with consumerism—for example,
traveling to romantic getaways so that soul mates can commune with
each other in a beautiful place.[4] Some of the single women portrayed
in this book have been able to combat the powerful cultural messages
connecting travel to the romantic couple by taking wonderful trips

with friends, by themselves, or with a group. But agreeing with all these arguments against the soul-mate ideal, and having positive experiences as single women, does not mean that we can easily relinquish the idea that finding a permanent soul mate will increase our happiness.

Indeed, many of the new single women I portray, while crafting satisfying intimate and sexual/sensual lives, have not completely relinquished the hope that they might find an enduring romantic partnership. They do not focus on the search for one, and they are open to unconventional alternatives that do not necessarily involve cohabitation or marriage, but they have not completely discarded this ideal, which has become deeply embedded in our psyches. The subtle allure and tenacious hold of the ideal of a romantic couple are seen in a personal example narrated by Jane Ganahl, a journalist for the *San Francisco Chronicle* and a divorced single mother who writes a weekly column on single life. Ganahl recounts going to a college reunion in her fifties and reconnecting with her sophomore roommate, Melissa, who has been married for twenty-three years. Melissa said that Ganahl seemed so happy now. Ganahl responded: " 'Do I? I guess it's because single life really agrees with me at last. It took a long time before I thought of it as a privilege, not a prison.' " But Melissa reminded Ganahl that even in college " 'It's what you always said you wanted. You said monogamy would never work for you and you always wanted to be single.' " Ganahl was astonished to hear that she had said that.[5] Like the women in this book, Ganahl saw the acceptance of her single life as a struggle to free herself from the cultural conditioning that she needed to be coupled to be happy.

The New Single Woman was criticized for challenging the coupled ideal even before its publication. A senior editor for a large publisher, after characterizing my "analysis of the emergence of this new breed of more self-assured, generally satisfied single women" as "both impressive and heartening," rejected my book proposal because it would not reach a large enough market. In her assessment, "the readership for books on relationships for women is powerfully dominated by those promising to help single women—or unhappy married women

—find satisfying relationships." She continued, "The message that they may well not need to do so and will still be able to create a happy, fulfilling life seems to be one that cuts too deeply against the grain."

Probably the idea presented here that is most "against the grain" is the possibility of separating intimate relationships from sexual ones and sometimes severing both from family ties. I argue for many types of intimacy and love and different ways of expressing sexuality.[6] "There is sexual intimacy and there is emotional intimacy, and the two may or may not go together," writes the psychiatrist Ethel Person. "There is the intimacy of kin, of lovers, of friends and the intimacy of those who work together closely."[7] I do not envision that many single women today will take Delia and Angie's relationship as a model and live together as intimate friends but nonromantic significant others and at the same time have a sexual partner with whom they do not cohabit or share family ties. Their life, however, is just a step beyond the more common occurrence of divorced and ever-single women who live with their children, confide in their friends, and have a noncohabiting lover. It is also only one step away from those married women who stay with their husbands for a shared family life while having their most intimate bonds with friends and seeking sexual satisfaction outside their marriage.

Nor do I think many women will be able to emulate Myra Detweiler's ability to find sexual satisfaction with one man and intimacy with another while maintaining a family tie with a third. But many of us (whether single, coupled, or in between) must admit that our intimate sharing, our sexual expression, and our family ties don't always fit neatly together. More single women can envision a life (and some are already leading it) where they maintain a committed sexual-intimate tie without cohabitation or marriage or where they engage in sensuous celibacy. We all must resist cultural commentators who tell us that our relationships are superficial, immature, unhealthy, pathetic, and bad, that only deep intimacy with a soul mate is *real* love, the only way to bring spirituality into our love life.

New single women are not isolated individuals but are enmeshed in networks of friends and extended family, networks that provide both intimacy and support. The autonomy these single women value is sustained by a web of relationships. Their friendship networks incorporate coupled and married women and provide them with security in case of divorce, the death of a partner, or severe illness. Through such networks, both single and coupled women gain alternative sources of secure intimacy. Thus, new single women support, rather than threaten, marriage, coupled life, and community.

I do not see middle-class single women as *victims* of capitalism, patriarchy, individualism, consumerism, the disintegration of the family, or a culture of divorce, although all these forces, I'm sure, play a role in everyone's life. One might see the increase in the numbers of single women as being related to the "stalled revolution"[8] between women and men, but this would not explain single lesbians. Rather, I see feminism as a positive influence, opening the benefits of American individualism to women, but in a way that promotes both women's autonomy and new forms of connection. The ties provided by networks of friends and extended family may be "looser"[9] than those of the traditional couple or the nuclear family, but they offer both more support to communities and individual variations in lifestyles.

All the women in my study made a series of individual choices that led them to a single life. Although their alternatives were sometimes painful and always limited by social forces beyond their control, they were glad to have choices, and, except in a few cases, they do not regret them. New economic opportunities for women since 1970 and cultural changes, especially those inspired by feminism, made these choices possible, even though neither provided a cultural map on how to live as a single woman. On a psychological level, single women had the strength to forge new paths, some because of the support of their cohesive families of origin, and others because of the character traits they gained from a struggle with poverty or from surviving disruptive family forces when they were young.

I reject not coupled life but the idea that it is the only and best way to live. I accept that some single women would prefer the daily closeness, touching, and routine of living as a couple. But I want it to be recognized that not everyone wants to be coupled, especially in traditional ways. Nor do I deny the attraction of romance, but let's expand our conceptions of it. I like what Barbara Lazear Ascher writes in *Isn't It Romantic? Finding the Magic in Everyday Life.* "Romance is structured yearning," she writes. "In the romantic moment, we gather and focus that yearning in order to connect with something outside ourselves, believing against all odds that such connection is possible." But Ascher has an expansive notion of romantic connection. "The romantic quest can be embarked upon solo," she writes. "It doesn't call for a significant other, great beauty, pulsating sexuality, a new dress, or complex planning. Its only requirements are the courage of an available heart and freedom of imagination."[10] Ascher gives a wonderful description of the romance involved in bird-watching. In this, and in other passions—like Nancy Dean's for flamenco dancing—we see "something eternal in our desire for connection and exaltation, for a sense of wonder and our compulsion to give it expression."[11]

The separation of intimacy, sexuality, and family ties that I found in the lives of mature single women has also been noticed among teenagers and young adults today. Often, they do not limit their sexual experimentation and search for intimacy to a steady girlfriend or boyfriend. They don't date. Rather, they socialize (hang out) with a network of friends, share intimately with a few friends (often both male and female), and have sexual encounters (sometimes with friends) that are brief, safe, and do not involve romantic expectations or commitment. Such casual sexual encounters are called hookups and may involve anything from kissing to oral sex to intercourse.

In a national survey of college women, 91 percent of them said that hookups happen very often or fairly often at their colleges.[12] Eighty-one percent of these college women said that "men at my college generally treat women with respect," 88 percent were "happy with the social scene" at their college, and 96 percent "have a clear sense of what I should do and should not do in my romantic/sexual interactions."[13] These young women are similar to those who tell researchers that they are looking for a soul mate. This disjunction between their ideals and their actions supports my thesis that the search for a soul mate rationalizes single life for women in their twenties and thirties, but in a way that does not give cultural sanction to long-term singleness.

Despite the college women's satisfaction with these new social practices and their feelings that they were not ready to make a serious commitment given the years of education and career preparation that lay ahead of them, the sociologists who conducted the study were disturbed because, in their view, these new college norms "undermined the likelihood of achieving the goal of a successful future marriage." I, however, see their behavior as a rehearsal for more diverse types of intimate and sexual relationships. Such experiences, I believe, will make young people more flexible and better able to find happiness in a number of possible settings, including both coupled and single life and in-between modes. What they need, however, is cultural support for this complexity, not the simplistic and misleading notion that they should hold out until they find a soul mate.

Even more controversial is the decrease among teenagers in coupled dating, which has been replaced by socializing with friends while having casual sexual hookups with friends and others. A May 30, 2004 article by journalist Benoit Denizet-Lewis, titled "Friends, Friends with Benefits and the Benefits of the Local Mall" and published in the *New York Times Magazine,* was advertised on the cover with the phrase "Whatever Happened to Teen Romance?" The author emphasized the difference between the opinions of almost all the adult experts cited in the article, who judged hooking up as harmful to teenagers, especially to girls, and the views of the one hundred teenagers he interviewed. Although admitting that exploitative sex exists among the young, as it does among their elders, Denizet-Lewis defended the students' views:

> For all the efforts to make teenagers aware of the dangers of hookups, many of the high school students I spoke to shrugged off the idea that hooking up is ultimately a bad thing. As they see it, if

they're not going to marry for another ten years, why not focus on other things (friendships, schoolwork, sports) in high school? And if they're not hurting anyone and not getting anyone pregnant, what is the harm in a little casual fun? The truth is, teenagers may spend less of their time hooking up than adults think they do —for many of them, friendships have become the most important part of their social lives.

Yet in giving voice to all the experts who bemoan the decline of more serious relationships, who see these teenagers as shallow, and girls especially as denying their real desires for deep intimacy, Denizet-Lewis leaves his article open to varying interpretations.

On June 13, 2004, the *New York Times Magazine* published a series of letters in response to the article. Several writers found the article sad: "The individuals portrayed were very lonely, emotionally disconnected and, underneath it all, depressed." Another woman had a positive reaction: "These youngsters are smarter than we were. Most of them instinctively recognize that 'dating' and 'going steady' in high school are hypocritical code words for sexual experimentation. Does anyone remember my generation's version of romance— intertwined bodies in parked cars obscured by steamy windows?" The most interesting letter, however, expressed the most ambivalence:

> Your article made teenagers seem, well, almost wise. Several things were particularly memorable. First, the use of condoms as the rule seemed exceptionally responsible. Second, most rational adults would agree that high school is no place for romantic relationships.... Third, the tremendous benefits of having close friends of the opposite sex ... will pay compound interest over a lifetime. Fourth, the direct parallel between not "dating" someone from your school and not dating someone from the office was impressive. Fifth, the teenagers are right to think that there is no need to get all "couply" in high school or even college. There is time for that. Still, there are those who, in the face of tremendous peer pressure, heed some inner voice to submit to the highs and lows of

a committed relationship.... They do not seem to be shunned by their peers, but almost admired, though perhaps from a distance, as offering an alternative model.

So this male letter writer, while admiring the ability of youth to separate their sexuality from a coupled relationship, and to partake of the intimacy offered by friendship, in the end comes back to the superiority of a committed relationship. I would not be surprised to find him advocating a soul-mate ideal.

Our culture today presents contrasting and conflicting views to youth and to all of us—upholding the romantic couple, now raised to the ideal of finding a soul mate, on the one hand, and giving some recognition to the diversity of ways to find love, sexual pleasure, and secure and familial ties, on the other. I hope, therefore, that the lives examined in this book will contribute to the cultural dialogue, one that broadens and enriches our options for ways to lead a satisfying life. No longer will the fear of being a single woman motivate women's decisions.[14] Life outside a couple, life without a soul mate, whatever its problems and limitations, will be one that can be lived with love, dignity, respect, purpose, spirituality, and joy.

ACKNOWLEDGMENTS

My greatest debt is to the women who agreed to participate in this study, talking to me two, three, sometimes four times over the course of eight, nine, ten years, opening up intimate, sometimes painful, details of their lives. I thank you all. The analysis is mine, however, one with which you may or may not agree.

This book probably would not have been written, certainly not in this form, were it not for the constant support of my writing group for more than five years. I thank especially Gayle Greene and Ilene Philipson, who participated from the beginning to the end, but also Barbara Epstein, Sherry Keith, and Mardi Louisell. These women read draft after draft of book proposals and chapters, urging me to improve my writing and sharpen the analysis. Their emotional and sometimes heated debates over the content reinforced for me their avowals that this was an important topic. I thank other friends who read part of the manuscript at various points and gave me helpful feedback: Wini Breines, Ellen DuBois, Judy Grether, Naomi Katz, Kathleen Lilley, Sasha Lilley, Glenna Matthews, Carolyn Saarni, and Alice Wexler. In the late 1980s and early 1990s, when I started thinking about singleness, Myrna Goodman and Kris Montgomery—then students and now colleagues—as research assistants, helped me find literature and focus the questions. In addition, I benefited from the teaching and suggestions of Lindsey Crittenden, an instructor of the excellent extension course on creative nonfiction writing at the University of California, Berkeley, and from the comments of students in her spring 2004 class. The enthusiasm, sharp insights, and efficiency of Gayatri Patnaik, my editor at Beacon Press, pushed this manuscript into print.

For their continued interest in and support of my work, I thank the following colleagues and friends: Marty Bennett, Ann Berlak, Deanne Burke, Michael Burowoy, Christine Cobough, Myrna Cozen, Alice Echols, Victor Garlin, Barbara Heyns, Elsa Johnson, Claire Kahane, Elaine Leeder, Claudia Robbins, Cindy Stearns, and Devra Weber.

I wish to acknowledge the institutional support I received for my study of single women. In 1994 the National Endowment for the Humanities awarded me a summer research grant that funded my initial interviews. Subsequent research grants from Sonoma State University—a faculty incentive award in 1994–95 and a research mini-grant in 1996–97—helped pay for transcriptions and additional research assistance. In 1997 I received a Radcliffe Research Support Grant to use a collection at the Murray Research Center at Harvard University. Although I decided to omit the historical component that was based on this research, it helped shape my perspective. My participation as a visiting scholar at the Center for Working Families at the University of California, Berkeley, between 2000 and 2002 encouraged me to restart my study. The collegial environment created by the center's directors Arlie Hochschild and Barrie Thorne, their interest in my work, and positive responses from others to a presentation I gave there increased my commitment to the project. "Friendship Networks and Care," the working paper I wrote for the center in the fall of 2001, became the basis for chapter 9 of this book. In a workshop for the center on how social scientists can improve their writing, Deirdre English inspired me to work on my prose. Since 2003, I have benefited from being a visiting scholar at the Institute for the Study of Social Change at the University of California, Berkeley, and from the support of its director, Rachel Moran. I thank, too, Jean Wasp, the media relations coordinator at Sonoma State University for her interest in and promotion of my work.

In 2000 I discovered and then became a supporter of the American Association of Single People (AASP). Its dedicated director, Tom Coleman, helped me find statistical data and assured me that there was an audience out there. Through AASP, I met Bella DePaulo. An e-mail correspondence with her, in which we shared ideas on writing and teaching about singleness, helped sustain me.

Finally, I thank my son, Marc. His arrival in 1981 began my transition to the satisfying life of a new single woman. His move out of our house in 2000—even though he still remained very much a part of my life—gave me the space—psychological and physical—to write this book.

INTRODUCTION

1. Subjects' names and some identifying characteristics have been changed, but all quoted words are their own.

2. Langford 1999, 28. For a historical perspective, see Gillis 1996, chapter 7.

3. The poll results are reported in "The State of Our Unions, 2001: Who Wants to Marry a Soul Mate?" by the National Marriage Project at Rutgers University, 2001, available on their Web site at http://marriage.rutgers.edu.

4. Roeper 2004.

5. For the original interviews, I defined *single* as anyone who was not married, including those in long-term cohabitations. Later I decided to study only those single women who were not currently cohabiting, although many had in the past. Fourteen women from the original study are not included here because they had married or were in long-term cohabitations, and there are five I was unable to locate.

6. Private communication by Thomas Coleman, director of the American Association for Single People, based on calculations from the 2000 U.S. Census.

7. The median age for first marriages is now higher than at any other time in the twentieth century (twenty-five for women and twenty-seven for men).

8. All data are from the 2000 census.

9. These statistics are cited in Rumblow 2002.

10. These data were compiled from the Population Reference Bureau and the Social Science Data Network by the American Association of Single People. See "Marital Sta-

tus and Earnings for Women," *Unmarried America* 1, no. 4 (Summer 2000): 7. Available online at www.unmarriedAmerica.com.

11. These figures are from Vicky Lovell, "40-Hour Work Proposal Significantly Raises Mother's Employment Standard," Publication no. D457, Institute for Women's Policy Research, June 2003, 7. See http://www.iwpr.org.

12. Koller 1990, 185.

13. The term *competent loner* and the focus on personality traits are by social scientist E. Mavis Hetherington and John Kelly (2002, chapter 5). Barbara Defoe Whitehead also assumes that a few women with distinctive personalities choose to be long-term singles. See *Why There Are No Good Men Left* (2003, 5). My perspective on who becomes a single woman is very different. Carolyn Heilbrun makes a good distinction between being single and being solitary. She contrasts Gloria Steinem, who was still single at age sixty-five, to herself: "Steinem, who lives alone, is not a solitary. I, who do not live alone and have lived with three children and a husband, am" (Heilbrun 1997, 52).

14. A number of quantitative studies of happiness (defined as having positive emotions and satisfaction with life) stress the importance of social relationships. Having friends is one of the most important—in some studies the most significant—sources of happiness. See Argyle 2001.

15. Orenstein 2000.

16. Ann Douglas, a Columbia University historian, was quoted by Phoebe Hoban, "Single Girls: Sex but Still No Respect," *New York Times,* October 12, 2002.

17. Orenstein 2000, 241.

18. Data from Eurostat, the European Union's statistical agency, show that in 2000 the marriage rate in the United States was 8.4 marriages per thousand and in the EU 5.1 overall. The highest rate in Europe (Portugal at 6.9) is lower than in the United States. But the U.S. divorce rate is also higher. In the United States there are 4.2 divorces per thousand, compared with 1.8 in the EU. Again, the highest rate in Europe (Switzerland at 2.9) is much lower than in the United States. These data were distributed by the Alternatives to Marriage Project, http://www.unmarried.org.

CHAPTER 1: "We Don't Have to Settle": Soul Mates and Singleness

1. The students had read several chapters in Reilly's *Women Living Single* (1996).

2. "The State of Our Unions, 2001," from the National Marriage Project at Rutgers University, available on their Web site at http://marriage.rutgers.edu.

3. Sociologist Eva Illouz postulates that sexuality has been subordinated in the culture of love throughout the twentieth century. See Illouz 1997, 5.

4. hooks 2000, 188.

5. Ibid., 175.

6. Schwartz 2001, 9.

7. Moore 1994, xvii.

8. Johnson 1999, 64.

9. Katz 2001, 59.

10. *New York Times Book Review,* July 28, 2002, p. 5.

11. Wallace 1998, 426.

12. Sociologist Norval Glenn states: "College educated women traditionally married about a year and a half later than other women, and that difference may have increased in recent years." "Hooking Up, Hanging Out, and Hoping for Mr. Right: College Women on Dating and Mating Today," a report for the Institute for American Values, 2001. For the report go to www.americanvalues.org.

13. Cagen's article was in the first issue of a new, small magazine that she started called *To Do List.* It was reprinted in the *Utne Reader* and discussed in the *San Francisco Chronicle* and other newspapers, and an Internet discussion group was set up in the Utne Reader Café.

14. Cagen expands these ideas in her book *Quirkyalone* (2004).

15. Orenstein 2000, 31.

16. Sociologist Neil Gross, in interviews with people in Los Angeles aged twenty-three to fifty-five, found similar ideals of deep intimacy. He discussed his preliminary findings in a talk entitled "The Code of Deep Intimacy," given at the Sociology Department of the University of California, Berkeley, on April 8, 2004. His evaluation of this code is quite different from mine.

17. According to *Newsweek* (March 3, 2003, p. 48), 24 percent of black women, as compared with 17 percent of black men, have ascended to the professional-managerial class.

18. In the mid-nineteenth century, finding a soul mate to marry became a popular cultural ideal among the U.S. middle class at a time when marriage was under attack as oppressive to women and more women remained single. See Berend 2000, 947–48.

19. See Epstein 1988; Baxandall 1998.

20. For a discussion of Firestone's views on marriage and those of other radical feminists in New York City in the late 1960s, see Baxandall 1998, 208–24.

21. Firestone 1970.

22. This chapter, "Love," was in Firestone 1970, 18.

23. Ibid., 17.

24. It is interesting to note that Firestone may have drawn on her negative evaluation of single women in the first wave of feminism to critique single feminist women in the late 1960s. She writes of women radicals and reformers of the early twentieth century: "They rushed into the young settlement movement, many of them giving their lives without reward—only to become the rather grim, embittered, but devoted spinster social workers of the stereotype" (Firestone 1970, 19–20).

25. Ibid., 26.

26. *Combat in the Erogenous Zone* was originally published in 1972 by Alfred Knopf. All references here are to the 1991 reissue by Harper-Collins, 101.

27. Ibid., 224.

28. Ibid., 216.

29. Ibid., 209.

30. Ibid., 222.

31. Ibid., xxxiii.

32. Bakos 1985.

33. Lewis 1990, 181.

34. Lee Reilly makes this point in chapter 8 of *Women Living Single* (1996).

35. See Jamieson 1998 and Giddens 1992.

36. Kitzinger 1996, 295.

37. Langford 1999, 91.

38. Anthropologist Mary Catherine Bateson, in *Full Circles, Overlapping Lives* (2000), discusses the lack of intimacy in many contemporary marriages (chapter 4).

39. For example, see Heilbrun 1988, chapter 4; and Sidel 1990, chapter 6.

40. See Oliker 1989.

41. See Fehr 2004, 9–26.

42. Pappano 2001, 162.

43. Pogrebin 1987, 35.

44. Sheehy 2000, 96.

45. Dowrick 1991, 244–45.

CHAPTER 2: Sex and the Single Woman

1. The epigraph is from Laumann, Ellingson, Mahay, Paik, and Youm 2004, 358.

2. See Schwartz and Rutter 1998, 45.

3. Michael, Gagnon, Laumann, and Kolata 1994, 116.

4. A 2003 survey (commissioned by the American Association of Retired People [AARP]) of 3,501 singles aged forty to sixty-nine found that 60 percent of single women had not had sexual intercourse in the previous six months (compared with 45 percent of men). See www.aarpmagazine.org. A 2001 survey comparing the sexual experiences of noncohabiting French women and men found that single Americans are more often without a sex partner but also have more sex partners than their French counterparts. The survey found that 78 percent of American women over the age of fifty and not living in a couple had had no sexual partner within the last year, compared with 52 percent of French women. See Good 2001.

5. Michael, Gagnon, Laumann, and Kolata 1994, 102.

6. Ibid., 119.

7. For a psychoanalytic perspective on how love and sex are individualized, see Chodorow 1994, chapter 3.

8. Laumann, Ellingson, Mahay, Paik, and Youm 2004, 356.

9. See the 2003 reissue of the 1962 classic by Brown, 103.

10. For an early analysis of women's sexuality as central to the sexual revolution of the 1960s and 1970s, see Ehrenreich, Hess, and Jacobs 1986.

11. Allyn 2000, 269.

12. Ibid., 100–101.

13. See Radner 1999, 8.

14. Brown 1993.

15. In a study of one hundred couples, the sociologist Pepper Schwartz found that those who had the closest and deepest intimacy (soul mates) tended to have less sex. She explains, "This very closeness and intimate friendship created a relationship that took away one of the reasons for sex—and one of the ingredients of passionate sex: the desire to bridge the gap of intimacy between partners, the desire to reduce or extinguish distance and hierarchy. . . . Couples could solve these issues through conversation and negotiation" (Schwartz 2001, 8–9).

16. For a discussion of the complicated mix of biological, social, and cultural factors that affect heterosexual and lesbian women's sexual lives after menopause, see Witnerich 2003.

17. Cline 1993, 8.

18. Hall 1995, 15–27.

19. Williams 1999, 35.

20. This quote is from an interview with Tiefer by Moira Brennan (Brennan 1999, 64).

21. Zeidenstein 1999.

22. Deveny 2003; Flanagan 2003; Rothblum and Brehony 1993.

23. Tiefer 1995; Escoffier 2004; Weeks, Holland, and Waites 2003.

24. Baumeister, Catanese, and Vohs 2001, 269.

25. Ibid., 256.

26. Loulan 1993, 68.

27. Canadian author Marian Botsford Fraser and U.S. author Marcelle Clements found that most celibate single women conceive of themselves as being between relationships; they do not see celibacy as a positive choice. See Fraser 2001, 193; Clements 1998, 258–59.

28. Williams 1999, 25–27. See also Cline 1993, 21; Keller 1999; Greer 1992; Collette 1993, 59–64; and Abbott 1999, epilogue.

29. Loulan 1993, 64.

30. Psychotherapist Ethel S. Person affirms that women's sexual agency can increase their autonomy (2002, 134).

31. Cline 1993, 91–103.

32. The deficit of male partners for older women is due to a higher mortality rate for men, higher remarriage rates among men, and the fact that men tend to marry younger women. See Mahay and Laumann 2004, 132.

33. Williams 1999, 21; Cline 1993, 14.

34. Michael, Gagnon, Laumann, and Kolata 1994, 165. Another survey of adults over the age of forty-five, which was conducted by the AARP, found that 77 percent of women without partners said that they did not masturbate (Jacoby 1999, 44). Ethel Spector Person, in another study on sexual fantasy, found that young adults with the most sexual experience also made the most use of sexual fantasy. She concluded: "erotic fantasies cannot be viewed as compensation for lack of sexual experience" (Person 1999, 255).

35. Williams 1999, 21. But sexually active women like Myra and Dorothy can foster self-development through their sexual agency. Why a sexual relationship undermines

self-realization for some women and fosters these personal traits in others is a question for further psychological exploration.

36. Ibid., 114.

37. Cline 1993, 118–21. Social theorist Anthony Giddens critiques modern society, which has confined passion to the sexual. See Giddens 1992, 201.

38. This is a pseudonym bearing no relation to any organization with the same name.

39. Claus 1990, 95.

40. Michael, Gagnon, Laumann, and Kolata 1994, 87.

41. Jacoby 1999, 43.

CHAPTER 3: Crafting Singular Lives

1. Such multiple, overlapping, and sometimes contradictory norms are not unusual, according to sociologists who study culture. See Swidler 2001.

2. These are fictitious names, and aspects of their identities have been changed.

3. Historian Ruth Rosen makes this point in *The World Split Open* (2000), part 1. For an example of a black woman from a working-class background who had the same reaction—rejecting her mother's life as a subordinate homemaker—see hooks 2002, chapter 2.

4. In a study of 125 childless single women, Yvonne Vissing found that those women who purposefully chose to be child free were "more confident of themselves and satisfied with their life outcomes" (Vissing 2002, 28).

5. Wilson 2001.

6. Entry of September 3, 1996, in "Single and Loving It," at Utne Reader Café, http://cafe.utne.com.

7. Architectural historian Alice T. Friedman found that a few well-off single women worked with some of the most famous architects to construct "an unexpectedly large number of the most significant and original houses built in Europe and America in the twentieth century" (Alice T. Friedman 1998, 15). She explains that these single women wanted to redefine domesticity: "As women heads of households—whether single, widowed, divorced, lesbian or in other sorts of unconventional living arrangements—they redefined domestic space to create room for a range of relationships that crossed boundaries prescribed by age, class, gender and sexuality. By choosing to build for themselves and their households, they made a radical statement about the value of their lives as independent women" (17).

8. Sarton 1973, 130.

9. Wellman 1999, 84. Wellman found that individuals in Canada and the United States,

on average, have 3 to 6 intimate ties, 5 to 15 significant but less strong ties, and approximately 1,000 acquaintances. Ibid., 85.

10. Putnam 2000, 278.

11. This is a pseudonym.

CHAPTER 4: "Nobody's Wife, Nobody's Mother, Nobody's Lover": Obstacles to Building a Satisfying Single Life

1. O'Faolain 1996. The memoir was published in the United States in 1998 as *Are You Somebody: The Accidental Memoir of a Dublin Woman.*

2. O'Faolain 1996, 105.

3. Ibid., 85–86.

4. Ibid., 128–29.

5. Ibid., 161.

6. Ibid., 192–93.

7. Reilly 1996, 149.

8. Lucas, Clark, Georgellis, and Diener 2003, 537.

9. There is evidence supporting the idea that forgiveness would help Beth be more content and make new friends. For a summary of this research on forgiveness, see Easterbrook 2003, chapter 8.

10. O'Faolain 1998, 178, 180.

11. Ibid., 188.

12. Ibid., 190.

13. Ibid., 206.

14. Ibid., 214.

15. O'Faolain 1996, 163.

16. Ibid., 172.

17. Ibid., 197.

18. Ibid., 163.

19. O'Faolain 2003.

20. Ibid., 263.

21. Ibid., 149.

22. Ibid., 160.

23. Ibid., 147, 149.

24. Ibid., 14.

25. Ibid., 152.

26. Ibid., 170.

27. Ibid., 247.

28. Ibid., 232.

29. Ibid., 233.

30. Ibid., 236, 235.

31. Ibid., 192, 61.

CHAPTER 5: Becoming a Whole Person: Autonomy and Long-Term Singleness

1. Franzen 2001, 378.

2. For more than twenty years, feminist philosophers and psychologists have debated whether autonomy is an appropriate goal for women. Starting in the 1980s, a group of feminist psychologists associated with the Stone Center at Wellesley College, following the leadership of Jean Baker Miller, argued that a separate (autonomous) self was a male concept, resulting from an individualistic society. The Stone Center psychologists believed that autonomy should not be seen as a hallmark of healthy human development. They argued that rather than viewing maturity as the evolution of a separate, individuated, well-bounded self, growth should be measured by the ability to create and sustain relationships. They developed the concept of self-in-relation and stressed the importance of empathy. These psychologists elevated an attribute that women develop by caring for others to a desirable trait that everyone in society should aspire to cultivate. For more detail on the views of these psychologists, see Jordan et al. 1991 and 1997.

During the 1990s, feminist philosophers resuscitated the concept of autonomy by incorporating some of the Stone Center critique. They developed an ideal of relational autonomy, which examined how individuals can acquire the skills of self-definition and self-direction only through critical reflection upon, and making choices about, the social relationships in which they are embedded. See Meyers 1989; Mackenzie and Stoljar 2000; Marilyn Friedman 2003.

3. Psychologist Anthony Storr (1988) makes the point that intimate interpersonal relationships are not the only ingredient in human happiness and self-fulfillment.

4. A woman who prefers to be alone most of the time does better when coupled with

someone of a similar temperament, for in all probability she does not have the skills to create the complex social relations that sustain single life. See Rufus 2003.

5. For example, sociologist Beatriz Pesquera found that blue-collar, clerical, and professional Chicana workers gained a lot of self-confidence from their work, and the professionals also gained a strong sense of identity (Pesquera 2000).

6. Marilyn Friedman 1993, 121.

7. Diana Tietjens Meyers articulates seven types of skills that facilitate the process of self-determination for women. They are similar to those I have identified as necessary to building a viable single life. See Meyers 1989, 741–42.

8. Although I did not include single women in their twenties in my study, considerable evidence points to the importance of economic self-sufficiency before marriage as a new value for women as well as men, driving up the average age of marriage to almost twenty-five for women and twenty-seven for men (see National Marriage Project 2001). Although single women in their twenties now gain a stronger sense of self through work, they often are conflicted about how to combine autonomy and intimacy.

9. In general, I found more similarities than differences between never-married women and those who remained single after a divorce.

10. The best scholars who studied divorce found that women, more than men, often established a new sense of self after divorce and experienced life-transforming personal growth. See Hetherington and Kelly 2002, 5; Wallerstein and Blakeslee 1989, 279–80. In addition, see Apter 1995, 178.

11. A study in the 1990s of Mexican American high school students from poor families found that the parents valued education and tried to help their children achieve in school. Romo and Falbo 1996. Another study of Chicanas who earned a PhD found that their mothers were the major influence on their educational achievement. See Gandara 1996. Others have noted that traditions of female strength and resistance in Chicana families and communities were a major influence on the development of Chicana feminism. See Arredondo, Hurtado, Klahn, Najera-Ramierez, and Zavella 2003, 66.

12. Gloria Cuadraz, another Chicana in a California PhD program about ten years before Elena, has written about similar feelings. Of her experience in the early 1980s in the graduate program of the Sociology Department at the University of California, Berkeley, she wrote: "In graduate school I was not asked who I was or where I came from, but what school did I graduate from, and who had I worked for. In other words, 'who do you know; what are your professional connections.'" She couldn't share with her white, middle-class peers that she felt a responsibility to others besides herself, to her family and community (Cuadraz and Pierce 1994, 21–44).

13. A study of black professional women found that some of them also experienced conflict between their personal identity and what they did in a business world where work defines who you are. See Chambers 2003, 29.

14. Marilyn Friedman 1993, 202.

15. Ackelsberg 1983, 346.

16. Rubin 1985, 40–41.

17. Ibid., 56.

18. Sociologist Beatriz Pesquera found that professional Chicanas gained more of their identity from work than clerical or blue-collar-worker Chicanas, but that they also experienced the most anxiety and felt the most conflict between their work and personal lives (Pesquera 2000, 174).

19. Other Chicanas have written about their difficult experiences in competitive academic settings. See the personal accounts in Latina Feminist Group 2001.

20. Weiss (1973) sees isolation as only one source of loneliness.

21. Bernikow 1986, 10.

22. Ibid., 64.

23. Stephanie Dowrick, a therapist, in her book *Intimacy & Solitude,* distinguishes solitude from loneliness. A person enjoys solitude when she is comfortable with her own self and secure in her social connections. She holds on to these connections in her head, even when no one is there. She experiences solitude as a calm, restful, and relaxed state, where she can fulfill her own needs and have a respite from meeting the needs of others. In contrast, the lonely person is anxious and needy. She experiences herself as fragmented, incomplete, or invisible. She is not alone by choice and fears that she will always be alone. She feels she will be happy only if someone or something new comes into her life. She focuses on what she does not have, what is missing from her life. See Dowrick 1991, part 3.

24. Anthropologist Patricia Zavella, in studying the sexuality of Mexican American women born and raised in the United States and those who were born in Mexico and had spent at least part of their childhood there, discovered that both found it hard to talk about sex, perhaps because they "experienced childhood as a time when there was an overwhelming silence regarding sexuality" (Zavella 2003, 235).

25. Gloria Cuadraz, in Cuadraz and Pierce 1994, writes about how her working-class family, neighbors, and friends pressured her to say in graduate school when she was thinking of dropping out (34). Beatriz Pesquera (2000) found too that Chicana professionals felt a responsibility to be role models for their ethnic communities.

26. Adrienne Rich graduated from an all-girls high school in the late 1940s where many of the teachers were single. Rich writes: "They were vital individuals, defined not by their relationships but by their personalities, and although under the pressure of the culture we were all certain we wanted to get married, their lives did not appear empty or dreary to us. In a kind of cognitive dissonance, we knew they were 'old maids' and

therefore supposed to be bitter and lonely, yet we saw them vigorously involved with life" (Rich 1979, 238).

27. For a detailed description of how women lose their selves in marriage, see Heyn 1997.

28. Hewitt 1989, 202.

29. Bridges 2003, 167.

30. See Heyn 1997; Orenstein 2000, chapter 10; Reilly 1996, 10; and Griffiths 1995, 117.

31. Lessing 1994, 310.

32. Orenstein 2000, 28.

33. See Westkott 1986, chapter 5; and Eichenbaum and Orbach 1988, chapter 3.

34. Dowrick 1991, chapters 10 and 11.

35. Sarton 1973, 56.

36. Storr 1988, xii.

37. Ruddick 1977, 136.

38. MD and psychotherapist Ethel Person finds a "fundamental tension between intimacy and autonomy" (Person 2002, 116).

39. Ibid., 18, 19.

40. Literary critic and essayist Vivian Gornick analyzes the many contradictions between romantic love and self-knowledge. See especially her essay "Clover Adams," in Gornick 1997.

CHAPTER 6: "Will I End Up as a Bag Lady?" Childless Single Women

1. This observation was made by young women in their twenties who took my class on single women in 2002 and 2003.

2. These poll results are reported in National Marriage Project 2001.

3. See, for example, May 1995, 185; Gillespie 2003, 128.

4. Carolyn N. Morell, a married, childless woman, wrote *Unwomanly Conduct: The Challenges of Intentional Childlessness,* a 1994 study of only married, childless women. Laurie Lisle, a married, childless woman wrote *Without Child,* a 1996 book that focused mainly on married, childless women. Journalist Terri Casey, in her *Pride and Joy* (1998), included only six single women out of the twenty-five in her book, two of whom were widows in their seventies or eighties. British psychologist Jane Bartlett, in her 1995 book *Will You Be Mother,* wrote little about single, childless women. Yvonne Vissing, a

mother, interviewed 125 childless women but does not tell us how many are single and how many coupled. Although she includes some women who are single, most of her analysis pertains to coupled, childless women. See Vissing 2002.

5. Similarly, Carolyn Morell found that childless married women had few feelings of regret. See Morell 1994, 97.

6. A study of ninety single women between the ages of forty and fifty-five who were interviewed between 1990 and 1992 confirms what I found in my smaller study. Psychologists Carol Anderson and Susan Stewart found two types of childless single women —those who never really wanted to have children and those who, while they had envisioned becoming a mother, did not have trouble giving up this aspiration and turning their lives to other pursuits (Anderson and Stewart 1994, chapter 15).

7. Reilly 1996, 79.

8. Ibid., 78.

9. The census table is available at http://www.census.gov/population/wwwsocdemo/fertility.html.

10. May 1995, 12.

11. This divorced woman remarried during my study, so I did not include her here.

12. One of the most influential books was *Of Women Born* (Rich 1976). For a survey of feminist writing, see Snitow 1992.

13. Ireland 1993, 6.

14. Ibid., 132.

15. Gillespie 2003, 131.

16. Veronica Chambers, in a study of successful black women, noted how achievement at work was the most important element of these women's identity. "Like other American women, many of the 30-something and even 40-something women interviewed in this book are childless. Unlike the panicked portraits of professional women depicted in the media, the women I spoke to routinely expressed no sense of regret, no Lichtenstein-like cartoon horror of 'Damn, I forgot to have a baby.' For one, these women were all—in their own eyes and in the eyes of the people who surrounded them —successful.... There is still very much a feeling, in the community, that when a young black person succeeds, all ships rise" (Chambers 2003, 9).

17. In the late 1980s, a study of white professional, childless lesbians between the ages of thirty-six and forty-seven found that those "women who see having children as 'something that women do' have the most difficulty coming to terms with their decisions not to mother" (Lesser 1991, 89).

18. Megan 2000, 45.

19. Fisher 1992.

20. Psychologist Phyllis O. Ziman Tobin (with Barbara Aria) makes this point in her 1998 book *Motherhood Optional* (5).

21. Carolyn Morell found that the word *choice* was not an adequate description of how married women became childless. "Rather than a choice, or a decision, remaining childless was described as an ongoing practice and/or an outcome determined by a variety of personal and social circumstances" (Morell 1994, 49). Laurie Lisle too finds that many women drift into childlessness as a "result of many smaller decisions as well as chance, compulsions and circumstances (Lisle 1996, 57). Likewise, Yvonne Vissing writes that childlessness is "a product of accumulated events that interact over decades of life" (Vissing 2002, 129).

22. Vissing also makes this point (2002, 200). Morell notes too that childless women are often active in social movements that stress nurturing (for example, peace and environmental movements), and that without direct descendants they are more likely to give an inheritance to public causes rather than primarily to family members (Morell 1994, 82).

23. When I contacted Emily in 2004, she told me that her friends had decided to move, and she had bought the house she lived in with financial help from her parents. Emily still lives in the small unit, renting out the larger one in order to make the hefty mortgage payments, but she loves the security that home ownership provides her.

24. Gayle Greene, *Missing Persons,* unpublished memoir.

25. Klepfisz 2000, 19.

26. Ibid., 20.

27. Ibid., 21.

28. Casey 1998, 176.

29. Patenaude 1992, 38.

30. Schwartzberg, Berliner, and Jacob 1995, 120. Other research that finds similar results is cited by Morell (1994, 119); Lisle (1996, 237–41); Cain (2001, 141); and Lang (1991, chapter 15).

31. Morell 1994, 118.

32. Fisher 1992, 3.

CHAPTER 7: Without a Dad: Single Women as Mothers

1. Many studies find that mothers still spend much more time with their children than do fathers, even in intact families. A recent study found that mothers with six- to seven-year-old children spend twenty-two hours per week alone with their children, and fathers spend only two. For fifteen- to sixteen-year-olds, mothers spend twice as much time as fathers. See Golombok 2000, 16. See also Hochschild 1989 and 1997.

2. Sociologist Karen Hansen, in a study of white, dual-earner couples with children from a variety of class backgrounds, found that they all had networks that helped them parent in their "not-so-nuclear families" (Hansen, 2005).

3. Law scholar Martha Fineman makes this salient point (Fineman 1995, 147–48).

4. These statistics were collected by the Centers for Disease Control and Prevention and are available on-line at www.cdc.gov/nchs/fastats/unmarry.htm. In 2001, 28 percent of births to white, non-Hispanic women were out of wedlock, compared with 43 percent for Hispanic women and 68 percent for African American women.

5. Sugarman 2003, 17.

6. Centers for Disease Control and Prevention.

7. Dowd 1997, 5.

8. Sugarman 2003, 19.

9. Melissa Ludtke, who studied both upper-middle-class older single women who were mothers by choice and adolescent, poor single mothers, found this to be true of the former (Ludtke 1997, 240).

10. It is not clear whether teenagers raised by single mothers have more problems than those raised in heterosexual couples when the researcher controls for family income and degree of family instability and conflict. More and better studies are needed. One study compared twelve-year-old adolescents who were raised fatherless from birth by single heterosexual and lesbian mothers with adolescents of the same age and social class who were raised with fathers in heterosexual couples. It found no difference in the "level of emotional and behavioral problems, school adjustment, peer relationships or self-esteem." However, mothers in families without fathers reported more serious disputes and more losses of temper. Were the disputes really more serious, or did single mothers perceive them as such? See MacCallum and Golombok 2004, 1415.

11. In a 1990s longitudinal study of children raised by lesbian mothers compared with those raised by single, heterosexual mothers, many more of the adult children of lesbians considered their mothers (in the early 1990s) to be positive about their sexual identity, whereas "children brought up by non-married heterosexual mothers were more likely to report that their mother was negative about her nontraditional identity and preferred to be married." The gay rights movement seems to have given lesbian mothers a sense of entitlement and support that single, heterosexual mothers lack. Tasker and Golombok 1997, 67.

12. In a study of factors that fostered positive outcomes in postdivorce relationships between single mothers and their children, psychologists Barbara Golby and Inge Bretherton found that those single mothers who parented with confidence, authority, and flexibility had more resilient children who adapted well to divorce. They did not analyze why some divorced single women were able to parent this way whereas others were more insecure. But certainly a culture that stresses the negative outcomes for chil-

dren of divorce, and of single mothering in general, will not foster confidence in single mothers (Golby and Bretherton 1999, 237–69).

13. I know of no longitudinal study based on interview data that follow children of single mothers into their adult years. One longitudinal study did follow children raised by divorced lesbian mothers and divorced heterosexual single mothers from the age of ten into their twenties, but this was not really a study of single mothers. Almost all of the lesbian and heterosexual women had cohabiting partners during a considerable portion of their children's lives, so the authors admit that their findings are really most valid as a comparison of lesbian and heterosexual stepfamilies (Tasker and Golombok 1997).

14. Dowd 1997, 31.

15. British psychologist Susan Golombok surveys research that leads her to this conclusion (Golombok 2000, 23). She finds, in addition, that studies do find that fathers play more with their children than do mothers (17).

16. Kathryn Black, in her interesting study of how women who were inadequately mothered became good mothers themselves, gives many examples of children and adolescents who got support from extended family members, friends, and/or teachers to become resilient in the face of inadequate mothering. If such adults (independent of gender) can at least partly make up for absent and ineffective mothers, they certainly can step in for an absent father when an involved mother is present (Black 2004, 111–18).

17. Several studies have found that lesbian nonbiological coparents are more involved with the children in their household, and that children have a better relationship with them, than do children with stepfathers. In addition, lesbian coparents share parenting to a greater degree than do heterosexual parents. See Stacey and Biblarz 2003, 47–48. This article originally appeared in *American Sociological Review* 66 (2001): 159–83.

18. My family was not unusual. A 1980s study of attitudes toward single mothers found that single mothers who had adopted were viewed much more positively than those who had given birth (Mechaneck, Klein, and Kuppersmith 1988, 266).

19. My experience was not unique. See Miller 1992, 57–58.

20. This has now changed. In 2001, 32 percent of adoptions were by single women, of whom 55 percent were black. These statistics are from the U.S. Department of Health and Human Services' Children's Bureau, as quoted by Thomas-Lester (2003).

21. Ludtke too found that in the 1990s friends were very supportive of mature, middle-class women who had become single mothers (Ludtke 1997, chapter 4).

22. Feminist legal scholars have started to investigate the legal implications of single women using anonymous or known donors. See Dowd 1997, part 3; Jones 2002.

23. There are numerous books on new infertility technologies. Interested readers can find them in their library, bookstore, or online by typing "infertility." I don't recommend any particular ones, since the technology is changing so quickly that they may be out of date by the time *The New Single Woman* is published.

24. One of the single mothers whom Melissa Ludtke interviewed expressed one aspect of this autonomy for ever-single mothers—the ability to pass on their family name, something that traditionally women could not do (Ludtke 1997, 258).

25. Ludtke makes this point. Ibid., 161.

26. Ibid., 258. A longitudinal study in England of children who were raised from the beginning without a father by single, heterosexual mothers and lesbian mothers compared them with children of the same age (twelve) and social class (educated, affluent) who were raised by heterosexual couples. It found no differences in the warmth or ability to confide between mothers and children in all three types of families. However, "in fatherless families, children perceived their mothers as interacting more with them and as being more available and dependable" (MacCallum and Golombok 2004, 1415).

27. For more information on cohousing, go to the Web site www.cohousingco.com. The creators of the Web site have also published a book. See McCamant and Durrett 1994.

28. Morgan 1994, 168.

29. Silverstein and Rashbaum 1994, 30–31.

30. Pollack 1998, 82.

31. Biblarz and Raftery 1999, 321.

32. Pogrebin 1980, 143, 145.

33. Rich 1976.

34. Lazarre 1978, 165.

35. Chodorow 1978; Dinnerstein 1977.

36. The 1980s backlash against feminism had denigrated single career women and fomented movements against abortion rights and gay liberation, but it promoted motherhood. While the cultural themes about the pathology of matriarchy persisted in the background, single mothers were not given much notice (see Faludi 1991). Yet indirectly, the 1980s' backlash held bad news for both married and single mothers. The standards for middle-class mothering began rising in the 1980s, increasing the expectations for the *good* mother (for a discussion of how the media spread these rising expectations for motherhood, see Douglas and Michaels 2004). Such intense mothering required either a breadwinner for support or a cooperative and skilled coparent. The latter could be a soul mate who, in addition, would be an involved father for one's children.

An interesting example of how these two ideologies—the need for a father for the child and a partner for the mother—interact is seen in a study of single mothers who became pregnant by donor insemination. Sociologist Rosanna Hertz found that both lesbian and heterosexual women wanted to keep a known donor at a distance from their young children because they hoped to find a partner who would adopt the child and become a father or, in the case of the lesbian, a coparent. These single mothers could not conceive of more than two parents or of a stable partner who did not want to coparent (Hertz 2002).

37. Whitehead 1993.

38. Nancy R. Gibbs, "Bringing Up Father," *Time,* June 28, 1993.

39. Stacey 1998, 53. Stacey provides additional evidence on how the cultural emphasis on the impact of fatherlessness escalated in the 1990s.

40. See Hochschild 1989; Ann Crittenden 2001.

41. See Miller 1992; Silverstein and Rashbaum 1994. Pollack 1998. Biblarz, Raftery, and Bucur 1997. In addition, see Biblarz and Raftery 1999. In a private communication in 2004, Biblarz confirmed to me that his research, despite being published in two of the most prestigious sociology journals, had gotten little publicity. The so-called consensus view that growing up without a father is harmful to children was still repeated in 2002 in the first issue of a magazine created by the American Sociological Association to popularize scholarly research. See McLanahan 2002.

42. Sociologist Rosanna Hertz, in a study of single women who became pregnant through artificial insemination (using both known and unknown donors), found that many of these women too fantasized about finding a partner who would adopt their child and be a dad. See Hertz 2002. Melissa Ludtke gives an example of a single mother who started dating through personal ads with the sole purpose of finding a father for her two-year-old (Ludtke 1997, 374).

43. A 1980s study of women who chose to become single mothers found that those who were involved with the father at the time of conception were later more dissatisfied than those who did not know the father of their children. See Mechaneck, Klein, and Kuppersmith 1988, 279.

44. Biblarz, Raftery, and Bucur (1997) and Biblarz and Raftery (1999) compiled the research supporting this.

45. Ludtke 1997, 262.

46. In 2000 the U.S. Department of Justice found that 34 percent of sexual abuse of a juvenile under the age of eighteen was by a family member, almost always a male. See Snyder 2000, 10. Available online at http://www.ojp.usdoj.gov/bjs/. Other research indicates that children are more at risk of abuse if they live in a household with a male who is not their genetic parent. See Ganong and Coleman 2004, 155.

47. Starting in the mid-1990s, feminist legal scholars began to challenge the ideology that all children need to be raised with an involved father and to advocate legal protections for single mothers. See Polikoff 1996.

48. Sociologist Karen Hansen criticized the sociology of the family, which has focused almost exclusively on the nuclear family. She found that grandfathers and uncles played important roles in children's lives. When male friends were available, they did too, but

female friends were much more involved in the networks that helped couples parent their children (Hansen 2005, chapter 8).

49. Silverstein and Rashbaum 1994, 88.

50. Ibid., 85. Judith Stacey and Timothy Biblarz, in commenting on a number of studies of lesbian parenting, write: "Children who derive their principal source of love, discipline, protection and identification from women living independent of male domestic authority or influence should develop less stereotypical symbolic, emotional, practical, and behavioral gender repertoires" (Stacey and Biblarz 2003, 51).

51. Adoption is a complex issue, which I will not address in the text. I have never heard from Marco's birth mother, or from anyone in her family, although they have my name and phone number, which are still the same. Marco has a picture of his birth mother and a copy of his birth certificate. As a child we always talked openly about his being adopted, and he often told his friends about it. He always wanted to meet his birth family, and I assured him that he would as an adult. Now at twenty-three, he talks a lot about contacting them but is not yet ready to do so. He is most interested to find out if he has any half siblings and about the black Creole part of the family. He tells me he is glad he was adopted, although I suspect his feelings are more complex.

52. Ludtke 1997, 354, 348.

53. I hope my argument will spark more debate in her organization and others. See Mattes 1994, 162–66.

54. Other researchers have documented the importance of friendship networks and extended family for middle-class single mothers and their children. See the work of Rosanna Hertz (2002). One researcher found that middle-class mothers had more aid of this nature than poorer single mothers (Roschelle 1997, 153). Another sociologist confirmed the importance of support networks outside the nuclear family but found that they required a lot of effort to sustain (Nelson 2002, 225–49).

55. Karen Black too stresses the importance of support from friends for those mothers —single or coupled—who didn't have good role models in their own mothers (Black 2004, 184).

56. Hornby 1998, 75.

57. Ibid., 95.

58. Ibid., 299.

59. Dunne 2000.

60. I hope that other scholars will pursue some of these ideas, using a larger sample.

61. Bock 2000.

62. Ann Crittenden 2001, 201.

63. Sociologist Rosanna Hertz is one researcher conducting this kind of research. She is studying different types of self-sufficient single mothers. In addition to her 2002 article, see Hertz and Ferguson 1997 and 1998. The psychological research in Golby and Bretherton 1999 is another example of such research.

64. Traditionally, parenting by women relatives and fictive kin has played a large role in the African American community. See James 1993, 44–54. Researchers are beginning to investigate the complex extended family relationships that are possible when sperm donors are known or become known. See Sullivan 2004, chapter 7.

CHAPTER 8: The Cultural Divide and Social Continuum between Single and Married Women

1. This statistic is from the 2000 U.S. Census.

2. The most prominent family-values advocates include William Galston, Barbara Defoe Whitehead, Jean Bethke Elstain, David Blankenhorn, David Popenoe, and other scholars associated with the Institute for American Values in New York City.

3. These scholars and the Institute for American Values are still at the center of the marriage movement but are joined by the National Marriage Project at Rutgers University, the Religion, Culture and Family Project at the University of Chicago, and the Coalition for Marriage, Family and Couples Education in Washington, D.C.

4. These liberal allies include the scholars Robert Bellah, Norval Glenn, Mary Pipher, and Judith Wallerstein and the communitarian Amitai Etzioni.

5. The clearest statement of this new position is The Marriage Movement: A Statement of Principles (www.marriagemovement.org), which was issued in June 2000.

6. For a thorough discussion of the marriage movements policy proposals, see Stacey 2001.

7. Information about Waite's and Gallagher's political affiliations is discussed in a profile of Waite in an October 2003 article ("Healthy, Wealthy and Wed," by Amy M. Braverman) in the *University of Chicago Magazine*.

8. Waite and Gallagher 2000.

9. Waite and Gallagher pull together a number of statistical surveys to critique a famous 1970s study by sociologist Jessie Bernard, who argued that single women were in better mental and physical health than their married counterparts. See Bernard 1972.

10. Wallerstein, Lewis, and Blakeslee 2000; Hetherington and John Kelly 2002.

11. Danielle Crittenden 1999.

12. Heyn 1992 and 1997.

13. Heyn, for example, writes: "Depression rates among married women are triple that of their single (never married, divorced or widowed) female counterparts; severe neurosis among married women is three times that of single women" (Heyn 1997, 11).

14. Ibid., xiii.

15. Geller 2001, 72.

16. Ibid., 70.

17. Waite and Gallagher 2000, 76.

18. Ibid., 175.

19. Wallerstein, Lewis, and Blakeslee 2000, 288.

20. Ibid., 290.

21. Ibid., 58.

22. Ibid., 59.

23. Hetherington and Kelly 2002, 98.

24. Ibid., 105.

25. Ibid.

26. To my knowledge, Hetherington, unlike Wallerstein, does not lend her name and expertise to the marriage movement. But because her research is often used to counter Wallerstein, I have included my critique here, since I find similarities in how they stereotype single life.

27. Danielle Crittenden 1999, 64.

28. Ibid., 73.

29. Ibid., 69.

30. Ibid., 74.

31. Ibid., 75.

32. Heyn 1997, 77.

33. Ibid., 26

34. Ibid., 97.

35. Ibid., 186–87.

36. Ibid., 188.

37. Geller 2001, 3.

38. Ibid., 5.

39. Ibid., 69, 70.

40. Kipnis 2003, 103.

41. Ibid., 44.

42. Ibid., 23.

43. Ibid., 19.

44. Ibid., 20.

45. Ibid., 66.

46. Ibid., 31.

47. See the excerpt from her book *Against Love,* titled "Against Love: A Treatise on the Tyranny of Two," published in the *New York Times Magazine*, October 14, 2001.

48. Ibid., 84–92.

49. Glenn 1996, 31.

50. Edwards and Hoover 1974, 217.

51. Wartik 2002, 237.

52. Ibid., 238.

53. Miya-Jervis 2000, 286.

54. Graham 1997, 615.

55. For example, see Freeman 2002, preface; and Willis 2004, 16.

56. Martha Ackelsberg and Judith Plaskow, "Why We're Not Getting Married," www.CommonDreams.org, June 1, 2004.

57. Geller 2001, 381.

58. See Chandler 1991.

59. See Gerstel and Gross 1984.

60. For an example of a long-term, noncohabiting, and committed heterosexual relationship in one's twenties, see Marshall 2002.

61. Kennedy 2001.

62. Ibid., 78.

63. Sasha Cagen describes a similar relationship between two young heterosexual women that has lasted for more than six years (Cagen 2004, 112–13).

CHAPTER 9: Friendship Networks as a Source of Community and Care

1. Sociologist Margaret Adams, in *Single Blessedness,* a forgotten and out-of-print book published in 1976, found that rather than being lonely or isolated, women who were long-term singles had a top-ten network of friends and relatives upon whom they relied. She found that this number of friends permitted a broad spectrum of intimacy (Adams 1976, 87). The most contented women in my study too seemed to have eight to ten good friends. Sometimes a relative is also a friend.

2. Isaacs 1999, 176; Gilbert 1997.

3. See Putnam and Feldstein 2003, 2; Wellman 1999, xiv.

4. Wellman 1999, 84. Wellman found that individuals in Canada and the United States on average have 3 to 6 social close intimate ties, 5 to 15 that are less strong but still significant ties, and approximately 1,000 acquaintances (85).

5. See Fischer 1982, 102, 115, 128, 130; Putnam 2000, 96–97.

6. For support for this idea, see Allan 2001.

7. Wellman 1999, 32.

8. Ellen Goodman and Patricia O'Brien, in their 2000 book, *I Know Just What You Mean: The Power of Friendship in Women's Lives,* interviewed Johnetta Cole and Beverly Guy-Sheftall, two high-powered academic women friends in Atlanta, who pledged to each other that they would not move or they would move together. Both women were divorced single mothers for a while, but Johnetta remarried and Beverly did not (Goodman and O'Brien 2000, 256).

9. Fielding 1996, 20.

10. Quantitative studies have found that life satisfaction is strongly correlated with an extroverted personality, which for females means warmth and gregariousness. See Argyle 2001, 150.

11. Capossela and Warnock 1995.

12. Watters 2003, 38, 55.

13. Ibid., chapter 3.

14. In the early twenty-first century, single women and men in their twenties and thirties began to go beyond these geographically situated networks to create online friendship ties. A number of Web sites—friendster.com, everyonesconnected.com, tribe.net, and celebratefriendship.org—encourage people to post profiles of themselves and their friends and to get their friends to do the same. Individuals may then connect to friends of friends to the fourth degree (that is, to a friend of a friend of a friend of a friend). Originally established as a dating site on the assumption that friends of friends are more

likely to be good dates than strangers, these sites are used for other reasons too—to meet new friends, get help in finding a job, and other sorts of aid. Online networks that are locally based—like Craigslist.org in the San Francisco Bay Area—can interact with and reinforce other social networks (see Putnam and Feldstein 2003).

Researcher Danah Boyd draws attention, however, to some problematic aspects of such online friendship networks, noting that people have different criteria for friends and that these Web sites are easily infiltrated by fakers, who undermine trust and raise questions about the validity of connections (see Danah Boyd, Friendster and Publicly Articulated Social Networking, 2004, available on her Web site at www.zephoria.org/snt). Still, such sites encourage young people to think beyond their families and couples and find other sorts of supportive relationships.

15. Watters 2003, 39.

16. Cagen 2004, 113.

17. Ibid., 114.

18. In *Share the Care,* the book that Lynn used to organize a care network to support Wendy, the authors called their own caregiving network of friends "Susan's funny family." In a *New York Times* article about how singles in New York City dealt with the September 11 crisis, journalist Ginia Bellafante wrote of an "overriding importance of friendships." She went on to remark that single New Yorkers "create surrogate families out of friends" (Bellafante 2001). Many scholars and journalists in the 1990s commented on the importance of friendship networks in creating lesbian and gay communities, but most labeled such networks "chosen families" (see, for example, Weston 1991 and Preston and Lowenthal 1995). Only a few commentators questioned this tendency to conflate family and friendship (see Nardi 1999 and Weinstock and Rothblum 1996, chapter 1). Activists in the women's movement of the 1970s called each other sister and declared that "sisterhood is powerful." These so-called sisters were not kin but friends and comrades. Friendship networks, not kinship, banded feminists together (see Ackelsberg 1983, 339).

19. Rubin 1985, 5.

20. Ibid., 16.

21. Ackelsberg 2001, 1.

22. Sociologist Rosabeth Kanter distinguishes these communes from those founded in the United States in the nineteenth century: "Overwhelmingly, the grand utopian visions of the past have been replaced by a concern with relations in a small group. Instead of conceptions of alternative societies, what is emerging are conceptions of alternative families. Whereas communes of the past were described in books about socialism, communism and cooperation, communes today are increasingly discussed in books about the family (Kanter 1972, 165).

23. Zablocki 2000, 79.

24. Zablocki 1980, 132–33.

25. Ogilvy and Ogilvy 1971, 89.

26. In interviews in the 1990s with many veterans of communal experiments in the 1960s, Timothy Miller found that they now "prefer some level of private facilities and generally a combination of communal and individual features in their domestic lives" (Miller 1999, 241). Another book published in the mid-1990s also recognizes this reality. See Shaffer and Anundsen 1993.

27. Sociologist Hung C. Thai, in a study of second-generation Vietnamese American young adults, found that many "often reject the values of self-sufficiency, individualism and egalitarianism that are generally prevalent in mainstream U.S. culture" (Thai 1999, 56). For his subjects, "friendships, like family, are permeated by a sense of obligation, non-egalitarianism, and sharing of resources" (72). These young Vietnamese Americans did not like to borrow money from their "white" friends, because these friends expected to be paid back right away. Vietnamese friends did not have such a strict standard of give and take. I would not presume to argue my position in such a cultural context— one that may exist for other ethnic or immigrant groups in the United States.

28. Coontz 1992, 230.

29. Ellen Goodman and Patricia O'Brien, in *I Know Just what You Mean,* discuss how friendships enhance family life (2000, 442).

30. Jody Heymann, director of policy at the Harvard University Center for Society and Health, followed a representative sample of 870 adults across the United States, speaking to the participants every day for a week about circumstances that led them to cut back on paid work in favor of care work. She found that fully 24 percent of cutbacks were for the care of adults outside the immediate family, including other relatives, friends, and neighbors (Heymann 2000, 27).

31. The following is a sample of quantitative studies on care for gay men in the United States with HIV/AIDS. I thank sociologist Andrew London for providing me with these studies. G. Hart et al., "Gay Men, Social Support and HIV Disease: A Study of Social Integration in the Gay Community," *AIDS Care* 2, no. 2 (1990): 163–70; Heather Turner et al., "The Prevalence of Informal Caregiving to Persons with AIDS in the United States: Caregiver Characteristics and Their Implications," *Soc. Sci. Med.* 38, no. 11 (1994): 1543–1552; A. S. London et al., "The Integration of Informal Care, Case Management and Community-Based Services for Persons with HIV/AIDS," *AIDS Care* 10, no. 4 (1998): 481–503; Heather Turner et al., "Informal Caregiving to Persons with AIDS in the United States: Caregiver Burden Among Central Cities' Residents Eighteen to Forty-Nine Years Old," *American Journal of Community Psychology* 25, no. 1 (1997) 35–59; Linda Wardlaw, "Sustaining Informal Caregivers for Persons with AIDS," *Families in Society: The Journal of Contemporary Human Services* 75, no. 6 (1994): 373–84; Allen LeBlanc and Richard Wight, "Reciprocity and Depression in AIDS Caregiving," *Sociological Perspectives* 43, no. 4 (2000): 631–49; Heather Turner et al., "Sources and Deter-

minants of Social Support for Caregivers of Persons with AIDS," *Journal of Health and Social Behavior* 39 (June 1998): 137–51; Leonard Pearlin et al., "The Structure and Functions of AIDS Caregiving Relationships," *Psychological Rehabilitation Journal* 17, no. 4 (1994): 51–67.

32. Allen LeBlanc, Carol Anehensel, and Richard Wight, "Psychotherapy Use and Depression Among AIDS Caregivers," *Journal of Community Psychology,* 23 (April 1995): 127.

33. Crohan and Antonucci 1989, 133. Susan Crohan and Toni Antonucci conclude: "Because friends have more in common than family members, due to their shared cohort experiences, lifestyles and interests, they often serve to involve older persons in the larger society more than family relationships do" (135). These findings are supported by sociologist Arlie Hochschild's ethnographic study of a group of white, working-class widows living in a publicly subsidized small apartment building in the Bay Area in California in the early 1970s. Most of the thirty-eight women had strong family ties and family living nearby, but they preferred to live in their own apartment. On a day-to-day basis, they relied more on friends than family for social interaction, emotional support, and giving and receiving care. Much of the social interaction among the women—and the five men who lived there—was equal and reciprocal. They shared food, visits, and excursions to church and community events equitably. But Hochschild also found a number of instances of caregiving by younger, healthier residents for those residents who could not reciprocate. Within any network of friends, the care given to those who were more needy would be expected to be returned to the caregivers by others in the future (Hochschild 1973).

34. See Gouldner and Symons Strong 1987, 150–51.

35. Two books that address the problems between friends are Eichenbaum and Orbach 1987 and Isaacs 1999.

36. See Pogrebin 1987, 11.

37. The 1993 U.S. Family and Medical Leave Act provides twelve weeks of *unpaid* leave in firms of more than fifty employees to care for a newborn or for an illness or injury to oneself, child, spouse, or parent. The California Paid Family Leave Act, which took effect in June 2004, makes all employees who pay into the California Disability Insurance eligible for up to twelve weeks a year of partial wage replacement (55 percent, up to $840 in 2005) for family emergencies. Employees can take paid time off to care for a sick child, parent, grandchild, spouse, or domestic partner or to bond with a new child. The Healthy Families Act, introduced in the U.S. Senate by Senator Edward Kennedy in June 2004, still uses the language of family but has begun to recognize that caretaking may include a broader range of relationships. The bill provides for seven days of paid sick leave a year for full-time employees and a prorated amount for part-time employees. These paid days off can be used for one's own health needs or for "the purpose of caring for a child, a parent, a spouse, or any other individual related by blood or affinity whose

close association with the employee is the equivalent of a family relationship." Senate Bill 2520, p. 12.

38. Living wage ordinances in San Francisco, Oakland, and Berkeley include these provisions. The text of these ordinances can be found at http://www.livingwageresearch .org.

39. The Hotel and Restaurant Employees, local 2, in San Francisco negotiated paid time off in a contract with San Francisco hotels that can be used for any reason at the employee's discretion. For more information, visit http://www.aflcio.org/issuespolitics/ worknfamily. A number of unions representing workers at Kaiser Permanente bargained for Life Balance Days, five days off a year for balancing life and work responsibilities. These five days can be used for any purpose and can be donated to coworkers in need. See *Labor News for Working Families* 10, no. 2 (2002): 3, available at http://laborproject .org. SEIU local 715, in negotiations with Santa Clara County, California, won a voluntary reduced time policy under which members may request a reduction in their work hours of 1 percent, 2 percent, 5 percent, or 20 percent for up to six months. See Control over Work Hours: Bargaining Fact Sheet at http://laborproject.org.

40. For information on new policies as they evolve, see the Web site of the American Association of Single People—http://www.unmarriedamerica.com—and of the Labor Project for Working Families—http://www.laborproject.org.

CONCLUSION: Challenging the Soul-Mate Ideal

1. Robert Wuthnow writes that the loose connections in modern society lead people to seek the more intense relationship of soul mates (1998, 52–53). I go even further: Focusing on a soul mate, I believe, undermines these connections. British social theorist Mary Evans also stresses that romantic love is based on and promotes individualism (Evans 2003).

2. See Illouz 1997, 237.

3. Langford 1999.

4. Illouz 1997, chapter 3.

5. Ganahl 2004.

6. I do not agree with sociologist Arlie Hochschild that women who separate love from sex necessarily are assimilating male rules or are protecting themselves from emotional involvement and hurt, thus exhibiting what she calls a "cool modern idea of love" (Hochschild 2003, chapter 1).

7. Person 2002, 109.

8. The term "stalled revolution" is by Arlie Hochschild (Hochschild 1989).

9. "Loose connection" is Robert Wuthnow's term (Wuthnow 1998).

10. Ascher 1999, xiii.

11. Ibid., xvi.

12. Institute for American Values, "Major New Study: Hooking Up, Hanging Out, and Hoping for Mr. Right: College Women on Dating and Mating Today," press release, July 26, 2001. This is available at http://www.americanvalues.org.

13. Glenn and Marquardt 2001, 72–74.

14. Ethel Person finds the following: "What is prominent in the psychological life of many women is not penis envy, but fear of loss of love, which belongs with a cluster of traits frequently observed in women in our culture: dependency, fear of independence, fear of abandonment and of being alone, and unrelenting longing for a love relationship with a man. These characteristics do not derive from early development, as so many of the first generation of psychoanalysis supposed. They originate rather in the fear of being a single woman" (Person 2002, 227–28).

Abbott, Elizabeth. 1999. *A History of Celibacy.* New York: Scribner's.

Ackelsberg, Martha A. 1983. " 'Sister' or 'Comrades'? The Politics of Friends and Families." In *Families, Politics and Public Policy,* ed. Irene Diamond. New York: Longman Publishers.

————. 2001. "Families, Care and Citizenship: Notes toward a Feminist Approach." Paper presented at the annual meeting of the American Political Science Association.

Adams, Margaret. 1976. *Single Blessedness: Observations on the Single Status in Married Society.* New York: Basic Books.

Allan, Graham. 2001. "Personal Relationships in Late Modernity." *Personal Relationships* 8:325–39.

Allyn, David. 2000. *Make Love, Not War—The Sexual Revolution: An Unfettered History.* New York: Little, Brown.

Anderson, Carol M., and Susan Stewart. 1994. *Flying Solo: Single Women in Midlife.* New York: W. W. Norton.

Apter, Teri. 1995. *Secret Path: Women in the New Midlife.* New York: W. W. Norton.

Argyle, Michael. 2001. *The Psychology of Happiness* 2nd ed. New York: Routledge.

Arredondo, Gabriela F., Aida Hurtado, Norma Klahn, Olga Najera-Ramierez, and Patricia Zavella, eds. 2003. *Chicana Feminisms: A Critical Reader.* Durham: Duke University Press.

Ascher, Barbara Lazear. 1999. *Isn't It Romantic? Finding the Magic in Everyday Life.* New York: Harper Perennial.

Bakos, Susan Crain. 1985. *This Wasn't Supposed to Happen: Single Women over 30 Talk Frankly about Their Lives.* New York: Continuum Books.

Bartlett, Jane. 1995. *Will You Be Mother: Women Who Chose to Say No.* New York: New York University Press.

Bateson, Mary Catherine. 2000. *Full Circles, Overlapping Lives.* New York: Ballantine Books.

Baumeister, Roy F., Kathleen R. Catanese, and Kathleen D. Vohs. 2001. "Is There a Gender Difference in Strength of Sex Drive? Theoretical Views, Conceptual Distinctions, and a Review of Relevant Evidence." *Personality and Social Psychological Review* 5, no. 3.

Baxandall, Roz. 1988. "Catching the Fire." In *The Feminist Memoir Project: Voices from Women's Liberation,* ed. Rachel Blau DuPlessis and Ann Snitow. New York: Three Rivers Press.

Bellafante, Ginia. 2001. "Being Single in New York Is a Little Lonelier Now." *New York Times,* September 30.

Bengis, Ingrid. 1991. *Combat in the Erogenous Zone.* New York: Harper-Collins.

Berend, Zsuzsa. 2000. " 'The Best or None!' Spinsterhood in Nineteenth-Century New England." *Journal of Social History* 33, no. 4 (Summer).

Bernard, Jessie. 1972. *The Future of Marriage.* New York: World Publishing.

Bernikow, Louise. 1986. *Alone in America: The Search for Companionship.* Boston: Faber & Faber.

Bialosky, Jill. 2002. "How We Became Strangers." In *The Bitch in the House,* ed. Cathi Hanauer. New York: William Morrow.

Biblarz, Timothy J., and Adrian E. Raftery. 1999. "Family Structure, Educational Attainment, and Socioeconomic Success: Rethinking the 'Pathology of Matriarchy.' " *The American Journal of Sociology* 105, no. 2 (September).

Biblarz, Timothy, Adrian E. Raftery, and Alexander Bucur. 1997. "Family Structure and Social Mobility." *Social Forces* 75, no. 4:1319–1339.

Black, Kathryn. 2004. *Mothering without a Map: The Search for the Good Mother Within.* New York: Viking Press.

Bock, Jane. 2000. "Doing the Right Thing? Single Mothers by Choice and the Struggle for Legitimacy." *Gender and Society* 14, no. 1:62–86.

Brennan, Moira. 1999. "The Opposite of Sex: A Provocative Conversation about Sex and Society with a Sex Therapist Who Takes Nothing for Granted." *Ms.* (August/September).

Bridges, Lisa. 2003. "Autonomy as an Element of Developmental Well-Being." In *Well-*

Being: Positive Development across the Life Course, ed. Marc H. Bornstein et al. Matwah, N.J.: Lawrence Erlbaum Publishers.

Brown, Helen Gurley. 1962. *Sex and the Single Girl.* Reissued in 2003. Fort Lee, N.J.: Barricade Books.

————. 1993. *The Late Show: A Semiwild but Practical Survival Plan for Women over 50.* New York: William Morrow.

Cagen, Sasha. 2004. *Quirkyalone: A Manifesto for Uncompromising Romantics.* San Francisco: HarperSan Francisco.

Cain, Madelyn. 2001. *The Childless Revolution: What It Means to Be Childless Today.* Cambridge, Mass.: Perseus Publishing.

Caposella, Cappy, and Sheila Warnock. 1995. *Share the Care: How to Organize a Group to Care for Someone Who Is Seriously Ill.* New York: Simon & Schuster.

Casey, Terri. 1998. *Pride and Joy: The Lives and Passions of Women without Children.* Hillsboro, Ore.: Beyond Words Publishing.

Chambers, Veronica. 2003. *Having It All? Black Women and Success.* New York: Doubleday.

Chandler, Joan. 1991. *Women without Husbands: An Exploration of the Margins of Marriage.* New York: St. Martin's Press.

Chodorow, Nancy. 1978. *The Reproduction of Mothering.* Berkeley: University of California Press.

————. 1994. *Femininities, Masculinities, Sexualities.* Lexington: University of Kentucky Press.

Claus, Madeleine. "Baile Flamenco." In *Flamenco: Gypsy Dance and Music from Andalusia,* ed. Claus Schreiner. Portland, Ore.: Amadeus Press, 1990.

Clements, Marcelle. 1998. *The Impoverished Woman: Single Women Reinventing Single Life.* New York: W. W. Norton.

Cline, Sally. 1993. *Women, Passion and Celibacy.* New York: Carol Southern Books.

Collette, Lin. "Creating a Separate Space: Celibacy and Singlehood." In *Single Women: Affirming Our Spiritual Journey,* ed. Mary O'Brien and Clare Christie. Westport, Conn.: Bergen & Garvey.

Coontz, Stephanie. 1992. *The Way We Never Were: American Families and the Nostalgia Trap.* New York: Basic Books.

Crittenden, Ann. 2001. *The Price of Motherhood: Why the Most Important Job in the World Is Still the Least Valued.* New York: Henry Holt.

Crittenden, Danielle. 1999. *What Our Mothers Didn't Tell Us: Why Happiness Eludes the Modern Woman.* New York: Simon & Schuster.

Crohan, Susan, and Toni Antonucci. 1989. "Friends as a Source of Social Support in Old Age." In *Older Adult Friendship: Structure and Process,* ed. Rebecca G. Adams and Rosemary Blieszner. Newbury Park, Calif.: Sage Publications.

Cuadraz, Gloria H., and Jennifer L. Pierce. 1994. "From Scholarship Girls to Scholarship Women: Surviving the Contradictions of Class and Race in Academe." *Explorations in Ethnic Studies* 17, no. 1:21–44.

Damsky, Lee, ed. 2000. *Sex and Single Girls: Straight and Queer Women on Sexuality.* Seattle: Seal Press.

Denizet-Lewis, Benoit. 2004. "Friends, Friends with Benefits and the Benefits of the Local Mall." *New York Times Magazine,* May 30.

Deveny, Kathleen. 2003. "We're Not in the Mood." *Newsweek,* June 30, 41–48.

Dinnerstein, Dorothy. 1977. *The Mermaid and the Minotaur: Sexual Arrangements and Human Malaise.* New York: Harper & Row.

Douglas, Susan J., and Meredith W. Michaels. 2004. *The Mommy Myth: The Idealization of Motherhood and How It Has Undermined Women.* New York: Free Press.

Dowd, Nancy E. 1997. *In Defense of Single-Parent Families.* New York: New York University Press.

Dowrick, Stephanie. 1991. *Intimacy & Solitude.* New York: W. W. Norton.

Dunne, Gillian A. 2000. "Opting into Motherhood: Lesbians Blurring the Boundaries and Transforming the Meaning of Parenthood and Kinship." *Gender and Society* 14, no. 1:11–35.

Easterbrook, Gregg. 2003. *The Progress Paradox.* New York: Random House.

Edwards, Marie, and Eleanor Hoover. 1974. *The Challenge of Being Single.* New York: New American Library.

Ehrenreich, Barbara, Elizabeth Hess, and Gloria Jacobs. 1986. *Re-making Love: The Feminization of Sex.* New York: Doubleday.

Eichenbaum, Luise, and Susie Orbach. 1988. *Between Women: Love, Envy and Competition in Women's Friendships.* New York: Penguin Books.

Epstein, Barbara. 1998. "Ambivalence about Feminism." In *The Feminist Memoir Project: Voices from Women's Liberation,* ed. Rachel Blau DuPlessis and Ann Snitow. New York: Three Rivers Press.

Escoffier, Jeffrey. 2004. Foreword to *An Interpretation of Desire: Essays in the Study of Sexuality,* by John H. Gagnon. Chicago: University of Chicago Press.

Evans, Mary. 2003. *Love: An Unromantic Discussion.* Cambridge, England: Polity Press.

Faludi, Susan. 1991. *Backlash: The Undeclared War against American Women.* New York: Crown Books.

Fehr, Beverly. 2004. "A Prototype Model of Intimacy Interactions in Same-Sex Friendships." In *Handbook of Closeness and Intimacy,* ed. Debra J. Mashek and Arthur Aron. Mahwah, N.J.: Lawrence Erlbaum Publishers.

Fielding, Helen. 1996. *Bridget Jones's Diary.* London: Picador.

Fineman, Martha A. 1995. *The Neutered Mother, the Sexual Family and Other Twentieth Century Tragedies.* New York: Routledge.

Firestone, Shulamith. 1970. *The Dialectic of Sex.* New York: Bantam Books.

———, ed. 1970. *Women's Liberation: Notes from the Second Year.* New York: Radical Feminism.

Fischer, Claude. 1982. *To Dwell among Friends: Personal Networks in Town and City.* Chicago: University of Chicago Press.

Fisher, Bernice. 1992. "Against the Grain: Lives of Women without Children." *Iris* 12, no. 2 (Spring/Summer).

Flanagan, Caitlin. 2003. "The Wifely Duty." *The Atlantic Monthly* (January/February).

Franzen, Jonathan. 2001. *The Corrections: A Novel.* New York: Farrar, Straus & Giroux.

Fraser, Marian Botsford. 2001. *Solitaire: The Intimate Lives of Single Women.* Toronto: Macfarlane, Walter & Ross.

Freeman, Elizabeth. 2002. *The Wedding Complex: Forms of Belonging in Modern American Culture.* Durham: Duke University Press.

Friedman, Alice T. 1998. *Women and the Making of the Modern House: A Social and Architectural History.* New York: Harry N. Abrams.

Friedman, Marilyn. 1993. *What Are Friends For? Feminist Perspective on Personal Relations and Moral Theory.* Ithaca, N.Y.: Cornell University Press.

———. 2003. *Autonomy, Gender, Politics.* New York: Oxford University Press.

Ganahl, Jane. 2004. "Somehow Becoming Who You Always Wanted to Be." *San Francisco Chronicle,* October 10, F2.

Gandara, Patricia. 1996. "Chicanas in Higher Education: Implications for Policy." In *Strategic Interventions in Education: Expanding the Latina/Latino Pipeline,* ed. Aida Hurtado, Richard Figueroa, and Eugene E. Garcia. Santa Cruz: University of California.

Ganong, Lawrence H., and Marilyn Coleman. 2004. *Stepfamily Relationships: Development, Dynamics, and Interventions.* New York: Kluwer Academic/Plenum Publishers.

Geller, Jaclyn. 2001. *Here Comes the Bride: Women, Weddings and the Marriage Mystique.* New York: Four Walls Eight Windows Press.

Gerson, Kathleen. 2002. "Moral Dilemmas, Moral Strategies, and the Transformation of Gender: Lessons from Two Generations of Work and Family Change." *Gender and Society* 16, no. 1 (February).

Gerstel, Naomi, and Harriet Gross. 1984. *Commuter Marriage.* New York: Guilford Press.

Giddens, Anthony. 1992. *The Transformation of Intimacy: Sexuality, Love and Eroticism in Modern Societies.* Stanford: Stanford University Press.

Gilbert, Susan. 1997. "Social Ties Reduce Risk of a Cold." *New York Times,* June 25.

Gillespie, Rosemary. 2003. "Childfree and Feminine: Understanding the Gender Identity of Voluntarily Childless Women." *Gender and Society* 17, no. 1 (February).

Gillis, John R. 1996. "The Perfect Couple." In *A World of Their Own Making: Myth, Ritual and the Quest for Family Values.* New York: Basic Books.

Glenn, Norval. 1996. "Values, Attitudes, and the State of American Marriage." In *Promises to Keep: Decline and Renewal of Marriage in America,* ed. David Popenoe, Jean Bethke Elshtain, and David Blankenhorn. Lanham, Md.: Rowman & Littlefield.

Glenn, Norval, and Elizabeth Marquardt. 2001. *Hooking Up, Hanging Out, and Hoping for Mr. Right: College Women on Dating and Mating Today.* New York: Institute for American Values.

Golby, Barbara J., and Inge Bretherton. 1999. "Resilience in Postdivorce Mother-Child Relationships." In *The Dynamics of Resilient Families,* ed. Hamilton I. McCubbin, Elizabeth A. Thomson, Anne I. Thompson, and Jo A. Futrell. Thousand Oaks, Calif.: Sage Publications: 237–69.

Golombok, Susan. 2000. *Parenting: What Really Counts?* Philadelphia: Routledge.

Good, Erica. 2001. "On Sex, U.S. and France Speak Same Language." *New York Times,* May 29.

Goodman, Ellen, and Patricia O'Brien. 2000. *I Know Just What You Mean: The Power of Friendship in Women's Lives.* New York: Simon & Schuster.

Gornick, Vivian. 1997. *The End of the Novel of Love.* Boston: Beacon Press.

Gouldner, Helen, and Mary Symons Strong. 1987. *Speaking of Friendship: Middle-Class Women and Their Friends.* New York: Greenwood Press.

Graham, Katharine. 1997. *Personal History.* New York: Knopf.

Greer, Germaine. 1992. *The Change: Women, Aging and Menopause.* New York: Alfred Knopf.

Griffiths, Morwenna. 1995. *Feminisms and the Self: The Web of Identity.* New York: Routledge.

Hall, Marny. 1995. " 'Not Tonight, Dear, I'm Deconstructing a Headache': Confessions of a Lesbian Sex Therapist." In *Lesbian Erotics,* ed. Karla Jay. New York: New York University Press.

Hanauer, Cathi, ed. 2002. *The Bitch in the House.* New York: William Morrow.

Hansen, Karen. 2005. *Not-So-Nuclear Families: Class, Gender and Networks of Care.* New Brunswick, N.J.: Rutgers University Press.

Heilbrun, Carolyn. 1988. *Writing a Woman's Life.* New York: Ballantine Books.

———. 1997. *The Last Gift of Time: Life beyond Sixty.* New York: Ballantine Books.

Hertz, Rosanna. 2002. "The Father as an Idea: A Challenge to Kinship Boundaries by Single Mothers." *Symbolic Interaction* 25, no. 1:1–31.

Hertz, Rosanna, and Faith I. T. Ferguson. 1997. "Kinship Strategies and Self-Sufficiency among Single Mothers by Choice: Post Modern Family Ties." *Qualitative Sociology* 20, no. 2:187–209.

———. 1998. "Only One Pair of Hands: Ways That Single Mothers Stretch Work and Family Resources." *Community, Work & Family* 1, no. 1:13–37.

Hetherington, E. Mavis, and John Kelly. 2002. *For Better or for Worse: Divorce Reconsidered.* New York: W. W. Norton.

Hewitt, John P. 1989. *Dilemmas of the American Self.* Philadelphia: Temple University Press.

Heymann, Jody. 2000. *The Widening Gap: Why America's Working Families Are in Jeopardy and What Can Be Done about It.* New York: Basic Books.

Heyn, Dalma. 1992. *The Erotic Silence of the American Wife.* New York: Turtle Bay Books.

———. 1997. *Marriage Shock: The Transformation of Women into Wives.* New York: Villard Books.

Hochschild, Arlie Russell. 1973. *The Unexpected Community: Portrait of an Old Age Subculture.* Berkeley: University of California Press.

———. 1989. *The Second Shift: Working Parents and the Revolution at Home.* New York: Viking Press.

———. 1997. *The Time Bind: When Work Becomes Home and Home Becomes Work.* New York: Metropolitan Books.

———. 2003. *The Commercialization of Intimate Live: Notes from Home and Work.* Berkeley: University of California Press.

hooks, bell. 2000. *All about Love: New Visions.* New York: William Morrow.

———. 2002. *Communion: The Female Search for Love.* New York: William Morrow.

Hornby, Nick. 1998. *About a Boy.* New York: Riverhead Books.

Illouz, Eva. 1997. *Consuming the Romantic Utopia: Love and the Cultural Contradictions of Capitalism.* Berkeley: University of California Press.

Ireland, Mardy S. 1993. *Reconceiving Women: Separating Motherhood from Female Identity.* New York: Guilford Press.

Isaacs, Florence. 1999. *Toxic Friends / True Friends: How Your Friends Can Make or Break Your Health, Happiness, Family, and Career.* New York: William Morrow.

Jacoby, Susan. 1999. "Great Sex: What's Age Got to Do with It?" *Modern Maturity* (September/October).

James, Stanlie M. 1993. "Mothering: A Possible Black Feminist Link to Social Transformation?" In *Theorizing Black Feminisms,* ed. Stanlie M. James and Abena P. A. Busia. New York: Routledge: 44–54.

Jamieson, Lynn. 1998. *Intimacy: Personal Relationships in Modern Societies.* Cambridge, England: Polity Press.

Johnson, Pamela. 1999. "Intimacies." *Essence,* no. 5 (September).

Jones, Bernie D. 2002. "Single Motherhood by Choice, Libertarian Feminism, and the Uniform Parentage Act." *Texas Journal of Women and the Law* 12:419–49.

Jordan, Judith V., et al., eds. 1991. *Women's Growth in Connection: Writings from the Stone Center.* New York: Guilford Press.

———. 1997. *Women's Growth in Diversity: More Writings from the Stone Center.* New York: Guilford Press.

Kanter, Rosabeth Moss. 1972. *Commitment and Community: Communes and Utopias in Sociological Perspective.* Cambridge, Mass: Harvard University Press.

Katz, Dian. 2001. "Are You in Love or Just Fulfilling a Need?" *Lesbian News* 27, no. 1 (August).

Keller, Wendy. 1999. *The Cult of the Born-Again Virgin.* Deerfield Beach, Fla.: Health Communications.

Kennedy, Pagan. 2001. "So—Are You Two Together?" *Ms.* 77 (July).

Kipnis, Laura. *Against Love: A Polemic.* New York: Pantheon Books.

Kitzinger, Celia. 1996. "Toward a Politics of Lesbian Friendship." In *Lesbian Friendships: For Ourselves and Each Other,* ed. Jacqueline S. Weinstock and Esther D. Rothblum. New York: New York University Press.

Klepfisz, Irena. 2000. "Women without Children; Women without Families; Women Alone." In *Bearing Life: Women's Writings on Childlessness,* ed. Rochelle Ratner. New York: Feminist Press of the City University of New York.

Koller, Alice. 1990. *The Stations of Solitude.* New York: Bantam Books.

Lang, Susan S. 1991. *Women without Children: The Reasons, the Rewards, the Regrets.* New York: Pharos Books.

Langford, Wendy. 1999. *Revolutions of the Heart: Gender, Power and the Delusions of Love.* New York: Routledge.

Latina Feminist Group, The. 2001. *Telling to Live: Latina Feminist Testimonies.* Durham: Duke University Press.

Laumann, Edward O., Stephen Ellingson, Jenna Mahay, Anthony Paik, and Yoosik Youm, eds. 2004. *The Sexual Organization of the City.* Chicago: University of Chicago Press.

Lazarre, Jane. 1978. *On Loving Men.* New York: Dial Press.

Lesser, Ronnie C. 1991. "Deciding Not to Become a Mother." In *Lesbians at Midlife: The Creative Transition,* ed. Barbara Sang, Joyce Warshow, and Adrienne J. Smith. San Francisco: Spinsters Book Company.

Lessing, Doris. 1994. *The Golden Notebook.* New York: Harper Collins.

Lewis, Karen Gail. 1990. "Single Heterosexual Women through the Life Cycle." In *Women in Context: Toward a Feminist Reconstruction of Psychotherapy,* ed. Marsha P. Mirkin. New York: Guilford Press

Lisle, Laurie. 1996. *Without Child: Challenging the Stigma of Childlessness.* New York: Ballantine Books.

Loulan, JoAnn. 1993. "Celibacy." In *Boston Marriages: Romantic but Asexual Relationships among Contemporary Lesbians,* ed. Esther Rothblum and Kathleen Brehony. Amherst: University of Massachusetts Press.

Lucas, Richard E., Andrew E. Clark, Yannis Georgellis, and Ed Diener. 2003. "Reexamining Adaptation and the Set Point Model of Happiness: Reactions to Changes in Marital Status." *Journal of Personality and Social Psychology* 84, no. 3.

Ludtke, Melissa. 1997. *On Our Own: Unmarried Motherhood in America.* Berkeley: University of California Press.

MacCallum, Fiona, and Susan Golombok. 2004. "Children Raised in Fatherless Families from Infancy: A Follow-up of Children of Lesbian and Single Heterosexual Mothers at Early Adolescence." *Journal of Child Psychology and Psychiatry* 45, no. 8.

Mackenzie, Catriona, and Natalie Stoljar, eds. 2000. *Relational Autonomy: Feminist Perspectives on Autonomy, Agency and the Social Self.* New York: Oxford University Press.

Mahay, Jennar, and Edward Laumann. 2004. "Meeting and Mating over the Life Course." In *The Sexual Organization of the City,* ed. Edward O. Laumann, Stephen Ellingson, Jenna Mahay, Anthony Paik, and Yoosik Youm. Chicago: University of Chicago Press.

Marshall, Jen. 2002. "Crossing to Safety." In *The Bitch in the House,* ed. Cathi Hanauer. New York: William Morrow.

Mattes, Jane. 1994. *Single Mothers by Choice: A Guidebook for Single Women Who Are Considering or Have Chosen Motherhood.* New York: Times Books.

May, Elaine Tyler. 1995. *Barren in the Promised Land: Childless Americans and the Pursuit of Happiness* New York: Basic Books.

McCamant, Kathryn, and Charles Durrett. 1994. *Cohousing: A Contemporary Approach to Housing Ourselves.* 2nd ed. Berkeley, Calif.: Ten Speed Press.

McLanahan, Sara. 2002. "Life without Father: What Happens to the Children?" *Contexts* (Spring): 35–44.

Mechaneck, Ruth, Elisabeth Klein, and Judith Kuppersmith. 1988. "Single Mothers by Choice: A Family Alternative." In *Women, Power and Therapy,* ed. Marjorie Braude. New York: Harrington Park Press.

Megan, Carolyn E. 2000. "Childless by Choice." *Ms.* (October/November).

Meyers, Diana T. 1989. *Self, Society and Personal Choice.* New York: Columbia University Press.

Michael, Robert T., John H. Gagnon, Edward O. Laumann, and Gina Kolata. 1994. *Sex in America: A Definitive Survey.* Boston: Little, Brown.

Miller, Naomi. 1992. *Single Parents by Choice: A Growing Trend in Family Life.* New York: Plenum Press.

Miller, Timothy. 1999. *The 60s Communes: Hippies and Beyond.* Syracuse, N.Y.: Syracuse University Press.

Miya-Jervis, Lisa. 2000. "A Celibate Sexpot Ties the Knot." In *Sex and Single Girls: Straight and Queer Women on Sexuality,* ed. Lee Damsky. Seattle: Seal Press.

Moore, Thomas. 1994. *Soul Mates: Honoring the Mysteries of Love and Relationship.* New York: Harper Perennial.

Morell, Carolyn N. 1994. *Unwomanly Conduct: The Challenges of Intentional Childlessness.* New York: Routledge.

Morgan, Robin. 1994. "Raising Sons." In *Feminist Parenting: Struggles, Triumphs and Comic Interludes,* ed. Dena Taylor. Freedom, Calif.: Crossing Press.

Nardi, Peter. 1999. *Gay Men's Friendships: Invisible Communities.* Chicago: University of Chicago Press.

National Marriage Project. 2001. "The State of Our Unions, 2001: Who Wants to Marry a Soul Mate?" Rutgers University.

Nelson, Margaret. 2002. "Single Mothers and Social Support: The Commitment to, and

Retreat from, Reciprocity." In *Families at Work: Expanding the Boundaries,* ed. Naomi Gerstel, Dan Clawson, and Robert Zussman. Nashville: Vanderbilt University Press: 225–49.

O'Faolain, Nuala. 1996. *Are You Somebody? The life and Times of Nuala O'Faolain.* Dublin: New Island Books.

———. 1998. *Are you Somebody: The Accidental Memoir of a Dublin Woman.* New York: Henry Holt.

———. 2001. *My Dream of You.* New York: Riverhead Books.

———. 2003. *Almost There: The Onward Journey of a Dublin Woman.* New York: Riverhead Books.

Ogilvy, Jay, and Heather Ogilvy. 1971. "Communes and the Reconstruction of Reality." In *The Family, Communes and Utopian Societies,* ed. Sallie TeSelle. New York: Harper & Row.

Oliker, Stacey. 1989. *Best Friends and Marriage.* Berkeley: University of California Press.

Orenstein, Peggy. 2000. *Flux: Women on Sex, Work, Kids, Love, and Life in a Half-Changed World.* New York: Doubleday.

Pappano, Laura. 2001. *The Connection Gap: Why Americans Feel So Alone.* New Brunswick, N.J.: Rutgers University Press.

Patenaude, Michelle. 1992. "On Not Having Children." In *Childless by Choice: A Feminist Anthology,* ed. Irene Reti. Santa Cruz, Calif.: Her Books.

Person, Ethel Spector. 1999. *The Sexual Century.* New Haven: Yale University Press.

———. 2002. *Feeling Strong: How Power Issues Affect Our Ability to Direct Our Own Lives.* New York: William Morrow.

Pesquera, Beatriz M. 2000. " 'Work Gave Me a Lot of Confianza': Chicana's Work Commitment and Work Identity." In *Las Obreras: Chicana Politics of Work and Family,* ed. Vicki Ruiz. Los Angeles: UCLA Chicano Studies Research Center.

Pogrebin, Letty Cottin. 1980. *Growing Up Free, Raising Your Child in the 80s.* New York: McGraw-Hill.

———. 1987. *Among Friends: Who We Like, Why We Like Them, and What We Do with Them.* New York: McGraw-Hill.

Polikoff, Nancy D. 1996. "The Deliberate Construction of Families without Fathers: Is It an Option for Lesbian and Heterosexual Mothers?" *Santa Clara Law Review* 36, no. 2:375–94.

Pollack, William. 1998. *Real Boys: Rescuing Our Sons from the Myths of Boyhood.* New York: Random House.

Preston, John, and Michael Lowenthal, eds. 1995. *Friends and Lovers: Gay Men Write about the Families They Create.* New York: Dutton.

Putnam, Robert D. 2000. *Bowling Alone: The Collapse and Revival of American Community.* New York: Simon & Schuster.

Putnam, Robert D., and Lewis M. Feldstein. 2003. *Better Together: Restoring the American Community.* New York: Simon & Schuster.

Radner, Hilary. 1999. Introduction to *Swinging Single: Representing Sexuality in the 1960s,* ed. Hilary Radner and Maya Luckett. Minneapolis: University of Minnesota Press.

Reilly, Lee. 1996. *Women Living Single: Thirty Women Share Their Stories of Navigating through a Married World.* Boston: Faber & Faber.

Rich, Adrienne. 1976. *Of Women Born: Motherhood as Experience and Institution.* New York: W. W. Norton.

———. 1979. *On Lies, Secrets, and Silence.* New York: W. W. Norton.

Romo, Harriet, and Toni Falbo. 1996. *Latino High School Graduates: Defying the Odds.* Austin: University of Texas Press.

Roeper, Richard. 2004. "Lighten Up, Married Folks: Being Single Isn't So Bad." *Chicago Sun-Times,* January 20.

Roschelle, Anne. 1997. *No More Kin: Exploring Race, Class & Gender in Family Networks.* Thousand Oaks: Sage Publications.

Rosen, Ruth. 2000. *The World Split Open: How the Modern Women's Movement Changed America.* New York: Viking Press.

Rothblum, Esther D., and Kathleen Brehony, eds. 1993. *Boston Marriages: Romantic but Asexual Relationships among Contemporary Lesbians.* Amherst: University of Massachusetts Press.

Rubin, Lillian. 1985. *Just Friends: The Role of Friendship in Our Lives.* New York: Harper & Row.

Ruddick, Sara. 1977. "A Work of One's Own." In *Working It Out,* ed. Sara Ruddick and Pamela Daniels. New York: Pantheon Books.

Rufus, Anneli. 2003. *Party of One: The Loners' Manifesto.* New York: Marlowe.

Rumblow, Helen. 2002. "Young Women Today Less Likely to Remarry Than Were Their Moms." *Washington Post,* July 26.

Sarton, May. 1973. *Journal of Solitude.* New York: W. W. Norton.

Schwartz, Pepper. 2001. *Everything You Know about Love and Sex Is Wrong: Twenty-five Relationship Myths Redefined to Achieve Happiness and Fulfillment in Your Intimate Life.* New York: Perigee.

Schwartz, Pepper, and Virginia Rutter. 1998. *The Gender of Sexuality.* Thousand Oaks, Calif.: Sage Publications.

Schwartzberg, Natalie, Kathy Berliner, and Jacob Demaris. 1995. *Single in a Married World: A Life Cycle Framework for Working with the Unmarried Adult.* New York: W. W. Norton.

Shaffer, Carolyn R., and Kristin Anundsen. 1993. *Creating Community Anywhere: Finding Support and Connection in a Fragmented World.* New York: Putnam Publishing Group.

Sheehy, Sandy. 2000. *Connecting: The Enduring Power of Female Friendship.* New York: William Morrow.

Sidel, Ruth. 1990. *On Her Own: Growing Up in the Shadow of the American Dream.* New York: Penguin Books.

Silverstein, Olga, and Beth Rashbaum. 1994. *The Courage to Raise Good Men.* New York: Viking.

Snitow, Ann. 1992. "Feminism and Motherhood: An American Reading." *Feminist Review,* no. 40 (Spring): 32–51.

Snyder, Howard N. 2000. *Sexual Assault of Young Children as Reported to Law Enforcement: Victim, Incident and Offender Characteristics.* Washington, D.C.: Bureau of Justice Statistics.

Stacey, Judith. 1998. "Dada-ism in the Nineties: Getting Past Baby Talk about Fatherlessness." In *Lost Fathers: The Politics of Fatherlessness in America,* ed. Cynthia R. Daniels. New York: St. Martin's Press.

———. 2001. "Family Values Forever." *The Nation,* July 9, 26–30.

Stacey, Judith, and Timothy J. Biblarz. 2003. "(How) Does the Sexual Orientation of Parents Matter?" *American Sociological Review* 66 (2001): 159–83.

Storr, Anthony. 1988. *Solitude: A Return to the Self.* New York: Free Press.

Sugarman, Stephen D. 2003. "Single-Parent Families." In *All Our Families: New Policies for a New Century,* ed. Mary Ann Mason, Arlene Skolnick, and Stephen D. Sugarman. 2nd ed. New York: Oxford University Press.

Sullivan, Maureen. 2004. *The Family of Woman: Lesbian Mothers, Their Children, and the Undoing of Gender.* Berkeley: University of California Press

Swidler, Ann. 2001. *Talk of Love: How Culture Matters.* Chicago: University of Chicago Press.

Tasker, Fiona, and Susan Golombok. 1997. *Growing Up in a Lesbian Family: Effects on Child Development.* New York: Guilford Press.

Thai, Hung C. 1999. "Splitting Things in Half Is So White!" Conceptions of Family Life and Friendship and the Formation of Ethnic Identity among Second Generation Vietnamese Americans." *Amerasia Journal* 25, no. 1.

Thomas-Lester, Avis. 2003. "Black Singles Taking Adoption Option." *Washington Post.* Reprinted in *Seattle Times,* February 18.

Tiefer, Lenore. 1995. *Sex Is Not a Natural Act and Other Essays.* Boulder, Colo.: Westview Press.

Tobin, Phyllis O. Ziman, with Barbara Aria. 1998. *Motherhood Optional: A Psychological Journey.* Northvale, N.J.: Jason Aronson.

Vissing, Yvonne. 2002. *Women without Children: Nurturing Lives.* New Brunswick, N.J.: Rutgers University Press.

Waite, Linda J., and Maggie Gallagher. 2000. *The Case for Marriage: Why Married People Are Happier, Healthier, and Better Off Financially.* New York: Broadway Books.

Wallace, Michele. 1998. "To Hell and Back: On the Road with Black Feminism in the 1960s and 1970s." In *The Feminist Memoir Project: Voices from Women's Liberation,* ed. Rachel Blau DuPlessis and Ann Snitow. New York: Three Rivers Press.

Wallerstein, Judith, and Sandra Blakeslee. 1989. *Second Chances: Men, Women and Children a Decade after Divorce.* Boston: Houghton Mifflin.

Wallerstein, Judith, Julia Lewis, and Sandra Blakeslee. 2000. *The Unexpected Legacy of Divorce: A 25 Year Landmark Study.* New York: Hyperion Books.

Wartik, Nancy. 2002. "Married at 46: The Agony and Ecstasy." In *The Bitch in the House: 26 Women Tell the Truth about Sex, Solitude, Work, Motherhood and Marriage,* ed. Cathi Hanauer. New York: William Morrow.

Watters, Ethan. 2003. *Urban Tribes: A Generation Redefines Friendship, Family and Commitment.* New York: Bloomsbury Press.

Weeks, Jeffrey, Janet Holland, and Matthew Waites, eds. 2003. *Sexualities and Society: A Reader.* Cambridge, England: Polity Press.

Weinstock, Jacqueline S., and Esther D. Rothblum. 1996. *Lesbian Friendships: For Ourselves and Each Other.* New York: New York University Press.

Weiss, Robert. 1973. *Loneliness: The Experience of Emotional and Social Isolation.* Cambridge, Mass.: MIT Press.

Wellman, Barry, ed. 1999. *Networks in the Global Village.* Boulder, Colo.: Westview Press.

Westkott, Marcia. 1986. *The Feminist Legacy of Karen Horney.* New Haven: Yale University Press.

Weston, Kath. 1991. *Families We Choose: Lesbians, Gays, Kinship.* New York: Columbia University Press.

Whitehead, Barbara Defoe. 1993. "Dan Quayle Was Right." *The Atlantic Monthly* (April): 47–84.

————. 2003. *Why There Are No Good Men Left: The Romantic Plight of the New Single Woman*. New York: Broadway Books.

Williams, Donna Marie. 1999. *Sensual Celibacy*. New York: Fireside Books.

Willis, Ellen. 2004. "Can Marriage Be Saved? A Forum." *The Nation*, July 5.

Wilson, Craig. 2001. "Singleness Not the Same as Not Settled." *USA Today*, October 23.

Witnerich, Julie A. 2003. "Sex, Menopause, and Culture: Sexual Orientation and the Meaning of Menopause for Women's Sex Lives." *Gender and Society* 17, no. 4 (August): 627–42.

Wuthnow, Robert. 1998. *Loose Connections: Joining Together in America's Fragmented Communities*. Cambridge, Mass.: Harvard University Press.

Zablocki, Benjamin D. 1980. *Alienation and Charisma: A Study of Contemporary American Communes*. New York: Free Press.

————. 2000. "What Can the Study of Communities Teach Us about Community?" In *Autonomy and Order: A Communitarian Anthology*, ed. Edward W. Lehman. New York: Rowman & Littlefeld.

Zavella, Patricia. 2003. "Talkin' Sex: Chicanas and Mexicanas Theorize about Silences and Sexual Pleasures." In *Chicana Feminisms: A Critical Reader*, ed. Gabriela F. Arredondo, Aida Hurtado, Norma Klahn, Olga Najera-Ramierez, and Patricia Zavella. Durham: Duke University Press.

Zeidenstein, Sondra. 1999. "The Naked Truth." *Ms.* (August/September).